MORE ADVANCE PRAISE FOR
GOD AND HIS DEMONS

"*God and His Demons* picks apart the teachings and practices of organized religions with characteristic wit, humor, and incision: vintage Parenti."
—Jacques R. Pauwels, author of *Beneath the Dust of Time*

"Michael Parenti is always provocative and brilliant, so his examination of theocracy is as groundbreaking as his previous books on history, the media, and democracy. This book is a long-overdue examination of topics ranging from fast-track saints to money plunderers and theocratic psychotics. It should be read by every American concerned with the preservation of our civil society."
—Lauren Coodley, author of
California: A Multicultural Documentary History

"Pharisees and charlatans beware. In *God and His Demons*, veteran scholar Michael Parenti turns pen to sword with acumen and rapier wit, slaying the sacred cows of organized religions. *God and His Demons* is vintage Parenti. A great book, much needed, which will hopefully be widely read. Parenti defiles the true religious defilers like no one else can—with stunning underreported facts, a wry smile, and world-class wit."
—Mickey Huff, associate professor of history,
Diablo Valley College, and coeditor of *Censored 2010*

"Michael Parenti's *God and His Demons* is wonderfully irreverent, institutionally challenging, and humanizingly relevant—a recommended read for believers, agnostics, and atheists."
—Peter Phillips, professor of sociology,
Sonoma State University,
and editor of Project Censored yearbooks

GOD
AND HIS
DEMONS

MICHAEL PARENTI

GOD

AND HIS

DEMONS

 Prometheus Books
59 John Glenn Drive
Amherst, New York 14228–2119

Published 2010 by Prometheus Books

Inquiries should be addressed to
Prometheus Books
59 John Glenn Drive
Amherst, New York 14228–2119
VOICE: 716–691–0133
FAX: 716–691–0137
WWW.PROMETHEUSBOOKS.COM

14 13 12 11 10   5 4 3 2 1

Library of Congress Cataloging-in-Publication Data

Parenti, Michael, 1933–
    God and his demons / by Michael Parenti.
        p. cm.
    Includes bibliographical references and index.
    ISBN 978–1–61614–177–6 (cloth : alk. paper)
    1. Good and evil. 2. God. 3. Christianity. 4. Religion. I. Title.

BJ1401.P37 2010
200—dc22

2009047806

Printed in the United States of America on acid-free paper

*Dedicated to the memory of
Giordano Bruno, 1548–1600*

CONTENTS

PART I

ALL IN THE BIBLE

1

UP FROM HEAVEN

> **I do not feel obliged to believe that the same God who endowed us with sense, reason, and intellect has intended us to forgo their use.**
>
> —GALILEO GALILEI

Since time immemorial, human beings have sought relief from the slings and arrows of outrageous fortune and the brutish uncertainties of a seemingly indifferent universe. Keenly aware of their vulnerability to infirmity and natural catastrophe, and often heartlessly victimized by other humans, they have beseeched their gods to bring them respite and wreak vengeance upon their enemies.

Even those who live with some measure of comfort and security face an inevitable mortality. Regardless of how they strive on earth, whatever the monuments they build to themselves, their ultimate fate on this planet is eternal nonexistence—an anticipation that is neigh impossible for many to countenance. So they choose to anticipate perpetual reincarnation into this world, or they fashion gods who will usher them into *la vita eterna*, an endless celestial bliss of a kind so sorely wanting in our terrestrial existence.

Along with the fear of death is the fear of life. To modern dwellers as well as primitives, the world is beset by unpredictable forces that are stronger than we. Many such forces are perceived as the willful expression of gods (or a single god) who need to be propitiated and enlisted in our cause.

This does not mean that all religious experience is but a compensation for human travail. There are other reasons people have looked to the heavens. Our intelligence invites us to ponder the nature of cosmic existence, to be awed by the miracle of life itself and the boundless wonders of the universe. On questions of cosmology, physics begins to sound like metaphysics, as mysteries are confronted that once were the exclusive province of religion. Did the universe have a beginning? Where did it come from? What is its ultimate fate? How are we attached to it? Is there some purpose or intent?

The greatest of physicists, Albert Einstein, was one of those who pondered these imponderables: "Try and penetrate with our limited means the secret of nature," he said, "and you will find that, behind all the discernible laws and connections, there remains something subtle, intangible and inexplicable. Veneration for this force beyond anything that we can comprehend is my religion."[1] Another great physicist, Stephen Hawking, resorts to a theological idiom to express a scientific effort. His book on landmark mathematical achievement is titled *God Created the Integers*.[2]

Perhaps the great German philosopher Georg Wilhelm Friedrich Hegel was right. In the beginning there was the world spirit, the *Weltgeist*, moving in unconscious creation, bringing forth cosmic energy that eventually objectified itself in the form of matter. From matter there evolved conscious matter in the form of life, and from conscious life came self-consciousness—the ability of consciousness to reflect upon its own nature in highly complex abstracted form—which, as far as we know, is a distinct property of human beings. What a remarkable thing the universe is that it would engage in this process of self-realizing (in both senses of the word) its own existence, a universe that creates a part of itself to study the rest of itself. As Hegel said, "It is in the nature of the *Geist* [spirit] to have itself as its object."[3]

To most philosophical materialists, questions about the existence of a spiritual realm are valueless, part of the unanswerable mysteries of existence. To religious believers they are self-evident: the mysteries are themselves manifestations of their deity's wonders. Human beings have fashioned numerous gods and goddesses over the centuries, many of whom have slipped into oblivion along with the societies that produced them.

In Western theism two basic traditions prevail. There is the god of rational totality, immutable and cosmic, impersonal and without deliberate demands, a pure creative force with an evolving design: Hegel's "self-manifesting" spirit. Then there is the Judeo-Christian god, "the Lord our God," also known as Yahweh or Jehovah, and other personalized godheads who act directly and anthropomorphically upon history with moods of love, jealousy, favoritism, and judgmental rage.

In our culture it is the latter type of god who seems to have the widest following by far, bolstered by regiments of conservative fundamentalists who conjure up images of *Him* (never *Her* or *It*) as the Almighty Patriarch and Protector, Winner of Wars, Punisher of Impiety, and Divine Dispenser of Rewards to those who adore him. It is this god and his intolerant, furiously proselytizing, and often corrupt and evil adherents who are the object of my critical attention in the pages ahead (which is not to say that all believers are corrupt and evil).

IN SEARCH OF SACRED SECULARISM

This book is not the work of a militant atheist bent on divesting the faithful of their sometimes comforting and sometimes terrifying beliefs. There are many believers who adhere to a merciful and just god, and who summons their pious precepts in support of social justice, peace, and economic democracy. As might the best of secular progressives, the religious progressives oppose the exploitative and irresponsible power inflicted upon the many by the superprivileged few throughout so much of the world. In addition, they do not try to bludgeon the rest of us with their convictions. Instead they show themselves tolerant of those who have neither taste nor talent for the supernatural. Such believers might find much to agree with in the pages ahead. In any case, they are not the people I am struggling against.

I do not much care whether people believe in one god or another or none at all. Of more interest is knowing how decent they might be as people and how committed they are to social justice, egalitarian reform, personal freedom, and environmental sustainability. Still, their religious views should not be a matter of total indifference to us, especially when they are wedded to reactionary political agendas. Those who attempt to impose their autocratic beliefs upon the entire society with the force of law become the enemies of personal liberty and a danger to our prospects for an open society. At this remove in time, the theocratic threat appears as lively as ever. We who are deeply devoted to secular democratic values should feel much troubled by the exploitative and totalitarian proclivities manifested by reactionary religionists of all stripes.

I began writing this book years ago in response to the intolerant religious forces that were emerging in the United States and other parts of the world. The project was put aside several times because of other tasks and deadlines. Unfortunately, the issues addressed herein are as compelling today as when first I broached them—if not more so.

Born in New York City of an Italian American working-class family, I was raised a Roman Catholic, served as an altar boy (never molested), and for a while even contemplated becoming a priest, mostly because I innocently assumed that priests had a sure ticket to *paradiso* and would never have to suffer the everlasting bonfire. I left the church at about the age of fifteen or so, accompanied by no great ringing of the welkin, just a quiet drifting away upon realizing that I would neither spend an afterlife romping joyfully with angels nor being tormented in the mean company of devils. It just no longer held true in my mind: all those fearsome sulfuric scenarios imposed by a god who, like some stern disciplinarian, was upset that I had done something untoward.

Years later, I began delving into religious thought, just as people might enjoy studying any mythology or belief system with a willing suspension of disbelief. One need not adhere to a religion in order to resonate to it. One can plunge into various theologies, taking them on their own terms, pondering their fantastical scripts and devotional goals. With my growing interest in history and the social sciences, I especially tried to get a sense of religion's enormous impact on secular society and how it repeatedly was used as an instrument of social control.

In those days I also wondered whether the universe might harbor secrets and meanings of a transcendent nature, offering an escape from the confines of the skin-encapsulated ego, a mystical experience of the Great Ineffable that some people like to label *God*. To this day I sometimes meditate and find myself contemplating the empyrean mysteries. Do my occasional feelings of near transcendence descend from a cosmic source? I rather doubt it. More inclined am I to suspect that "spiritual experience" originates someplace closer to home, being auto-induced, even if it feels splendidly otherwise.

Still, it is not all settled in my mind. In regard to what is broadly called the "spiritual" realm, I remain agnostic about certain things and disbelieve most everything else. What I do believe is that—beyond the thermal, solar, gravitational, nuclear, and other familiar energies—there may be forms of energy that are subjected in extraordinary ways to laws of nature not yet comprehended or even imagined by us. Such an unfinished thought should not ignite furious objections in anyone's heart, except perhaps the most orthodox scientists and religionists.

SAVE US, O LORD, FROM THOSE
WHO WOULD SAVE US

In regard to *organized religions*, it has been impossible to deny the strong surges of incredulity that can drench one's mind when confronted with certain narratives, some of which are dealt with in the chapters immediately ahead. As bad as they are, however, the improbable stories and strictures are nothing as compared to the monstrosities of actual religious institutional practice or *mal*practice; the lies, hypocrisies, and dispiriting criminal abuses perpetrated by the purveyors of a pompous piety and pretended purity; the parading of a shallow "spirituality" that cloaks a rampant material greed; the endless talk of a loving god by unloving personages; the heartless exploitation of bedraggled populations; the undemocratic complicity with privileged elites; and the shameless zeal and homicidal intolerance shown toward other creeds and nonbelievers.

How ironic that many religionists who presumably are so enhanced by their god's merciful ways can manifest such a murderous fury toward persons of alternative persuasions. We cannot completely divorce a belief system from that which is done in its name. A religion may profess the most elevating sentiments, but if it produces proselytes who kill nonbelievers or who rejoice in the death of the faithless, then this ought to blunt our enthusiasm. Religion is what the religious do. One frequently hears that we cannot reject an all-perfect doctrine because of its imperfect adherents. But how else can we decide the workable value of a belief system, save by the performance of its faithful acolytes?

Difficult it is to accept the sacred when it is so heavily besmirched by the profane, when it is vented by the meanest of spirits, breathing spite and hatred rather than mercy and love. As someone once said, "It's not God I have a problem with, it's his fan club." But the fans infect their gods with all their own pathological attributes so that the gods themselves do become part of the problem.

Played out in actual history, religion has proven to be more of a toxin than a tonic. A chronicle of all the cruelties and crimes committed in its name would fill more volumes than I could manage. So the record here is by necessity selective. Presented in this book is a two-pronged critique directed not only at the *beliefs* but also at the *practices* of organized religion, bringing us to the shabby side of faith and an understanding of the terrible wrongs committed in the name of one god or another. In fairness let it be said that of course wrongdoing is not the exclusive failing of religious hypocrites. But, as we shall see, they do seem to have more than their share of it.

2

THE GREAT EXTERMINATOR

> **I am halfway through Genesis, and quite appalled by the disgraceful behavior of all the characters involved, including God.**
>
> —J. R. Ackerley

That "old-time religion" is still very much with us and is having a considerable impact on US political life. Opinion polls show that large majorities of Americans believe in God, and large numbers also think the devil exists as a real entity. While membership in mainstream religious denominations has declined dramatically over the last thirty years, growing numbers of faithful embrace the enthusiasms of non-denominational fundamentalist megachurches and televangelist missions. Though frequently of modest income, many of these believers "vote their values" instead of their pocketbooks, supporting conservative political leaders who claim to be restoring God to public life while, along the way, giving huge tax cuts and subsidies to the superrich.[1]

GOD'S STENOGRAPHERS

What is it that people believe when they say they believe in God? In the United States we may presume that they have in mind the Judeo-Christian god, the deity most worshiped in Western society. The regnant source for him is the *Holy Bible*, sometimes referred to as "the Good Book." Some argue that the Bible is not to be taken literally. Over a century ago, Samuel Butler scornfully referred to that era when people believed that "every syllable of the Old Testament was taken down verbatim from the mouth of God."[2] Such certainty is still with us. Millions of faithful continue to hold that the Bible is a product of divine inspiration—even divine composition. After living thirty years in the Bible Belt, Gene Lyons reported that fundamentalist Christianity is as alive as ever, with its belief in "the historical and scientific accuracy of every syllable in the Bible."[3] Televangelist Jerry Falwell certainly agreed, maintaining that "the Bible is God's infallible, inerrantly inspired word. There are no mistakes in the Bible."[4]

Let us agree that God would not err when giving dictation; however, humans do err when *taking* dictation. They form differing impressions about what has been whispered to them in those moments of deep revelation, or thundered at them from the mountaintop or out in the lonely desert. Worse still, over the years and centuries their texts suffer excisions and insertions by various scribes. Nettlesome passages are rejected as apocryphal, not divinely inspired. Even texts categorized as sacred have been subsequently subjected to dubious reconstruction or mistaken transcription.

Of what sense is it to claim that the *original* script is divinely inspired given that we do not have any originals. All we have are error-ridden copies of copies of copies, and so forth, often produced centuries apart from each other, differing from one another in thousands of passages, recorded many times inaccurately by scribes who made honest mistakes because of ambiguities and abbreviations in the inscriptions, and damages in the parchment. Sometimes, to clarify a point, or suppress a theologically unacceptable passage, transcribers deliberately imposed revisions.[5]

As biblical scholar Bart Ehrman argues, how could all these words be absolutely and literally true and divinely inspired when in fact they contradict each other? "It would have been no more difficult for God to preserve the words of [the original] Scripture than it would have been for him to inspire them in the first place," Ehrman reminds us. If God wanted his people to have his divine message, surely he would have given it to them in some reliable and enduring form, and perhaps "in a language they can understand, rather than Greek and Hebrew."[6]

Speaking of language, the Bible is by now available in hundreds of different tongues, replete with all the variations and ambiguities that such translations invite. In English alone, a language that did not exist when God gave dictation, there are numerable biblical versions. Newly minted English translations of the Judeo-Christian Bible continue to appear, from which one can draw freshly honed inferences. All these editions have been produced by ordinary latter-day mortals drawing from wildly conflicting Greek, Latin, Hebrew, and English texts. If biblical wording is literally true, again we might ask, which set of words can we possibly be talking about?

In this book I utilize only the King James Version because it has so enriched our language and is the Bible most widely used by English-speaking Protestants. When today's Pentecostal preachers and fundamentalists talk about the Bible, it is the King James that they have in mind.[7]

It is not my intent to entertain the usual controversies regarding literal versus allegoric interpretations of the Bible. In this chapter and the two that follow, I treat the King James Bible exactly as the fundamentalist Jesus worshipers do, as the founding authoritative document of the Judeo-Christian creed, not as an allegory but on its own terms, *literally*, divinely ordained, just as it is taken today by millions of true believers. Many of the Bible's mind-boggling events, however, will be passed over: Adam's procreative rib, Cain finding a wife out of nowhere, Jonah spending a long weekend in a whale's digestive tract, Joshua lengthening the day by making the sun—not the earth—stand still, Moses being handed the tablets directly from the Big Guy in the Sky, Elijah taken up to heaven in a whirlwind, and so forth.

Of interest to us here are the larger questions: What does the Bible really tell us about the god that so many people worship? What social, moral, and political values does this god represent in word and deed?

NO PERFECTIONIST

Alexander Dumas *fils* once remarked that if God had to live in the misery that many humans endure, he would kill himself. Indeed, why would a purportedly just and loving deity create such a hurtful world? Think of all the suffering, death, and natural disasters. Consider human beings, purportedly Yahweh's "highest creation"; why are so many of them capable of the lowest deeds?

The religionists argue that humans themselves are culpable, for they *choose* to commit these wicked acts of their own free will. But if humans are God's creation, does he not bear some responsibility for what he has rendered? Why would an omnipotent, all-perfect divinity create such flawed creatures capable of conducting themselves in unspeakable ways? Aware of their dismally faulty design, why would he then endow them with free will so they might elect to afflict others? This is not to say that all people are evil, but there are more than enough who do hurtful things: murderers, torturers, rapists, molesters, abusers, swindlers, exploiters, profiteers, warmongers, oppressors, and enslavers—some of whom even think well of themselves for the doing.

So the Judeo-Christian god fashioned a bipedal creature endowed with the potential for every kind of knavery, who preys upon fellow humans and other animals often with little regard for the misery inflicted. Indeed, the misery inflicted is sometimes part of the gratification. In sum, this omnipotent, omniscient, all-perfect deity is himself no perfectionist. He might have done better had he taken more than six days to put the universe together. As one wit put it, God is an underachiever.

Being omniscient, God knows everything that has happened and will happen. He does not have to wait to see how the future plays out, as do we. He knows all things through all of time. So when he first created humans, he must have been fully aware of the crimes and horrors they would commit—often in his name. As Bertrand Russell argued, before God created the world he foresaw all the pain and misery that it would contain; therefore he is responsible for it all.[8]

Am I being overly harsh on the Almighty? I think not. If we repair to the Bible, we discover that Yahweh himself felt that the world he had fashioned was a botched job. Appalled by the prevalence of wickedness among human beings, he repented of his work scarcely ten generations after the Creation: "that he had made man on the earth . . . it grieved him at his heart."[9] Apparently he is neither omnipotent nor omniscient in what he creates and anticipates. So Yahweh, the god of the Holy Bible, wishing to start with a clean slate, destroyed all the Earth's population and all the animals and other innocent living creatures in a great flood, sparing only Noah and his family, who found grace in the Lord's eyes.

The Bible does not explain what was so exceptional about Noah and his immediate kin that they alone were appointed to survive and repopulate the world. Surely there were other decent beings among the world's multitude, including blameless infants and toddlers and even some unoffending adults. Why did Yahweh indiscriminately annihilate all? And why did he kill all the innocent animals, except for the pairs ushered into Noah's ark? Having bungled the Creation, Yahweh did even worse with the Deluge, which might better be called "the Overkill."

Another touchy issue left untouched by the faithful themselves: If Noah and his virtuous family were the only humans to survive the flood, then they were obliged to indulge in incestuous relations in order to get procreation rolling again. Here was a gene pool almost as limited as the one found in the Garden of Eden. Perhaps because of all this inbreeding, the descendants of Noah's family have turned out to be no better than the descendants of Adam and Eve.

There is something even more troublesome about the Judeo-Christian god that too often goes unnoticed. Not only did he create a world filled with natural catastrophes and people capable of rapacious abominations, but *he himself is no stranger to unspeakable mass murder.* All this is recorded in painful detail in the Holy Bible itself.

ALMIGHTY SERIAL KILLER

Of the many wars and massacres inspired by the Lord our God, I shall offer only a sampling. Looming large is the aforementioned Deluge, the most horrific and totalistic mass murder ever chronicled in any history, religion, or mythology. The Deluge seems to have had an unsettling effect on Yahweh himself, for after the waters receded and he saw what he had wrought, he entered into a covenant with Noah and every surviving creature in his ark, pledging never again to destroy the earth with flood—though saying not a word about what he might do with fire, quake, or pestilence.[10]

Indeed, not too many generations later, the Lord used one of these loopholes for his next act of mass murder, raining down brimstone and fire upon Sodom and Gomorrah, killing the unoffending humans in those cities simply because he disapproved of their lifestyle.[11] Mass murder is one of Yahweh's favorite pastimes. He smites the innocent men of Bethshemesh, numbering over 50,000, because a few of them had peered into a sacred vessel of the Lord.[12] Yahweh launched other mass attacks, obliterating city walls and palaces with missiles of fire from heaven. In one instance, an angel of the Lord smote 185,000 men, "and when they arose in the morning, behold, they were all dead corpses."[13] The Lord also rained down fire upon the walls of Damascus, Gaza, Tyrus, Edom, and a number of other locales because of their unspecified transgressions.[14]

Mass murders are committed also by God's favorites on earth under his command and often with his direct assistance: "For the Lord your God is he that goeth with you, to fight for you against your enemies, to save you."[15] Yahweh orders the Israelites to invade other nations and enslave their inhabitants. The lands that resist shall be set upon without mercy, "And when the Lord thy God hath delivered it into thine hands, thou shalt smite every male thereof" while the women, children, and all the city's spoils "thou shalt take unto thyself."[16]

In the battle against the Midians, God instructs Moses to kill all the men and male children and every woman who was not a virgin. "But all the women children, that have not known a man by lying with him, keep alive for yourselves"[17]—an unsettling heavenly mandate if ever there was one from a god who ordains war, conquest, mass murder, enslavement, and child rape.

Often not even the virginal "women children" are spared. On one occasion the Lord instructs the Israelites to "save alive nothing that breatheth: But thou shalt utterly destroy them, namely the Hittites, and the Amorites, the Canaanites, and the Perizzites, the Hivites, and the Jebusites; as the Lord thy God hath commanded thee."[18] Add to this hit list the killing of Og, the king of Bashan and all his people.[19] God also helps Moses kill Sihon, king of Heshbon, and lay waste to all his cities, killing every man, woman, and child.[20] The same fate is delivered upon the Benjamites and all their cities.[21] All of them deserve to die for worshiping false gods.

To the Israelites God gives "the heathen for thine inheritance, and the uttermost parts of the earth for thy possession. Thou shalt break them with a rod of iron; thou shalt dash them in pieces like a potter's vessel."[22] God commands Saul to "utterly destroy" the Amalekites, "spare them not; but slay both man and woman, infant and suckling." On one icky occasion, when his Israelites route and butcher the Philistines, they deliver two hundred Philistine foreskins to King Saul.[23] What he did with this war prize we best not speculate. With God's approval, King David and his troops conquered several nations, left no survivors, and plundered all their possessions.[24]

There is a popular Negro spiritual that celebrates how "Joshua fit the battle of Jericho." Left unsung is what Joshua's soldiers did after "them walls come a-tumbling down." In fact, they slaughtered every living creature then burned Jericho to the ground, salvaging only the silver, gold, and other riches to be "put into the treasury of the house of the Lord."[25]

This reference to the Lord's treasury reminds us that the Holy Bible sometimes reads like the book of Mammon, brimming with approving references to material wealth: vast herds, treasures, landholdings, precious metals, pearls, shekels, temples, and slaves ("servants"). "The hand of the diligent maketh rich," we are instructed.[26]

Yahweh has little tolerance for democratic dissent. When two hundred and fifty Israelites, renowned in the congregation, gather in opposition to Moses and Aaron (God's favorites), an angry Yahweh casts down a fire that consumes them all. He dispatches other dissidents in the congregation by sending them "down alive into the pit, and the earth closed upon them."[27] Following his Lord's example, the prophet Elijah slew a whole slew of competing prophets.[28] One could go on and on with examples of divinely inspired carnage. Not without reason did Moses joyfully cry, "The Lord is a man of war."[29] We criticize some US presidents for trying to act like God. Equally unsettling is when God acts like some US presidents.

There are those who feel best when serving a severely powerful overlord, the object of their genuflection whom they not only can adulate but also *fear*, as in the expression "a God-fearing man." In the eyes of some worshipers, God's enormously destructive capacity serves only to make him all the more awesomely potent and deserving of devotion. They embrace him not primarily because he is all merciful and all loving but because he is all powerful; indeed, he is worshiped as *the Almighty*.

3

THE GREAT ABOMINATOR

> **It ain't those parts of the Bible that I can't under-
> stand that bother me, it is the parts that I do
> understand.**
>
> —MARK TWAIN

The god who presides over the Judeo-Christian belief system bears a disquieting resemblance to those imperfect creations known as human beings. This suggests that either he really did fashion us in his own image or we fashioned him in ours.

SACRED SADISM

One of Yahweh's troubling features is his unbecoming penchant for sadistic play. He seems to take much gratification in blood-letting ceremonies, including the ritual sacrifices of innocent animals. Being judged as having no souls and no feelings worthy of the name, animals can be slaughtered individually or en masse. In the Bible they are burned, cursed, dismembered, devoured, or cast into the abyss.[1] In a word, they can be treated just as horridly as humans. Along with sword, pestilence, and famine, untamed creatures are one of Yahweh's "four sore judgments" that deliver death and destruction.[2] "I will send wild beasts among you which shall rob you of your children and destroy your cattle and make you few in number."[3] The "noisome beasts" are to be feared, hated, and exterminated. Domesticated animals are to be harnessed, beaten, eaten, worked to death, traded off as possessions, or sacrificed to one's god.

Sometimes the sacrifice of animals is simply not enough to placate Yahweh. There was the time he ordered Abraham to make a *human* sacrifice of his only child, Isaac. The sorrowful Abraham takes his son into the woods, binds the terrified boy, and places him on a sacrificial altar. As he readies his blade, an angel appears and calls off the whole thing. Just joking. Yahweh only wanted to test Abraham's loyalty.[4]

There was the time Yahweh allowed Lot and his wife and two daughters to escape Sodom, but he warned them not to look back upon the city as he destroyed it. Was he ashamed of this act of mass murder? Lot's wife could not resist a peek, and for this peccadillo God ended her life by turning her into a pillar of salt.[5] A pillar of salt? It cannot be said that this particular deity lacks a sense of humor.

His megalomaniacal moods can devolve into scatology, as when he tells some priests that if they do not "give glory unto my name," he will put a curse on them and "spread dung upon your faces."[6] He delivers other inventive torments: "I will bring up sackcloth upon all loins, and baldness upon every head."[7]

Yahweh does not broach disobedience to parental authority. There was the son who would not heed his parents, preferring to give himself over to gluttony and drink. God orders that he be stoned to death by all the men of the city, none of whom dare suggest that the punishment might be just a tad too harsh.[8] Generally parents are advised to "Withhold not correction from the child: for if thou beatest him with the rod, he shall not die. Thou shalt beat him with the rod and shalt deliver his soul from hell."[9]

On occasion Yahweh's retributions seem ill placed, to say the least. King David arranges to have one of his devoted commanders, Uriah, killed in battle; a number of his other valiant soldiers also perish in the setup. This allows David to marry Uriah's beautiful wife, Bathsheba, with whom he already has been carrying on an adulterous affair. To register his displeasure, God leaves the errant David and Bathsheba untouched but murders their innocent newborn baby.[10]

One wonders why Yahweh's present-day fundamentalist believers are so upset about abortion, equating it with the killing of children and claiming that it violates biblical dictate. As we saw in the previous chapter, butchering innocent babes (actual infants, not fetuses) is a common and much-encouraged practice in the Holy Bible. God ordered the slaughter of all children and adults among the Midians, Hittites, Canaanites, and numerous other peoples. Psalms 137 addresses the "daughter of Babylon, who art to be destroyed" with "Happy shall he be, that taketh and dasheth thy little ones against the stones." So why all the fuss nowadays about doing away with a fertilized ovum?

God is capable of killing one's most treasured love on the sheer basis of a bargain struck. Jephthah, "a mighty man of valor," promises—as a form of sacrifice—to kill whomever issues forth from his house to greet his return, if only God will assure him of victory against the Ammonites. Jephthah does smite the Ammonites "with a very great slaughter." But when he returns home, the first person to come out to greet him is his only child, his beloved daughter, a reception he might have sensibly anticipated. God holds him to his vow, and the brokenhearted Jephthah eventually reduces his own daughter to a burnt offering in grisly homage to a bloodthirsty deity.[11]

DOING A JOB ON JOB

One of the cruelest instances of torment and murder involves God's brutalization of his devoted servant Job. Presiding over a prosperous household, Job is a man "perfect and upright" who "feared God and eschewed evil" and regularly made burnt offerings.[12] Then one day the Lord Almighty feels a need to brag to Satan about how perfectly devoted is Job. But the devil taunts him, asking how can he be sure that Job really loves him, given that God has blessed the man with every earthly good thing. Do away with all that Job has "and he will curse thee to thy face."[13]

Acting much the insecure schoolboy responding to a dare, Yahweh sends marauders to slaughter all of Job's oxen, asses, and camels, and murder all the innocent servants who were tending these vast herds. He delivers fire from heaven to burn up all Job's sheep as well as the shepherds who were tending them. Warming to his task, Yahweh then musters up a great wind that destroys the house in which Job's seven sons and three daughters were dining, killing them all. Job is staggered yet stays firm in his devotion to his maniacally homicidal godhead.[14] Some people try to cover up for God. Thus the phrase "poor as Job" is explained in one reference book this way: "The allusion is to Job being deprived by Satan of everything he possessed."[15] In fact, it was God, not Satan, who reduced Job to penury.

Yahweh finally realizes that he has fallen for Satan's ploy: "thou movedst me against him, to destroy him without cause." But Satan, who obviously is the superior strategist, now professes to be unimpressed by Job's devotion and ups the ante, telling God to inflict pain and sickness upon Job's own person; then surely Job "will curse thee to thy face." Too dimwitted to back off from this vile game, God delivers Job unto the devil to do what he wants short of killing him. Satan afflicts Job "with sore boils from the sole of his foot unto his crown." Mourning for the loss of his children, his servants, and his possessions, and now physically tormented beyond endurance, Job longs for death.[16]

"The patience of Job" is a familiar expression in our language, but truth be told Job does not suffer patiently and quietly. He cries out for death with "the bitterness of my soul" and for some understanding of the afflictions that have beset him.

He angrily asks God, why does he "shine upon the counsel for the wicked?"[17] An excellent question that goes unanswered.

God eventually comes to his senses and stops the sadistic contest, but even then he cannot refrain from repeatedly reminding Job of how powerful is the Lord—as if the beleaguered wretch needed further persuasion. God then restores Job's seven sons and three daughters to life (there is no mention about resurrecting the servants and shepherds).[18] He also rewards Job with money, gold, and herds that are double the number he previously possessed, a kind of victim compensation.

DEATH TO THE SINNERS

Let us consider some of the "abominations" against which the Judeo-Christian god continually inveighs.

Blasphemy really infuriates the Almighty. It is a capital offense. He orders Moses to have the congregation execute a young man because he took God's name in vain. Anyone "that blasphemeth the name of the Lord, he shall surely be put to death, and all the congregation shall certainly stone him."[19]

Violating the Sabbath is an infraction that can bring death if God is feeling out of sorts. Thus when the Israelites found a man gathering sticks on the Sabbath, they took him into custody to decide what to do, at which point the Lord told them to stone him to death, a command that was swiftly carried out.[20]

Idolatry is so frequently and furiously condemned in the Bible as to leave no doubt that the Judeo-Christian god is a jealous god. Such things as graven images, alien religious rites, and false prophets cause Yahweh to deliver death upon those who "serve other gods."[21] He even instructs his faithful to kill their own siblings and spouses if they proselytize on behalf of other deities.[22]

Intolerance and xenophobia are among God's more pronounced attributes. "I am a great King, saith the Lord of hosts, and my name is dreadful among the heathen."[23] Foreigners, nonbelievers, and other abominators who neither observe his laws nor enter into his covenant are to be slated for mass extermination or enslavement: "the heathen that are round about you; of them shall ye buy bondmen and bondmaids."[24] This is the punishment for all nations that fail to keep "the feast of tabernacles."[25]

Disobedience to God's commands carries unforgiving consequences. When Eve ate of the tree of knowledge, God relegated her and every other woman to unhappy subjugation: "I will greatly multiply thy sorrow and thy conception; in sorrow thou shalt bring forth children; and thy desire shall be to thy husband, and he shall rule over thee." And to Adam who also disobeyed: "in sorrow shalt thou eat of it all the days of thy life . . . in the sweat of thy face shalt thou eat bread till thou return unto the ground."[26]

God delivers plague and death upon the Israelites themselves when they stray. The "wicked"—a term used tirelessly in the Bible—are those who violate the Judaic law by engaging in activities on the Sabbath, by eating pork or shellfish, by wearing garments of mixed weave (linen and wool together), or by not lighting the right candles at the right time. But when people heed God's commandments and observe all his ritual laws, he assures them: "I will put none of these diseases upon thee, which I have brought upon the Egyptians."[27]

Adultery is punishable by death. A man who sleeps with another's wife shall be put to death along with the woman.[28] When a certain king abducts Sarah, Abraham's wife, God threatens to kill him and his entire family, even though the other family members presumably were not involved in the crime.[29] Getting the message, the king restores Sarah to Abraham unmolested.

Homosexuality is a capital crime in the Almighty's eyes. If a man lies with another man, the Lord says, "both of them have committed an abomination: they shall surely be put to death; their blood shall be upon them."[30] Remember all of Sodom and Gomorrah were destroyed because a goodly number of the inhabitants indulged in same-sex liaisons.

Apparently homosexual rape is far worse than heterosexual rape. Before Yahweh destroyed Sodom, two male angels visited Lot and dined with him. It was not long before the men of Sodom surrounded the house and demanded that Lot hand over his guests to them so that they might take their pleasure of the newcomers who, being angels, were probably beauteous. To protect his guests and stave off the crowd, Lot offered to hand over his two virgin daughters to the sexual predators! Fortunately, the angels saved the day by afflicting the men with blindness so that they could not find their way into Lot's house. Yahweh uttered not a word of reprimand to Lot for offering up his daughters to be gang-raped.[31]

The early church fathers and theologians, who laid the foundation of Christianity, had no difficulty discarding or downplaying most aspects of Judaic law, but they zealously embraced the Old Testament's denunciations of homosexuality. The entire Bible makes only eight mentions of homosexuality while offering numerous injunctions against the unfair distribution of wealth. "Yet no Christian tribunals have ever been set up to ferret out and burn exploitative landowners and financiers as they repeatedly did with homosexuals. . . . God punishes all those who sin, but for homosexuality, God punishes entire cities."[32]

Cross-dressing is another deviancy that greatly upsets the Lord—though one would think he might have more important things with which to occupy himself. "The woman shall not wear that which pertaineth unto a man, neither shall a man put on a woman's garment: for all that do so are abomination unto the Lord thy God."[33] During the nineteenth century, a number of state governments within the United States touted religiously inspired laws that made cross-dressing a crime.

Masturbation seems to be a capital crime in Yahweh's book. He is as phobic about masturbation as any seventeenth-century Puritan or nineteenth-century psychiatrist. There is the notorious case of Onan, who was struck dead by the Lord for spilling his seed on the ground.[34] Use it and you lose it.

Fornication, even of the heterosexual variety, is punishable by death under certain circumstances. If the daughter of a priest "profane herself by playing the whore . . . she shall be burnt with fire."[35] Likewise, when a betrothed virgin is taken by another man, both shall be stoned to death, "the damsel because she cried [out] not."[36] No thought that the damsel might have been terrified into silence by the threats of her rapist. (This attitude is still with us today in many parts of the world where rape victims are banished, whipped, jailed, or killed for being "complicit" and "soiled.")[37] If a man sleeps both with his wife and her mother, all three "shall be burnt with fire" so "that there be no wickedness among you."[38]

Rape, like murder, is one of those acts that really *is* an abomination in my mind. But in the Bible, rape, like murder, seems to be not all that abominable when the victims are plucked from enemy populations. Earlier we noted how the Almighty instructed Moses to "keep alive for yourselves" all the virginal Midian "women children."[39] Elsewhere God lays down a general mandate on how to handle "a beautiful woman" taken in war. Drag her away from her family and her people and make her your captive, strip her of her alien garments, shave her head, pare her nails, lock her in your house for a full month while she weeps and wails for her parents, then rape her into matrimonial submission. But if, after you have forcefully taken her as your wife, you find that you "have no delight in her," you can "let her go whither she will" rather than sell her for money.[40]

Slavery—including sexual slavery—is not an abomination in the Bible; if anything, it is sanctioned. Slaves are one of the regular forms of war booty that go to God's victorious Israelites. Slavery is often disguised in the Bible because slaves are regularly described as "servants." A man can "sell his daughter to be a maidservant," betrothed to a master or his son.[41] She, of course, has nothing to say about these arrangements. It also is quite all right to "liveth carnally" with a "bondmaid" (female slave), even one who is promised to someone else. She will be seriously whipped for it, but neither she nor the male fornicator will be put to death "because she was not free."[42] The male escapes all punishment because he is raping a mere slave.

Sexual mutilation by circumcision is an abomination (in my book) that Yahweh greatly *esteems*. In the days of Abraham, God carved a covenant with his Chosen People, the Israelites, to be observed by circumcising every male infant.[43] The foreskin, a mobile sheath with thousands of nerve endings, is cut back and torn off the penis, causing loss of blood, severe pain, and a hurtful healing period. In the worst cases, there can be recurrent bleeding and infection, or the blade might slip and the infant's appendage is slashed, disfigured, or rendered dysfunctional. Infants and toddlers in Egypt, Iran, Nepal, and other countries have died from loss of blood or other complications due to circumcision.[44]

In Europe circumcision is relatively rare, practiced mostly by those of Judaic and Islamic persuasion. In the United States it is common even among the Gentile population. Two-thirds of newborn US males are subjected to this involuntary and unnecessary form of surgery, in what amounts to a multimillion-dollar medical practice. In recent years, increasing numbers of Americans have refused to have their male babies sexually mutilated, regardless of what Jehovah and others might urge.

For more than a century, medical authorities—proving themselves to be even more deranged than religious authorities—hailed circumcision as a cure for masturbation, bedwetting, tuberculosis, asthma, epilepsy, and even speech impairments. Recently, removal of the foreskin has been thought to diminish the likelihood of syphilis, cervical cancer, and AIDS. In fact, studies have shown that circumcision offers no reliable protection from sexually transmitted diseases or any other disease. Condoms are a superior and less-damaging recourse.[45]

SELECTIVE ENFORCEMENT

In sum, were we to live literally by God's eternal and unchanging word as recorded in the Bible, we would have to execute homosexuals, adulterers, fornicators, and masturbators. We would have to stone to death those offspring who are given to drink or gluttony, or who disrespect their parents. We would have to kill rape victims who fail to cry out loud enough and exterminate people who violate the Sabbath. We would be obliged to execute those who take the Lord's name in vain or who proselytize for other deities or who have been labeled a witch. We would need to slice and tear the foreskins off all male infants; assassinate family members if they take up with false gods; suppress all other religions because they are ipso facto erroneous; instruct the millions held in involuntary servitude around the world to serve their enslavers faithfully because all authority stems from God; and launch genocidal military attacks against heathen nations that do not honor the one true deity of the West.

We also can feel free to sell our daughters into domestic servitude and treat family members like mortal enemies should they encumber our own religious development in any way. We may own slaves captured from nearby nations (not just Mexico but even Canada). But we dare not taste shellfish or pork, and we must avoid all contact with women on the days they are menstruating, though it is not always easy to tell when that might be.[46]

One unsettling thought: among us there are believers prepared to do many of these very things were they to acquire sufficient power and opportunity. Today's Bible-thumping reactionaries, however, betray glaring inconsistencies when money comes into play. In 2005, Senator Charles Grassley, a Republican from Iowa, opposed abortion and same-sex marriage because the Bible supposedly mandated such prohibitions. (In fact, the Bible does not mention abortion or same-sex marriage.) Yet the senator believed that the Bible's unequivocal and repeated condemnation of *usury* was of no great moment—even though passages from Deuteronomy, Exodus, Leviticus, and Nehemiah explicitly prohibit the charging of interest on loans.[47]

No matter. Grassley was a key sponsor of a bill that allowed credit card companies and banks—which already were posting soaring profits—to charge the kind of usurious lending fees and interest rates that would keep borrowers in debt servitude for most of their lives. People fall into serious debt because of medical expenses, college tuition loans, job loss, or divorce—and not usually because of self-indulgent shopping sprees. With astronomical interest rates of 30 to 40 percent and endless fees charged by credit card companies, a debt can accumulate with a momentum all its own, faster than the interest can be paid.[48]

When an organization of socially conscious Christian lawyers challenged Senator Grassley for promoting such usurious legislation, the senator responded, "I can't listen to Christian lawyers because I would be imposing the Bible on a diverse population."[49] As already noted, he and his cohorts manifest no hesitation about imposing their sectarian biblical mandates on a diverse population in regard to abortion and same-sex marriage. Only when it comes to safeguarding the obscene profits of their corporate campaign contributors do certain lawmakers suddenly become proponents of secular pluralism.

Modern-day fundamentalist Christians not only ignore inconvenient biblical strictures but also make claim to ones that do not exist. With the Bible as their moral guide, how did certain Protestant denominations arrive at the notion that drinking liquor was a moral offense against the Lord? The Bible lays down no prohibition against alcohol. Proverbs 31:6–7 reads, "Give strong drink unto him that is ready to perish, and wine unto those that be of heavy hearts. Let him drink, and forget his poverty, and remember his misery no more." Jesus went out drinking with his apostles, as we all know. In Luke 12:19 we are told to "eat, drink, and be merry," and in various other places in the Bible we are urged to drink and enjoy.[50] Yet through much of the nineteenth and twentieth centuries, citing the Bible as its inspiration, the Christian temperance movement waged war against alcohol consumption.

SHAFTS OF LIGHT IN THE BOOK OF DARKNESS

As we have seen, the Bible is a horrific chronicle of carnage and atrocity, but it does not speak with one tongue. If anything, it houses a cacophony of contradictory voices. Along with the tribal imperialism and clannish wars, there are sporadic utterances about international peace. Recall the famously inspiring passage from Isaiah 2:4, "[T]hey shall beat their swords into plowshares, and their spears into pruning hooks: nation shall not lift up sword against nation, neither shall they learn war any more."

Along with the ethnic cleansing and genocidal xenophobia, there is the occasional egalitarian acceptance of strangers.[51] Along with the crass celebrations of autocracy and wealth, there are calls for justice and concern for the poor. Isaiah repeatedly voices egalitarian messages such as: "Learn to do well; seek judgment [justice], relieve the oppressed . . ." And "Woe unto them that decree unrighteous decrees . . . to take away the right from the poor of my people."[52] From Psalms 82:3 we hear, "Defend the poor and fatherless; do justice to the afflicted and needy." And passages like Nehemiah 9:31 tell us that God is "gracious and merciful."

Still, how do we measure the fair and loving side of Yahweh's words and works against his many darker deeds? What would we say of a man who was known among his co-workers and neighbors to have a kindly side but who also turned out to be a mass murderer? Would we decide that his occasional words of love and mercy and his charity work for the indigent made up for the time he spent dismembering people in his basement? Surely such criminal violence would weigh more heavily in our minds than his sympathetic utterances about peace and poverty. If true of an ordinary mortal, all the more so for a god who purportedly lights our way. Sad to say, too much in the Bible leans toward autocracy, violence, cruelty, and mayhem.

In sum, we cannot excise whole passages of Scripture that celebrate the deity's murkier messages. Just as we credit religion for its advocacy of mercy and charity, so might we criticize it for the exploitation and bloody oppression perpetrated in its name. The god of the Holy Bible—so much adored in the United States and elsewhere—is ferociously vindictive, neurotically jealous, intolerant, vainglorious, punitive, wrathful, sexist, racist, xenophobic, homophobic, sadistic, and homicidal. As they say, it's all in the Bible.

Beware of those who act in the name of such a god. Were we to encounter these vicious traits in an ordinary man, we would judge him to be in need of lifelong incarceration at a maximum-security facility. At the very least, we would not prattle on about how he works his wonders in mysterious ways.

4

THE OTHER FACE OF OUR SWEET SAVIOR

Man is the only animal that has the true religion—several of them.

—MARK TWAIN

At first glance it seems that once the Almighty converted to Christianity in the New Testament, he mended his ways. Gone is the usual smiting and laying waste of cities. Instead we have Jesus' much-vaunted Sermon on the Mount, blessing those who are meek and merciful, who hunger after righteousness and are the peacemakers. He tells us we must learn to turn the other cheek, love our enemies, and love our neighbors as ourselves. He counsels tolerance and forbearance: "Judge not, that ye be not judged." Here at last is a savior endowed with a gratifying message of love and peace.[1] But a closer reading of the Gospels reveals a more disquieting profile.

NEW TESTAMENT, OLD DEITY

For all his reputation as a loving pacific deity, Jesus actually manifests traits that are much like the intolerant, vainglorious

Yahweh. He repeatedly describes himself as the sole source of salvation: "the only begotten Son of God," "the light of the world," and "the prince of this world."[2] And "ye shall see heaven open, and the angels of God ascending and descending upon the Son of man."[3] He calls himself "the bread of life"; "I am the way, the truth, and the life: no man cometh unto the Father, but by me."[4] He brushes aside the notion that he is merely one of the prophets. Unequivocally he declares, "I and my Father are one," and "I am the Son of God."[5]

Jesus warns his followers not to be deceived by the "false Christs and false prophets" who try to seduce "even the elect."[6] To those who would study the preaching of Jonas and the wisdom of Solomon he offers himself as "greater than Jonas," and "behold, a greater than Solomon is here."[7] A resurrected Jesus announces to his disciples the imperial mission of the coming Christianity: "All power is given unto me in heaven and in earth. Go ye therefore, and teach all nations. . . . Teaching them to observe all things whatsoever I have commanded you."[8]

Jesus designated as his "enemies" those who spurn the idea "that I should reign over them." He orders his followers to bring such nonbelievers to him "and slay them before me."[9] Any community that refuses to accept his message will meet a fate more horrendous than that which beset Sodom and Gomorrah. Woe unto whole cities such as Chorazin, Bethsaida, and Capernaum that reject his "mighty works" and fail to repent, for they "shalt be brought down to hell."[10]

No one in the Bible dwells so persistently on the fiery torments of hell as does Jesus Christ. Those who offend Jesus "shall be in danger of hell fire" and cast "into the furnace of fire: there shall be wailing and gnashing of teeth"; many shall be "cast into everlasting fire," and cannot hope to "escape the damnation of hell"; "into the fire that never shall be quenched," to be "tormented in this flame"; and "thy whole body shall be cast into hell."[11] He repeatedly damns those who do not embrace him as the one true savior: "Ye serpents, ye generation of vipers, how can ye escape the damnation of hell?" Those who are skeptics "are of your father the devil." "Depart from me, ye cursed, into everlasting fire, prepared for the devil and his angels." And "if a man abide not in me, he is cast forth [like a withered branch] into the fire."[12]

Not even trees escape his ire. On one occasion, feeling hungry, he approached a fig tree only to find that it bore no fruit, for the season had not yet begun. Jesus delivers an angry curse: "No man eat fruit of thee hereafter forever," and the helpless tree withered and died by the following morn.[13]

To this day, preachers and worshipers refer to Jesus' "unconditional love." But is it really so unconditional? Is it really love? More often, anticipating Calvin, he voices a language of fatal and intolerant retribution. Most of humankind, he foretells, shall pass through the broad gates to destruction. Only a few, "the elect," will find the narrow path that leads to eternal life.[14] No one can achieve eternal life except through him, and those who can are relatively few in number, "for many be called, but few chosen."[15]

Jesus frequently focuses on Satan, whom he treats as a powerful rival, a "murderer" and "liar." The everlasting fiery punishment is tended by "the devil and his angels." Jesus exorcises a host of devils from one man and channels them into a herd of swine, causing the blameless creatures to stampede to their death.[16] Various women also are healed of evil spirits by Jesus, including one "Mary called Magdalene, out of whom went seven devils."[17] Jesus orders his disciples to do nothing less than "raise the dead, cast out devils," and when they are unsuccessful in their efforts, he rebukes them angrily, saying that were they of greater faith, nothing would be impossible.[18]

What determines whether one shall enjoy endless bliss in heaven or eternal agony in the unquenchable fires of hell? It is all a matter of belief. But belief in what? It is not always clear what are the religious tenets and theology that Jesus is putting forth to the multitude. He often speaks in parables that are neither lucid nor consistent.[19] When his disciples question why he uses parables, he floats a strikingly elitist explanation: "Because it is given unto you to know the mysteries of the kingdom of heaven, but to them it is not given. . . . Therefore speak I to them in parables: because they seeing see not; and hearing they hear not, neither do they understand."[20]

Make no mistake, the important thing for salvation is not that his listeners apprehend his message but that they possess unquestioning faith in him. Those whosoever believe in him "should not perish, but have everlasting life"; while "he that believeth not is condemned already, because he hath not believed in the name of the only begotten Son of God."[21] Jesus labored under the illusion that life on earth was swiftly coming to an end. "For nation shall rise against nation, and kingdom against kingdom: and there shall be earthquakes . . . famines and troubles" that "are the beginning of sorrows."[22] Worldly attachments were of no great moment "for the kingdom of heaven is at hand," and "This generation shall not pass, till all these things be fulfilled."[23]

Along with an eternal afterlife, Jesus promises the faithful that they will develop supernatural powers in this life. "In my name shall they cast out devils" and "speak with new tongues. They shall take up serpents; and if they drink any deadly thing, it shall not hurt them; they shall lay hands on the sick, and [the sick] shall recover."[24] If they "have faith and doubt not" they shall be able to remove a mountain and cast it into the sea; "nothing shall be impossible unto you."[25]

HOME WRECKER

Were we to learn of Christianist values only through the diatribes of present-day fundamentalists, we might conclude that Jesus focused primarily on sex, abortion, homosexuality, and family values. In fact, aside from a few denunciations of "lust," he has relatively little to say about sex. He does denounce "this adulterous and sinful generation,"[26] but he forgives an adulteress who is about to be stoned—though he admonishes her to "go, and sin no more" and has not a word of blame for her male accomplice.[27] He is definitely against adultery and divorce, and he seems to equate the two, as when saying that whoever marries someone who is divorced "committeth adultery."[28] But he never condemns or even mentions homosexuality or abortion. Strangely, he gives an approving nod to eunuchs, especially those who deliberately castrate themselves so that they can be "eunuchs for the kingdom of heaven's sake."[29]

Even more striking, Jesus manifests little interest in family values or filial attachments, having neither married nor fathered any children, as far as we know. He demands that his disciples and other followers cast aside their families and give devotion only to him: "a man's foes shall be they of his own household. He that loveth father or mother more than me is not worthy of me: and he that loveth son or daughter more than me is not worthy of me."[30] But those who abandon their families "for the kingdom of God's sake" shall receive manifold repayment in this world and everlasting life in the world to come.[31]

In the impending struggle for the one true faith, Jesus chillingly predicts that "the brother shall deliver up the brother to death, and the father of the child: and the children shall rise up against their parents, and cause them to be put to death."[32] And "If any man come to me, and hate not his father, and mother, and wife, and children, and brethren, and sisters, yea, and his own life also, he cannot be my disciple."[33] Most certainly Jesus was not a family man. In his demands for personal loyalty and dedication, he sometimes sounds more like a cult leader who wages war against the competing loyalties posed by the families of his followers.

Jesus treated his own kin with something less than civility. Informed that his mother and siblings were waiting at the edge of a gathered crowd, hoping to speak to him, he responded, "Who is my mother? and who are my brethren?" He then stretched out his hand toward his disciples and exclaimed, "Behold my mother and my brethren!"[34] On another occasion, Jesus and his disciples were invited to a wedding feast. His mother, Mary, who happened to be there, mentioned to him that they had no wine, to which he responded rudely, "Woman, what have I to do with thee?"[35]

What has Jesus to do with women in general? He acknowledges them only when they are performing some act of subservience, such as anointing his head with oil and his feet with ointment, or washing his feet with water or with their tears, then wiping his feet with their hair. He tells his disciples, "This woman since the time I came in hath not ceased to kiss my feet," and for this, "Her sins, which are many, are forgiven."[36]

Even more revealing is what Jesus does *not* say about women. He does not say wives should have the same rights in regard to marriage and divorce as their husbands and should not have to submit to patriarchal rule. He seems to accept the idea that a groom can have many brides. He does not say that women have a right to play an active role in congregational preaching and spreading the word of God.

It can be argued that Jesus was a product of his day; he shared the male supremacist convictions of ancient times, hence we should not judge him by anachronistic modern standards. This would be a strange defense to erect for the Christ whose divinely inspired wisdom is supposedly timeless and universal, transcending the historic limitations of place and culture. In any case, his attitude toward women is not all that outdated. To this day every major religion is still run mostly by men, from a male-driven perspective, in service to godheads that are almost always male.

THE SOCIAL PYRAMID

As with gender, so with class. Jesus presents a mixed record regarding his egalitarianism. To his credit he denounces the scribes and Pharisees for their avarice and hypocrisy, and he predicts that "a rich man shall hardly enter into the kingdom of heaven."[37] He advises the rich to give away all their possessions to the poor (thereby reducing themselves to poverty), a suggestion that few have taken seriously down to this day, least of all the rich. Jesus himself does not press the matter.

He is hailed for driving out the moneychangers and small merchants from the temple because they sullied his "house of prayer."[38] The job of the moneychangers was merely to convert the various currencies into official coinage. And the small merchants were selling doves and other animals deemed appropriate as sacrificial offerings within the temple. Neither moneychangers nor merchants were doing anything particularly pernicious or dishonest.[39]

As for the lowest of the low, Jesus never urges those locked in servitude to rebel against their masters. He does not urge the poverty stricken to mobilize against the opulent hierarchy. His precursor, John the Baptist, tells the working poor to "be content with your wages."[40] Jesus has no problem with that. He reminds the poor that "the servant [slave] is not greater than his lord."[41] He accepts the notion that masters have a right to render whippings whenever a servant's performance is not up to snuff. The servant who knowingly disobeys his lord "shall be beaten with many stripes," while the servant who performs poorly but without deliberate disobedience "shall be beaten with few stripes."[42]

Repeatedly in his parables, he accepts the master-servant relationship as a legitimate one. He holds in high regard "the faithful and wise servant" who conscientiously tends to his lord.[43] He does not encourage the leveling of ranks; rather, he instructs people to accept their station in the existing social order. When attending a wedding, for instance, one should not sit oneself in the highest room "lest a more honorable man than thou" come claim the seat.[44]

Those at the bottom of the social pyramid do not win his special regard. When one of his many female admirers pours precious ointment on his head, some of his apostles complain that the ointment might have been sold for a handsome sum and the money then given to the poor. Jesus dismisses their concern, reminding them that they will always have the poor with them, "but me ye have not always."[45] As the incident suggests, he accepts poverty as an unavoidable social condition of no great urgency.

Jesus repeatedly heals "great multitudes" of all manner of disease[46]—except the disease of poverty. Listen as he celebrates his accomplishments: "The blind receive their sight, and the lame walk, the lepers are cleansed, and the deaf hear, the dead are raised up, and the poor have the gospel preached to them."[47] There is no miraculous reversal for that last group. The poor are not rescued from their plight; they must content themselves with preachments.

Paul and the other apostles, along with early church fathers such as St. Augustine, St. Ambrose, and St. John Chrysostom, offer us the same ready acceptance of the existing conditions of slavery, wealth, and poverty. The famed third-century church theologian Origen reveals just the kind of class bigotry one might expect from a high-ranking churchman: "Not even a stupid man would praise the poor indiscriminately; most of them have very bad characters."[48]

We are told to obey worldly authority, including that of emperor, king, and governors, for all authority stems from God.[49] Slaves are instructed by St. Paul to "count their own masters worthy of all honor"[50] and "be obedient to them that are your masters . . . with fear and trembling, in singleness of our heart, as unto Christ."[51] And St. Peter tells slaves that they must "be subject to your masters with all fear," not only to good and kindly overlords but also to the harsh and adverse.[52]

A popular passage from Galatians 3:28: "there is neither bond nor free, there is neither male nor female: for ye are all one in Christ Jesus," is often mistaken for an egalitarian avowal. It signifies quite the opposite. Paul is simply dismissing worldly inequalities as being of no great moment, urging his followers to focus on the higher, ethereal equality we presumably enjoy in God's eyes. One's station in life matters not, for God loves all equally as one—but with a love that leaves earthly hierarchies intact, no matter how unjust they be.

SELF-INFLICTED WOUNDS

The Heavenly Father of the New Testament perpetrated something untoward that not even old Jehovah dared to do. He
impregnated an innocent maiden so that she might bear him a
son. But he did it so deftly as to allow her to remain a virgin,
which perhaps is a mitigating factor, aside from being an
impressive feat.[53] After the virginal birth of Jesus, Mary went
on to conceive at least two more children with Joseph, presumably the old-fashioned way.

One enormous crime in the New Testament is not even
defined as a crime but is the very crux of salvation theology: the
crucifixion of Jesus, as decreed by God himself. None of the
usual burnt offerings or sacrificial lambs will do in this instance.
Nothing less than the brutal flogging and murder of the deity's
only begotten son by humans allows these same humans to
qualify for redemption and eternal life. Had Jesus been left
unharmed to finish his ministry in peace, presumably we all
would still be denied entrance to paradise. So we owe his
vicious tormentors and murderers a hearty thanks; indeed, we
owe the Christ-killers our eternal salvation. It is never explained
why God could not have freely granted us redemption and salvation, assuming we were deemed worthy of it, without con-
triving to have some of us brutalize and murder his son.

Finally, let us make some mention of that most visionary—
some would say hallucinatory—book in the New Testament,
the Revelation of St. John the Divine. In Revelation we are forewarned of the horrific mass killings that will be delivered upon
great numbers of humankind—including the infidels, abominators, whoremongers, sorcerers, and idolaters—as they are cast
into the lake of fire and brimstone, when "the great day of
[God's] wrath is come."[54] So Christianity's last momentous act
brings global carnage and eternal torture to billions of nonbelievers and "sinners." For this we can thank our loving, merciful, Father-and-Son deity.

Elsewhere in the New Testament, with the frothy and fanatical St. Paul leading the charge, we have much the same furious Old Testament–like denunciations of idolatry, fornication, homosexuality, and "fleshly lusts."[55] Women are forbidden to teach, adorn themselves, speak in church, or visit friends. They must live in fearful and chaste subjugation to their husbands and whatever other men who might enjoy dominion over them.[56]

In regard to national groups, Jesus himself wavers between an egalitarian universality and an ethnocentric tribalism. We all know the parable he tells of the Good Samaritan, who selflessly aids an Israelite who has been robbed and beaten by brigands.[57] The message is a laudable one of universal brotherhood: the Samaritan is to be loved as a neighbor and an equal. (Samaritans were a rival heretical sect that separated from Judaism generations earlier.)

On other occasions, however, Jesus sounds like a Judaic supremacist, as when he scorns a courteous Samaritan woman, for "ye worship ye know not what: we know what we worship: for salvation is of the Jews."[58] When he sends forth his twelve disciples, he commands them to avoid the Gentiles and the Samaritans. "But go rather to the lost sheep of the house of Israel."[59] When a frantic Canaanite mother tearfully begs Jesus to rescue her daughter who is grievously vexed by a devil, he brushes her aside, for she is a Gentile. He explains allegorically that he cannot take the bread of children (Israelites) and cast it to dogs (Gentiles). "Truth, Lord," she says, "yet the dogs eat of the crumbs which fall from their masters' table." Impressed by what he suddenly takes to be her deep devotion, Jesus relents and heals her daughter.[60]

MAKING CLAIM TO THE "REAL" JESUS

Partisans of different stripes try to lay hold to the legacy of Jesus, a figure whom everyone seems to admire. Proponents of liberal Christianity and others of a humanistic bent frequently hail Jesus as the purveyor of peace, love, and kindness. Reformminded Christians see Jesus as a great social reformer. There are leftists who claim that Jesus was himself a revolutionary or at least a radical of some sort. Others seem convinced that he was in love with and married to Mary Magdalene or some other woman. Some suggest that he avoided women because he was gay all the way.

All contenders for his mantle refashion him in their own image, quick to assert that the Scriptures have been tampered with and therefore give an unreliable picture of Jesus.[61] Ergo, the argument goes, the Jesus who comes down to us in the Bible is not a reliable one. How true, but that is the Jesus who is worshiped and hailed as savior, he who reigns over Christianity as described in the New Testament—the only Jesus we have. No other sources give us a definitive profile. We can only imagine what the historical Jesus stood for, assuming he stood for anything other than his self-promoted place next to his heavenly father.

As we have seen, the biblical Jesus is occasionally capable of expressing mercy and tolerance. He does not share the fundamentalists' obsession with homosexuality and is downright hostile toward family commitments. He is largely indifferent to existing class and gender oppressions. He persistently talks of hellfire and damnation, and repeatedly insists that *only through him* can salvation be attained. He is brimming with scornful intolerance for those who are not ready on blind faith to embrace his grandiose claim to be soon reigning over heaven and earth alongside "my Father." His ultimate vision is of an impending apocalypse, with its slaughter of the multitude and rapturous deliverance of the elect few.

Given all this, the biblical Jesus qualifies quite well as founder and forerunner of an intolerant Christianity that rode into power on the back of the Roman Empire, holding sway for the better part of two millennia. Today there are millions of devotees who eagerly await Judgment Day, convinced that they number among the Chosen who will ascend into heaven while looking back gleefully at the libertines and liberals writhing and screaming in the lake of fire for all eternity. Nice people these soldiers of Christ, lovers of the divine.

WHO KILLED JESUS AND ALL THOSE OTHER JEWS?

Religious intolerance . . . was inevitably born with the belief in one God.

—SIGMUND FREUD

In the spring of 2004, Hollywood actor Mel Gibson made a movie titled *The Passion of the Christ*, an unsparing rendition of Jesus' final torment, graphically depicted with a bloody flogging scene that seemed to run longer than *Gone with the Wind*. The film was all the rage among fundamentalist worshipers. Less enthusiastic viewers denounced it for implicitly blaming the Jews for Jesus' crucifixion. Gibson blithely defended his movie by claiming Holy Scripture as his infallible guide. "It's all in the Bible," he assured us.

COLLECTIVE AND INHERITED GUILT

Gibson was a member of a schismatic Latin-rite Catholic sect purveyor of murky ultra-rightist politics. Whether or not intended, his film resurrects the age-old image of the Jew as Christ-killer, a charge that presumably was put to rest by Vatican Council II in 1965 when Roman Church prelates explicitly repudiated the notion of Jewish culpability.

If we rely on Scripture to settle this question, we end up with a mixed and inconsistent record, as is often the case. The first three Gospels (Matthew, Mark, and Luke) indicate that the Jewish "multitude" endorsed the sermons of Jesus, the maverick preacher, and even provided some protection for him, causing the elders and Pharisees to tread cautiously: they "sought to lay hold on him, but feared the people."[1] None of this is mentioned in the film. Instead Gibson presents Pharisees and commoners as of one mind, all thumbs down on the man from Galilee.

No doubt, most of those who plotted against Jesus were Jewish, but so were those who supported him; so were his apostles who went forth and spread his word, and, for that matter, so was Jesus himself. Indeed, except for the Roman occupiers, virtually everyone in the neighborhood was Jewish. To say therefore that "the Jews killed Jesus" makes no more sense—or maybe less—than to say that "the Jews loved and followed Jesus."

The Roman occupiers must have looked with suspicion upon Judaism's nationalistic teaching of a Messiah who someday would lead a triumphant rebellion by God's Chosen People. If the Romans went after Jesus, it was because they feared he might be playing the Messiah, inciting the impoverished multitude against imperial rule. All the temple priests of Judaea were appointed by the Romans. Given their privileged positions, they must have experienced some of the same discomfiture about Jesus, as did their imperial masters.

Devout Jews doubtless found it difficult to acknowledge Jesus as the Messiah. He bore no resemblance to a mighty Judaic king who would throw off the oppressor and deliver an entire people. Jesus was a relatively powerless itinerant with a handful of disciples, all lower class like himself, occasionally followed by a bedraggled crowd.

It was St. Paul and his following who declared Jesus to be not only the Messiah but God himself. They insisted that he had assumed a temporary terrestrial embodiment so he could sacrifice himself in a painful and humiliating death, thus bringing salvation to all those in the world who believed in him. This was too heady a narrative for many Jews (and pagans) to embrace.

It has been suggested that the early church, taking its cues from Paul, put the blame for Jesus' death squarely on the Jews rather than on the Romans in hope of currying favor with the empire. Paul busied himself confecting a new monotheism tailored for the Gentile world.[2] He leveled salvos at the Jewish community on more than one occasion, referring to the "many unruly and vain talkers and deceivers, specially they of the circumcision."[3] He denounced "the Jews who both killed the Lord Jesus, and their own prophets, and have persecuted us [Gentiles]; and they please not God, and are contrary to all men."[4]

Paul refers to none of the actual events in Jesus' life (except his death and resurrection) probably because he knew next to nothing about them. He transformed Jesus from a Jewish preacher and prophet into a universal godhead, replete with grand scenarios of divine sacrifice and eternal salvation. And as part of this scenario, he fingered the Jews as the nonbelievers and executioners.

Unfortunately Paul is not the only scriptural source for the image of the Jew as Christ-killer. The Gospels of Matthew, Mark, and Luke refer rather precisely to Pharisees, scribes, elders, and priests as those who opposed Jesus. But in the fourth Gospel (falsely ascribed to the apostle John), the author, writing from a hostile perspective outside the Jewish world, rarely describes priests and scribes as the perpetrators and repeatedly accuses "the Jews" of seeking to kill Jesus.[5]

There also is the hard-to-believe scene, scripted in Matthew, and repeated in Gibson's film and in the countless Passion plays performed in churches for generations down to this day, in which the Roman governor Pontius Pilate washes his hands and utters the uncharacteristically noble and pacific concern that he be "innocent of this man's blood." Pilate is portrayed most sympathetically—and improbably—as a fair-minded official unwilling to kill a guiltless man. In reality, according to secular accounts, during his ten-year rule over Judaea, Pilate earned a reputation for rapacity, violence, and cruelty. That he would meekly acquiesce to a jabbering crowd and show himself "the more afraid"[6] is exactly contrary to what we know about him from contemporary sources. "Brutal crowd-control was his specialty."[7]

Furthermore, had the Jewish commoners dispatched Jesus, it would have been with stones or knives. Crucifixion was a distinctly Roman mode of execution, an elaborately torturous procedure regularly practiced in various parts of the empire, requiring the polished brutality of a small squad of trained soldiers. Jesus was mocked, scourged, and nailed naked to a cross by the Romans, "the ones with the real power."[8]

Perhaps the most incredible scene occurs in Matthew 27:24–25: Pilate hands Jesus over to the crowd and they shout, "His blood be upon us and our children." Would the congregated Jews really have taken leave of their senses to place homicidal guilt upon themselves and their progeny? Scripture not withstanding, only a grotesquely racist blood theory of *collective guilt* (all Jews of that era were responsible for his death) and *inherited guilt* (all Jews throughout history are responsible) can allow us to blame Jesus' death on tens of millions of people over the last two thousand years who had no part whatsoever in the incident. Even in those days, the temple elders who denounced Jesus were but a minuscule segment of the two million or so Jews in Palestine, most of whom probably never had any contact with him during his relatively brief ministry. The other three or four million Jews living in Antioch, Alexandria, Rome, Athens, and elsewhere had little sense of day-to-day happenings in Jerusalem, and doubtless never heard of the man from Nazareth, certainly not in AD 33.

JEW-HATING SAINTS

In the centuries that followed, the image of the Jews as Christ-killers was wholeheartedly embraced by church leaders. Papal proclamations, sermons, pastoral letters, and council edicts heaped contumely upon the Jews for having crucified Jesus and for refusing to embrace Christianity. St. Ambrose, archbishop of Milan, applauded the burning of a synagogue by a Christian mob: "there should no longer be any place where Christ is denied."[9] St. Augustine declared that the "true image of the Hebrew is Judas Iscariot, who sells the Lord for silver. The Jew ... forever will bear the guilt for the death of Jesus."[10] St. Jerome warned, "Jews are congenital liars who lure Christians to heresy. They should therefore be punished until they confess."[11] More than eight hundred years later, St. Thomas Aquinas considered it lawful and desirable "to hold Jews, because of their crime [killing Christ], in perpetual servitude."[12]

Jerome, Ambrose, Augustine, and Aquinas were not obscure friars. They were leading theologians, influential church fathers, all eventually canonized as saints whose teachings bestowed a respectability on Jew hating that carried into modern times.

During the Protestant Reformation, Martin Luther lashed out at the Jews for failing to flock to his purportedly improved version of Christianity: a "wicked, venomous and devilish thing is the existence of these Jews ... our pest, torment, and misfortune."[13] In a book titled *On the Jews and Their Lies*, Luther called for their forced deportation to Palestine and the burning of synagogues.

Numerous archeological findings in Italy and near Galilee, dating from the early centuries of Christianity, reveal the existence of closely related communities of Jews and Christians living together harmoniously.[14] Well into the Dark Ages (500–1000 AD), church authorities and state officials issued an unending stream of decrees denouncing the close social intercourse that existed between Christians and Jews. Generally, the commoners paid little heed to such directives. Christians socialized with Jews. "Business relations were markedly free and close, and there [were] many instances of commercial partnerships between adherents of the two faiths."[15]

The Jew as Christ-killer who allegedly indulged in secret

poisonings, ritual murder of Christian children, desecration of the sacred host, and other abominations "was entirely the creation of theological thinking. . . . The European peasant had to learn—and he learned slowly—that he was expected to equate the theological Jew with the neighbor whose friendship he enjoyed and with whom he worked and dealt."[16] The mass of people did not share the hierarchy's preoccupation with heretics and infidels. Nor did the peasantry have any great interest in Christianity itself, retaining for centuries a sub rosa attachment to magic, sorcery, and animistic pre-Christianist beliefs.[17]

Anti-Semitism was used repeatedly by ruling circles to distract the populace from their real grievances about land, taxes, and tithes. Better the people should storm the synagogue than wreak their fury upon the manor, the castle, the monastery, or the cathedral wherein resided their real exploiters, their fellow Christians. The officially proscribed Jew served as a convenient scapegoat, blamed for plagues, pestilence, poverty, famines, and other supposed manifestations of divine displeasure.[18]

Throughout Christendom, Jews were saddled with an array of legal and social disabilities that eventually stigmatized them in the eyes of Christians: special taxes, forced ghettoization, confiscation of property, and the burning of synagogues. Jews were banned from public office and most professions. They were forbidden to own farmlands or engage in export and import business. In various locales, authorities prohibited all social contact between Christians and Jews. There were occasions when Jewish children were forcibly removed from their families and handed over to Christian households or monasteries for conversion.

In 1215, at the initiative of Pope Innocent III, the Fourth Lateran Council adopted a series of measures against the Jewish population of Europe, including social ostracism and the wearing of a distinctive headgear that visibly branded Jews as a race of outcasts. But in countries like Spain, "no social class except the clergy showed any inclination to attack the Jews, who, owing to their intelligence and their industry, were contributing to the prosperity of the country," observes Malcolm Hay, himself a Gentile.[19]

By the early medieval period, church efforts at setting Christians against Jews were having the desired effect. Even then, the mobs that attacked and despoiled Jews often had to be prodded and incited by nobles and prelates who saw opportunities for expropriating Jewish property.

From the twelfth to fifteenth centuries, usually at the urging of higher clergy and nobility, Jewish communities were massacred in Germany, England, Hungary, Spain, and the Ukraine, and Jewish property and valuables were confiscated by the pogrom leaders.[20] On occasion, church authorities issued condemnations of anti-Judaic atrocities. But never was there a retraction of the theological ill will that incubated such violence.

By the fourteenth and fifteenth centuries conversion to Christianity was no longer a way to escape persecution. A prime target of the Spanish Inquisition were Jews who had converted. Thousands of *conversos* were burned at the stake by church inquisitors who treated "Jewish blood taint" as a contaminant irrespective of religious subscription, laying the grounds for the racialist anti-Semitism of Nazism. In Eastern Europe in the midseventeenth century, Jewish victims were flayed alive, roasted on coals, burned at the stake, or boiled in scalding hot water.

From the nineteenth century onward, after years of struggle, Jews began to gain emancipation in various countries. Toward the end of that century, the Italian government granted Jews equal rights in Italy, a law that Pope Pius IX vigorously and unsuccessfully opposed. To divert the Italian public's attention away from the anticlerical attacks of the day, Pius issued a series of anti-Jewish proclamations, while conservative Catholic publications throughout Europe launched Jew-baiting attacks.[21]

Former Jesuit theologian Peter de Rosa noted that, while the Roman Church published over one hundred official anti-Judaic documents over the centuries, not one papal encyclical or pastoral directive rings a positive note about the Jews.[22] Not until 1959, on orders from Pope John XXIII—described by *Encyclopedia*

Judaica as "the first pope to show a high personal regard for Jews and Judaism"—were passages about the "perfidious Jews" expunged from the Good Friday liturgy of the Roman Missal.

The Vatican has regressed since John XXIII. In 2008, Benedict XVI pronounced a new Good Friday prayer that included the following passage: "Let us pray for the Jews. May the Lord our God enlighten their hearts so that they may acknowledge Jesus Christ, the Savior of all men."[23]

PAVING THE WAY FOR ADOLF

The caricature of the wicked Jew propagated by popes, bishops, and saints over the centuries is replicated *mutatis mutandis* in Nazi propaganda. In *Mein Kampf* Adolf Hitler characterized his war against the Jews as a holy crusade: "I am acting in accordance with the will of the Almighty Creator; by defending myself against the Jew, I am fighting for the work of the Lord."

The Nazis incorporated not only Christianity's anti-Jewish preachments but its *practices*. It was the church that devised forced deracination, special taxes, exclusion from public office, bans on intermarriage, corralling Jews into ghettos, the wearing of yellow badges, defiling or burning down synagogues, looting and destroying Jewish homes and businesses, burning sacred and secular Jewish literature, and launching large-scale massacres. All these horrific Nazi practices had their time-honored antecedents in centuries of Christendom.

Well into the twentieth century, Catholic religious orders such as the Jesuits still imposed blood-purity regulations, prohibiting membership to anyone "descended of Hebrew or Saracen stock." Such strictures "are the ancestor of the Nazi Nuremberg laws."[24]

In the face of unspeakable Nazi atrocities during the Holocaust, Pope Pius XII remained silent. Supposedly Pius could not risk incurring the punitive retaliations that the Nazis might deliver upon Catholic churches and worshipers in Hitler's domain had he spoken out. But such concerns about retribution did not keep the pontiff from issuing vehement challenges against *Communist* governments and parties during the Cold War, including his 1949 excommunication of all Communist Party members throughout the world.[25] The Roman hierarchy could not abide the Reds but could cozy with the Nazis. Of the many German Catholics who were active players in the Holocaust, not a one was excommunicated, not even Hitler. As I. F. Stone observed, the Roman Church furiously denounced Marxism, both the social democratic and Communist varieties, "but everywhere it welcomed fascism—in Italy, in Germany, in Spain, in Austria, in Slovakia, and in Hungary."[26]

In 2000, Pope John Paul II issued a formal apology for the violence and injustices against people of other faiths committed or condoned by Roman Catholics over the past two thousand years. Turning to contemporary sins, he asked Catholics to decry secularism, ethical relativism, abortion, and indifference to poverty.[27] The pope made no reference to the *active collaboration* with Nazism practiced by many church leaders and other clergy, and the pronouncedly pro-Nazi church hierarchy in various places. In Croatia, Catholic clergy, including Franciscan monks, played a leading part in the forced conversions, torture, and mass extermination of Serbs, Jews, and Roma ("gypsies").[28] John Paul also left unmentioned the centuries of defamation and atrocity delivered upon Jewish populations by prelates, inquisitors, and church-inspired mobs.

Viewed in this historic context, the Holocaust is not the mysterious enormity it is sometimes made out to be. When the Nazis came along, their venomous message fell on ground well fertilized by Christianity's age-old war against the Jews. The many centuries of church-inspired anti-Judaic calumny and crime, continuing into modern times, helped lay the groundwork for the Holocaust itself. Against all this, a passing expression of regret from a pope seems like paltry recompense, little more than an attempt to put away past enormities without fully owning up to them.

As of 2005, in a series of lawsuits, concentration camp survivors accused the Vatican of concealing the funds plundered from Yugoslavia during the Second World War by Croatian Nazis. The Vatican was also charged with laundering assets looted by the Croatian Nazis from Holocaust inmates between 1941 and 1945, including dental gold removed from the bodies of victims. Vatican lawyers argued that the church was not liable because the Nazi Croatian regime's torture and extermination of hundreds of thousands of innocents did not violate any international law of that time.[29]

Along with the Vatican, many Protestant churches have a dismal record of collaboration with the Hitler regime. Prominent Protestant theologians and pastors enthusiastically hailed Nazism as the needed antidote to irreligious modernism. They urged all Germans to feel "responsible before God to assist the work of the Führer." Supporting Hitler "in all things" was a "God directed call."[30]

In sum, instead of engaging in ill-informed, movie-inspired debates about whether the Jews killed the first Christian, we ought to give serious attention to how and why the godly promoters of Christianity killed so many Jews.

PART II
DIVINE DESIGN?

6

WORKING HIS BLUNDERS IN MYSTERIOUS WAYS

In the secret of my heart I am in perpetual quarrel with God that he should allow such things to go on.
—MOHANDAS K. GANDHI (REFERRING TO WORLD WAR II)

How God treats his present-day devotees should give us pause. In many instances it is Job Redux. No matter how horrific life becomes, we are admonished to "trust in the Lord with all thine heart" for "he shall direct thy paths."[1]

BECAUSE HE LOVES US

Throughout the world, many faithful suffer the afflictions of natural catastrophe. Some even perish as a direct result of their devotional efforts. During the pilgrimages to Mecca, for instance, crowds of Muslim worshipers have been crushed to death in stampedes as they strive to get to the sacred site before sundown. In 1990, some 1,400 Mecca pilgrims were killed; in 2004, in a similar incident, 245 died; and in 2006, another 360 perished with about 1,000 injured. In response to that last stampede, Crown Prince Sultan bin Abdel Aziz declared, "We cannot stop what God has preordained. It is impossible."[2]

In 1966, at least 113 Hindu pilgrims, naked and smeared with ashes, perished in a snowstorm in the Himalayas while en route to worship a stalagmite believed to represent the phallus of the god Shiva. Of course, we can understand that our Judeo-Christian god might want to smite those who practice public nudity and worship the private parts of alien gods. But in another incident that same year, twenty-five *Christian* pilgrims, heading for a town in Brazil to celebrate the Virgin of Nazareth, drowned when their overcrowded craft sank. Thus did an omnipotent Jesus let perish these presumably decent folks who not only believed in him but also adored his mother.

After a massive tidal wave killed 3,000 people in Papua, New Guinea, a satirical newspaper, the *Onion*, offered an irreverent account of how God held a press conference to explain why it happened: "The Lord announced Monday that He killed the island villagers as part of His longtime 'moving in mysterious ways' policy, calling the natural disaster 'part of My unknowable, divine plan for mankind.'" The Lord could easily have released the same statement in regard to the more than 250,000 souls who perished in the Indian Ocean tsunami of December 2004, or in any number of other momentous catastrophes before and since.

Belief in a beneficent godhead is maintained in part through a process of *selective perception*. When over 22,000 people were killed in a 7.6-magnitude earthquake in Pakistan in 2005, one survivor, convinced that his god had saved him—and taking no notice of the thousands who perished—shouted "Allah is great."[3] In 2003, when a US space shuttle blew up in midair killing seven astronauts, thousands of pieces of wreckage rained down on East Texas. Fortunately no one on the ground was hurt. Many believers praised their god for watching over them. One marquee in Hemphill, Texas, read: "THANK YOU GOD. YOU PROTECTED US ALL HERE ON THE GROUND. YOU ARE AMAZING."[4] Not a word was proffered regarding God's less than amazing performance in regard to the astronauts.

When people survive a danger, they proclaim that their prayers have been answered. But when individuals perish, no one is likely to be quoted as bitterly remarking, "Our prayers went unanswered," and no news story is inclined to voice a lament about the futility of prayer. Instead, the faithful assure us that "God called the victim home to heaven." In short, the efficacy of prayer is nonfalsifiable. Whether it be survival or fatality, the outcome is taken as evidence of God's caring responsiveness.

The Christian god seems to be notably heedful of our prayers during wartime. A letter sent by US Air Force captain Donna Kohout to members of her church in Dillon, Colorado, tells of her experiences in the Iraq war: "I'm still praising God for the opportunity to . . . serve in the largest conflict of our day and to witness the wonders He was working at Prince Sultan Air Base in Saudi Arabia, where I lived." She mentioned various sites from the Bible over which she flew, including "the Garden of Eden." And it was "still nothing shy of a miracle" that the Iraqis failed to shoot down any of the planes that were attacking them. "Praise God for the safety He has provided to so many of us over the last several months."[5]

TEACHING US A LESSON

All this said, devotees sometimes see death and destruction as discharging directly—and deservedly—from a disapproving deity. Over the centuries, plague, pestilence, famine, and flood have been interpreted as signs of God's displeasure at our having failed to live according to his diktat. In 1675, Native Americans ("Indians") waged King Philip's War to roll back the English encroachment into New England. They killed hundreds of colonists and destroyed numerous settlements. The Puritans saw this catastrophe as divine punishment for their failure to convert the native heathens to Christianity and for conducting themselves in a less pious manner than the earlier generation of Calvinist settlers.[6]

In modern times the same mentality is much in evidence. Soon after the September 2001 attacks on the Pentagon and the World Trade Center, resulting in nearly three thousand deaths, the Christian evangelist Jerry Falwell decided (with his TV host Pat Robertson concurring) that the attacks were divine punishment upon America for harboring "the pagans and the abortionists and the feminists and the gays and the lesbians."[7]

The flood that destroyed the poorer neighborhoods of New Orleans in the wake of Hurricane Katrina in 2005 was welcomed by Republican congressman Richard Baker of Baton Rouge as a divine intervention: "We finally cleaned up public housing in New Orleans. We couldn't do it, but God did."[8] In a similar spirit, the mayor of Gulfport, Mississippi, proclaimed, "Property values are going to skyrocket here. All the unattractive stuff has been blown away. . . . God has come in and wiped the slate clean for us."[9]

The Katrina disaster was hailed by Pastor John Hagee (Senator John McCain's erstwhile minister) as punishment for New Orleans' sybaritic ways, including a planned "homosexual parade."[10] But how to explain the tornado in Iowa some years later that brought injury and death to Boy Scouts—noted for their antigay and antiatheist views? Hagee had an answer: while all natural phenomena represent God's "permissible will," he said, it is wrong to think that every natural disaster is the result of sin, for "no man on Earth knows the mind of God." Here is selective perception romping rampant. When God is killing libertines and queens in New Orleans, Hagee can read his divine mind with instant certitude. But when God rubs out superpatriotic Boy Scouts, it's all too mysteriously wondrous and beyond our puny comprehension.[11]

PETITIONING THE GREAT DECISION MAKER

Throughout the ages believers have been urged to place their faith in prayer. A wash of books and articles proclaim that prayer can heal, and religious faith can make people almost invulnerable to disease, as Jesus himself promised.[12] Between 2002 and 2005, the Bush administration spent over $2.3 million on "prayer research."[13] But a number of systematic studies—using randomized, double-blind clinical trials and published in reputable medical journals such as *Lancet, Mayo Clinic Proceedings,* and *Archives of Internal Medicine*—found no efficacy in prayer. In each case hundreds of coronary patients were prayed for but showed no superior survival rate than control groups that went without prayer. Some of these tests were conducted by medical investigators who themselves were enthusiastic about using prayer in conjunction with medical treatment.[14]

In any case, we might wonder why God would save only some of those who were prayed for while letting others die. Why would he be indifferent toward the lonely unfortunates who have no one to pray for them? Does God operate like some political officeholder, responding to only the more persistent lobbyists?

A still more deflating study published in *American Heart Journal* involved three random groups of heart patients: the group that knew it was being prayed for had a significantly *worse* complication rate than the other two, a backfire effect suggesting that patients who hear they are the object of prayer become anxious, expecting the worst, and this affects their health negatively.[15] This finding corroborates an earlier study released by the University of New Mexico, which found that alcoholics in rehab fared *worse* if they knew they were being prayed for.[16]

In any case, the healing power of prayer seems to apply only to those diseases and disabilities that have a potential for *natural* recovery. Nobody entertains the expectation that prayer will enable an amputee to grow a missing limb.[17] Nobody (these days) expects prayer to raise loved ones from the grave, even though Jesus reportedly did so for Lazarus and urged his disciples to emulate this feat.[18] But if prayer activates divine intercession, then why do we not ask an omnipotent god to resurrect loved ones? Or mend into perfect form a mangled body? Or replace a missing eye? Or undo all aging and restore everyone to youthful health and the ability to live vigorously for, say, three hundred years? Or undo a costly disaster that has destroyed many homes and lives? Calling upon supernatural powers through prayer, apparently, cannot achieve anything that does not have the potential to be achieved by natural means.

While prayer may not successfully summon divine intervention, it can sooth and comfort those who pray, thereby providing salutary results in some instances. There is occasional evidence suggesting that visualizations, meditation, meditative breathing exercises, repetitive chanting, and other such practices can have a healing effect on the person who is performing them by calming the mind, relaxing the body, improving circulation and respiration, and even strengthening the immune system in some way. The mind can have a telling effect upon the body, for better or worse, just as the body can have on the mind. But let us not confuse this *mind healing* or *psychic healing* and its limited indeterminate effects with the kind of *faith healing* that is said to come with intervention by a supernatural force exogenous to one's own mind and body, a force that supposedly can heal not only the supplicant but also all others who are being prayed for. The evidence for such accomplishments has yet to blossom.

Finally we must ask, would any deity worth its name really be so flattered by the ritualized devotionals of prayer as to dole out piecemeal cures for this or that person's ailments and adversities? The renowned twelfth-century rabbi Moses Maimonides felt it belittled God to endow him with human attributes. It was wrong to ring the welkin with our pedestrian pleas in hope of enlisting his intercession. God has no particularistic features, according to Maimonides. He reigns in munificent silence, and the reverence paid to him, if not exactly wordless, should never be freighted with mundane entreaties.[19]

The habit of treating fortunate human outcomes as proof of God's direct doings and evidence of the verity of one's own particular religion was criticized by none other than the famed six-

teenth-century essayist Michel de Montaigne. A devout Roman
Catholic and conservative monarchist, Montaigne nevertheless
loathed the cruel religious wars of his day. He disapproved of
those who impudently pretended to discern God's "holy unfath-
omable wisdom" at every juncture. "What I consider wrong is
our usual practice of trying to support and confirm our religion
by the success or happy outcome of our undertakings."[20] It
diminishes the magnitude of God, argued Montaigne, to presume that "heaven's infinity is passionately concerned with our
piddling distinctions."[21] Montaigne not withstanding, piddling
distinctions inflated into soul-saving sacramentals are the stock-
in-trade of many religious paladins.

THE FURIES OF FAITH

God's wonders never work more mysteriously—and deleteri-
ously—than in the propagation of religion itself. Religion is
widely credited with being the great progenitor of moral virtues,
but looking at the actualities of history we cannot help noticing
how frequently religions have served as instruments for promoting intolerance, autocracy, and atrocity. "When religion is
the ruling force in a society," writes James Haught, "it produces
horror. The stronger the supernatural beliefs, the worse the
inhumanity. . . . The 'Age of Faith' was an age of holy slaughter.
When religion gradually ceased to control daily life, the concept
of human rights and personal freedoms took root."[22]

The histories of Christianity and other major religions are
heavily laced with violence and repression. Religionists have
claimed a divine mandate to massacre rival denominations, with
each murder hailed as an act of moral cleansing in God's name.
During Christianity's first five centuries, for instance, far more
Christianists were killed by other Christianists than by the
Romans and their arena lions. Sectarian slaughter continued
through the ages, directed against one or another heresy, often
metastasizing into full-fledged wars as during the Reformation.[23]

In addition, there were the protracted hostilities waged against infidels. In 1099 Christianist crusaders purified the holy city of Jerusalem by slaughtering virtually every Muslim resident, causing one chronicler to rejoice: "Wonderful things were to be seen. Numbers of Saracens were beheaded. . . . Others were shot with arrows or forced to jump from the towers; others were tortured for several days, then burned in flames. In the streets were seen piles of heads and hands and feet. . . . It was a just and marvelous judgment of God." A century later, in the Third Crusade, when Richard the Lion-Hearted massacred the inhabitants of Acre, including women and children, another chronicler exulted, "They were slaughtered every one. For this be the Creator blessed!" With the death of every pagan, St. Bernard of Clairvaux insisted, "Christ himself is glorified."[24]

Nor does it get much better in the modern era. Hindus and Muslims have been murdering each other in India and Kashmir. Islamists and Christianists have attacked and killed each other in Nigeria, Egypt, and the Philippines, and as of 2006–2008 were locked in a full-blown civil war in Sudan. Muslim militants have killed teachers and burned schools in the southern region of Thailand, inviting violent retaliation upon Muslim communities by Buddhist vigilante groups. In a province in Indonesia, a long history of violence between Christianists and Islamists brought thousands of deaths, including the beheading of schoolgirls.[25] Intermittently over the last seven hundred years, the devotees of Christianity and Islam have been butchering each other in Abyssinia and throughout the Horn of Africa. For decades Protestants and Catholics murdered each other in Northern Ireland, and Jews and Muslims have been doing the same in Palestine. Even when religious rivalry is not the sole source of conflict—as when nationalism, imperialism, ethnicity, class, and language differences are mixed in—the furies of faith still bulk large in the bloodletting.

Whether or not fairly, Muslim extremists have been designated the most ferociously fanatical of religious killers. In Iraq, in the aftermath of the US invasion, Muslims engaged in protracted sectarian warfare against other Muslims, causing tens of thousands of deaths. And Muslims have slain nonbelievers in Egypt, Iraq, Iran, Afghanistan, Algeria, Palestine, and elsewhere.

In 1955, backed by the shah's army, Muslim militants launched a storm of murder, rape, and pillage in Iran against the defenseless Baha'i minority, a heretical offshoot of a branch of Muslim Shiites. The bloodletting resumed in the 1980s, with torture and executions inflicted upon many of Iran's 300,000 Baha'is, including women and teenage girls. As a chief Muslim judge explained, "The Iranian nation has determined to establish the government of God on Earth. Therefore, it cannot tolerate the perverted Baha'is, who are instruments of Satan and followers of the devil and of the superpowers."[26]

In 2007, the Yazidi, a religious sect situated in northern Iraq, were the object of repeated attacks by Muslim Kurds. When a Yazidi woman eloped with a Muslim man and converted to Islam, her family stoned her to death in order to "restore the family's honor." Mobs of Sunni Kurds used this incident to massacre scores of Yazidi. A month later, a Muslim woman was discovered associating with two Yazidi men, again inciting Sunni Kurds to attack Yazidi homes and businesses and destroy innocent lives. Then in August 2007, more than seven hundred Yazidi were annihilated by five synchronized truck bombings in what proved to be the worst massacre of the Iraq war.[27]

The Yazidi are neither Christian nor Muslim. They speak a variant of Kurdish and follow a set of beliefs that predate Islam. They are hated in part because they worship as a divinity the chief archangel, Peacock Angel (Melek Taus), otherwise known to the Muslims as Lucifer or Satan.

Muslims are sometimes the victims rather than the victimizers in the endless bloodletting perpetrated by those who say their hearts are filled with God's love. In 2002, for instance, the city of Ahmedabad in India was torn apart as gangs of Hindu zealots rampaged through Muslim neighborhoods, setting shops ablaze and slaughtering terrified people. By the time the butchery was over, perhaps as many as two thousand lay dead in one of the most calamitous religious pogroms in India since its independence in 1947. Entire families of Muslims were incinerated in their abodes by crowds of cheering armed Hindu extremists. Women were gang-raped and set afire. Children were hacked to death in front of their parents, who then met the same fate. Evidence suggests that the attacks did not just burst forth in a spontaneous fit. There was planning by the perpetrators with collaboration by police.[28]

Within the United States over the last two decades there have been violent and even homicidal incidents involving fundamentalist "soldiers of Christ" who have bombed or otherwise attacked hundreds of abortion clinics, killing several clinical workers and doctors, while injuring dozens more, including clients and visitors. Associated with a movement calling itself Christian Identity, Timothy McVeigh killed 168 innocent people in the Oklahoma City terrorist bombing of 1995. McVeigh went to his execution firmly believing that he had struck a blow against Jews, liberals, nonbelievers, and all those who supposedly had dislodged white Christian America from its spiritual moorings.[29]

Violence and death have never been far from religious ethos, promoted by those who believe they are carrying out their deity's mandate. It is perhaps forgivable, then, that many thinking persons are disinclined to praise the Lord for his wonders to behold.

7

JIFFY CREATION, DUBIOUS DESIGN

> That point of imperfection which we occupy—is
> it on the way *up* or *down*?
>
> —RALPH WALDO EMERSON

What is called "creationism" is the belief that in six days the Judeo-Christian deity created the universe and all the earthly species, including humans in finished form much as they exist today. For centuries this view prevailed throughout the Western world. Even after evolutionary science had emerged in the latter half of the nineteenth century, the scenario sketched in Genesis remained the only acceptable one for most of Christendom.

DINOSAURS FOR GENESIS

By the early twentieth century, Darwinian science enjoyed a more receptive hearing in US scientific and academic communities but not in the more homespun regions of the country. Even after the famous Scopes "monkey trial" of 1925, prohibitions against the teaching of evolution prevailed especially in that region known as the Bible Belt, the rural and small-town areas of the American South and Midwest. During the 1940s and 1950s conservative Christian publishers sold over a hundred thousand copies of books that denounced evolution and trumpeted Genesis. In 1965, forty years after Scopes, a school teacher in Tennessee lost his job for reportedly saying to students that the Bible was a collection of fairy tales. The 1980s and 1990s witnessed a resurgence of creationism teachings in various states. Reactionary religionists demanded that the subject of evolution be labeled as just a speculative theory with many factual gaps, and that creationism be taught alongside it or in its stead.[1]

Rather than riding regnant, modern evolutionary science seems to be barely hanging on in the arena of public opinion. A May 2007 Gallup Poll reported only 49 percent of the US public accepted evolution. Another survey found 42 percent of Americans held strict creationist views. Various school districts throughout the country have experienced furious dustups over the teaching of evolution.[2]

In 2005 a Museum of Earth History opened in Arkansas. It assured visitors that "dinosaurs and humans did co-exist." Creation museums in California and Kentucky pushed the same theme, with displays of mechanical juvenile Tyrannosaurus rexes cavorting among animatronic children clad in buckskin. One creationist asserted that Noah's ark is mistakenly represented as no bigger than a ferryboat when in fact it was "many times larger than the Titanic" and therefore able to house all the earth's species including dinosaurs, though most likely "baby dinosaurs." After Noah's ark ran aground in central Asia, some creationists explain, the surviving animals repopulated the other continents by floating across the oceans on the "billions of trees" uprooted by the Great Deluge.[3]

Of late there has emerged a more refined offshoot of creationism called *intelligent design* (ID). It argues that living organisms, being so splendidly constructed and irreducibly complex, could not have evolved haphazardly over the eons from more primitive forms but were precisely created in one fell swoop by a higher intelligence. In their assault on evolution, the creationists and ID protagonists summon an urgent refrain. To quote a statement by an anti-Darwinian school board in Dover, Pennsylvania:

> Darwin's Theory is [just] a theory. . . . The Theory is not a fact. Gaps exist in the Theory for which there is no evidence. . . . Intelligent Design is an explanation of the origin of life that differs from Darwin's view. . . . Students are encouraged to keep an open mind.[4]

Pope John Paul II allowed that modern research "leads to the recognition of the theory of evolution as more than a hypothesis."[5] But in 2007, his successor, Pope Benedict XVI, announced that "the theory of evolution is not a complete, scientifically proven theory." It can never be fully verified or disproved, and it "covers over its own gaps and does not want to see the questions that reach beyond the methodological possibilities of natural science."[6]

Out of step was the Vatican's chief astronomer, Rev. George Coyne, an American Jesuit, who stated that intelligent design "isn't science even though it pretends to be. If you want to teach it in schools, intelligent design should be taught when religion or cultural history is taught, not science." Shortly after such utterances, Father Coyne was removed as director of the Vatican Observatory by Pope Benedict.[7]

Benedict and the creationists almost have a point. There certainly are "gaps" in an evolutionary theory that is neither fixed nor final. But the same holds true of all scientific theories, be they in nutritional science, meteorology, astronomy, biology, geology, or physics. Science frequently produces theories that contain unanswered questions and invite varying interpretations.

SCIENTISTIC ARROGANCE VS. IMPERFECT SCIENCE

There are those who treat science itself as a sacred cow, seeing it as the alpha and omega of all human understanding. This is known as *scientism*, the belief that truth can be found only within the confines of conventionally recognized scientific opinion and methodology. Scientism relegates philosophy, the arts, aesthetics, and most other areas of human thought to a secondary status of subjective impression.

The *scientistic* thinker usually relies more on scientific *convention* than on scientific investigation. Recall how the best scientific minds of Europe's Enlightenment ridiculed the simple-minded peasants for reporting that rocks fell from the sky as they toiled in the fields. It was all just too improbable to be treated seriously—until enterprising individuals, remembering what science was really supposed to be, investigated and discovered fallen meteorites. The rigid scientistic nonbeliever, who already knows it all, seems like the mirror image of the rigid religious believer.

Truth be told, there are no fixed and final laws of science. Many scientific mavens do not even like the term *law*, preferring to speak of scientific *theories*. For it is in the nature of science—when practiced at its best—to keep everything accessible for further investigation and conceptualization. Triumphant scientific breakthroughs often open up additional areas of inquiry and puzzlement.

Be this as it may, an established body of science is not something to be dismissed out of hand just because it harbors unanswered questions. That a scientific theory is incomplete does not give us license to ignore all the evidence it has accumulated. The data provided by paleontology, geology, molecular biology, and other fields betoken a strong case for evolution and have yet to be explained away by the intelligent designers.

By its very nature, life depends on adaptability. This means that change, complexity, and development are inevitable components of the natural world. Not all organisms reproduce with uniform success. Reproductive capacity arises directly from how well creatures (including humans) are able to compete for resources, both against other species and against other members of the same species—and against conditions presented by the natural elements themselves. Competition is not the whole story. Cooperation within species—and symbiotic interaction between species—can induce evolvement. Given this infinitude of interactive forces, it would seem improbable for evolution not to be happening.

Indeed evolution continues before our very eyes as demonstrated by the recently discovered ways that viruses and other microbes acquire new traits and evolve into more virulent strains, sometimes in a matter of days.[8] Evolutionary theory explains the dramatic adaptability of viruses and bacteria; the Bible does not, nor do the intelligent designers.

MORE THAN SPECULATION

There is something else to be said about scientific theory. When intelligent designers insist that evolution is a *theory* and not a *fact*, they are juxtaposing theory and fact as two mutually exclusive and competitive concepts. This is a view commonly held by laypersons who know nothing about science, who assume that there are "hard facts" on the one hand and airy theories facilely spun out of one's head on the other. So we are admonished to stop "theorizing," to stop devising abstract speculations that by definition are more fanciful than factual.[9]

In both the natural and the social sciences, however, theory is something more than mere speculation. Theory is the generalizable distillation of empirical investigation, the *payoff* that comes from gathering and connecting a heap of pertinent facts. It takes facts to build a scientific theory, and it takes a theory to organize and make sense of the facts. Theories are valued for their explanatory power. A developed and confirmed theory is what science aims for. It is the gold standard of scientific inquiry. The theory of gravity and the theory of relativity are not lacking in facts just because they are theories. To dismiss something as *just* a theory and therefore not factual does not make sense from a scientific point of view. Theory is not all that "soft" and, for that matter, facts are sometimes not all that "hard" or firmly fixed.

Since scientific theories in all fields contain some unanswered questions, why is evolution singled out by the intelligent designers as the one gap-ridden speculative theory? The answer is glaringly evident: evolution is in direct collision with Genesis. If evolution is true, then the Bible's description of how God fashioned the world in six days and created humans in their present form seems much the fairy tale. And if Genesis is a fairy tale, then of what validity is the remainder of the divinely dictated tome that serves as the unerring fundament of Judaic-Christian belief?

The response offered by the scientific defenders of evolution is predictable and somewhat incomplete: "We have no way of testing and demonstrating the truth or falsity of non-natural spirit forces that are presumed to be acting in nature."[10] It would be nice if someday someone would add, "and neither do the intelligent designers." That is the real problem. Of course, scientists cannot move outside their fundamental paradigm and demonstrate divine causation, but neither can their creationist critics.

This is a crucial point because the burden of proof for intelligent design is on the designers. Where is their field work, their laboratory experiments, their observational reports and accumulated evidence measuring the effects of ID vectors on various natural forces and entities, all the things we would expect from a scientific inquiry interested in "hard facts"? This is the problem with teaching ID: What would you actually teach? How could you judge the reliability of what you teach? How do we determine what is or isn't evidentiary if one can postulate a priori an unseen supreme designer lurking behind everything? In the two decades since ID has emerged, it has generated no important experiments or insights into biology and has come to look less and less like a science and more and more like an extended polemic.[11]

Advocates of ID seem unaware of their own scientific illiteracy. One of them asserts that there is no evidence of a protracted evolution because "all the vertebrate groups, from fish to mammals appear [in the fossil record] at one time." Not true, British writer George Monbiot reminds us. The first fish fossils and the first mammal fossils are separated from each other by some 300 million years.[12]

ID proponents make much of the human eye. Given the intricacy and the delicate precision that enables it to perform its marvelous function, and "the purposeful arrangement of parts," the eye could never have developed from hit-and-miss mutation and natural selection, the argument goes.[13] If evolution were true, there would be fossils of particular animals without vision and others with varying degrees of eye development strung out across the ages, but "such fossils do not exist," the designers maintain. Such fossils *do* exist, Monbiot points out; the fossil record does indeed stretch across the ages with countless eyes "in all stages of development."[14]

Its proponents insist that ID is not religiously anchored; it requires neither miracles nor a creator. They avoid mention of the six-day jiffy creation and other biblical narratives. But if ID is not supernatural, then how does it act as a universalistic template for the natural sphere? Whence in this imperfect, unfinished world comes intelligent design's perfect and finished creative powers?

A divine designer that is reflected in nature yet transcends ordinary materiality and is antecedent to nature's laws is nothing less than "a supernatural designer."[15] We are back to Hegel's *Weltgeist*, which I find to be an inviting concept but one that cannot replace materialist science because it is outside the realm of that science—as is any spirit force.

The proponents of ID are centered at the Discovery Institute, a conservative think tank in Seattle funded by wealthy media mogul Philip Anschutz. They revealed their religiously motivated hand in their strikingly candid, in-house document, "The Wedge Strategy," written in 1999 and eventually leaked to the public. It states that the ultimate goal of intelligent design is "nothing less than the overthrow of materialism and its cultural legacies," replacing scientific materialism "with the theistic understanding that nature and human beings are created by God." The authors of "The Wedge Strategy" blame materialistic science for most of the world's evils. They accuse materialistic reformers of trying to "engineer the perfect society through the application of scientific knowledge," using "coercive government programs that falsely promised to create heaven on earth."[16] In sum, ID is neither a science nor a field of study; it is a refined fundamentalist preachment in service to an ultraconservative politico-economic agenda.

As for the creationists, it is not that they have questions about particular aspects of evolution, as might we all. Rather, they deny that it ever happened. They appear to be championing free speech and diversity of ideas when they urge that students be taught more than just Darwinism. Indeed, Darwin's theory of natural selection always struck me as a central but still limited explanation for evolution. However, the designers themselves are not interested in a pluralism of views. They do not want to supplement evolutionary theory; they want to replace it. Thus in 1999, while controlling the Kansas state board of education, they removed nearly all references to evolution from the curriculum. Such references were restored only after voters ousted the creationist bloc in 2001.

There are as many stories of how the world began and how it is held together as there are tribal mythologies and tales. The creationists believe in only the Genesis narrative, the one they would accord exclusive standing in school and society.

A DESIGN LESS THAN IMPRESSIVE

If the present world is intelligent design's finished work, why does so much of it look like *un*intelligent design? As noted earlier, the divine creator is an underachiever. When it comes to design he appears to be downright incompetent. Let us begin with the human body, whose physiology and morphology are often hailed as living proof of God's wondrous creation. Closer examination reveals that we are designed as quadrupeds but tipped upward to walk around on only two legs, with a spinal curvature that only partly compensates for the vertical pressure. "Perhaps," writes theologian Lisa Fullam, "the God of intelligent design has a special place in his plan for chiropractors."[17]

And what of the knee? Fullam asks. A simple hinge joint that sustains enormous stress, held together only by ligaments, a slipshod job destined to cause trouble even for many who are not athletes. To get more personal, consider mammalian testicles that dangle one's genetic legacy precariously outside the torso in a thin-skinned scrotum—all because sperm cells need to be kept cooler than the rest of the body. "Surely an intelligent designer could have figured out a way for testicles to work at body temperature, as ovaries do."[18]

Our prenatal development also testifies to the incompetence of the Great Designer. In the embryonic stage we sport gill sacs, tails, and a coat of apelike hair. Fortunately, most of us discard these charming accessories before birth. This bizarre ontogenetic recapitulation of the phylogenetic is readily interpreted in evolutionary terms but not readily understood if it is a product of intelligent design.[19] Another poorly rigged construction is the male urinary tract, which runs directly through the prostate gland. The prostate tends to expand with age, putting a squeeze on the urination process. This arrangement has failed to win the awe and admiration of older men.

Even more serious is the deficient design of the female pelvis, which causes hundreds of thousands of pregnant women around the world to suffer obstructed labor, resulting in obstetric ruptures that can lead to permanent incontinence, damage to the infant, or in some cases death for mother or child. Should we not also mention the erupting hemorrhoids, postpartum depression, and other emotionally challenging hormonal imbalances that childbirth can deliver.

Then there is the slipshod bottleneck that jams the human digestive and respiratory systems together around the pharynx, sending thousands of children and adults to the emergency room each year, some choking to death or suffering other injuries when food "goes down the wrong pipe."[20]

Speaking of bottlenecks, look again at the body's lower region and note how the eliminative and reproductive functions are crowded atop each other. Male ejaculation and urination pass through narrow lines within the same appendage. And inches away, in case you haven't noticed, on both men and women there lurks the anus. As the joke goes, God must be a civil engineer, for who else would situate a major waste disposal system adjacent to a prime recreational site?

And who designed that tormented morass known as our emotional and psychological makeup? How would we even begin to hardwire a more serviceable psyche so that it might be less typically human yet more humane?

Moving away from *Homo sapiens*, we might wonder if the wider world is designed any better. God seems to have an overmuch fondness for vermin, fleas, mosquitoes, ticks, rodents, and lethal viruses, not to mention storms, tornadoes, earthquakes, tidal waves, and other impressively designed disasters. Darwin himself was not impressed by what he uncovered. He complained of "the clumsy, wasteful, blundering, low and horridly cruel works of Nature." On another occasion he remarked, "I cannot persuade myself that a benevolent and omnipotent God would have designedly created the Ichneumonidae [parasitic wasps] with the express intention of their feeding within the living bodies of caterpillars."[21] On the world's design, I leave Sam Harris with the last word:

When we look at the natural world, we see extraordinary complexity, but we do not see optimal design. We see redundancy, regressions, and unnecessary complications; we see bewildering inefficiencies that result in suffering and death. We see flightless birds and snakes with pelvises. We see species of fish, salamanders, and crustaceans that have no functional eyes because they continued to evolve in darkness for millions of years. We see whales that produce teeth during fetal development, only to reabsorb them as adults. Such features of our world are utterly mysterious if God created all species of life on earth "intelligently"; none of them are perplexing in light of evolution.[22]

PART III

WHEN THE ETHEREAL BECOMES MATERIAL

8

MOTHER TERESA, JOHN PAUL, AND THE FAST-TRACK SAINTS

Saints are dead sinners, revised and edited.

—AMBROSE BIERCE

During his twenty-six-year papacy, Pope John Paul II elevated 483 individuals to sainthood, more saints than any previous pope. Just as he packed the College of Cardinals with ultraconservatives, so did he attempt to populate heaven's pantheon itself.

MUST WE ADORE HER?

One personage John Paul beatified but did not live long enough to canonize was Mother Teresa, the media-hyped Roman Catholic nun of Albanian origin who was courted by the world's rich and famous and showered with kudos for her "humanitarian work" with the poor. What usually went unreported were the vast sums she received from sometimes tainted sources, including a million dollars from convicted Wall Street swindler Charles Keating, on whose behalf she sent a personal plea for clemency to the presiding judge. When asked by the prosecutor to return Keating's gift because it was money he had stolen from small investors and depositors, she never did.[1] Teresa also accepted rich offerings from a Duvalier dictatorship whose wealth was siphoned from the Haitian public treasury.[2]

Her "homes" for the indigent in India and elsewhere, usually described in the media as "hospitals" and "clinics," were actually hospices in which seriously ill indigents were afforded a place to die.[3] One young doctor, Marcus Fernandes, was taken aback by the substandard conditions. He pointed out that many of the inmates were not dying from fatal diseases but suffering from malnutrition and could be saved if fed a modestly improved diet that included vitamin supplements. But he could not persuade Teresa, who showed no interest in medicine or in treating patients with vitamins. Dr. Fernandes also unhappily discovered that expensive medical equipment donated to Teresa was left to rust, completely unused.[4]

A disillusioned British volunteer at Teresa's Calcutta center concluded that the "standard of health care was atrocious." Jack Preger, a Catholic doctor who had worked with Teresa, reported that "needles for injections are simply rinsed in cold water after use and passed from one patient to the next. And patients with TB are not isolated, despite the highly contagious nature of the disease."[5] Wendy Bainbridge, a British nursing nun who had worked at mainstream hospices, was stunned by the squalor and lack of minimal amenities at Teresa's establishment. There were no aids to mobility, no toilet paper. "The toilet was an open gutter running behind the washroom and waste was washed away with a bucket of water."[6]

Dr. Robin Fox, later the editor of the prestigious medical journal the *Lancet*, wrote a sharp criticism of the medical practices at Teresa's Home for the Dying in Calcutta. He complained that suffering inmates were denied strong analgesics. Nuns and volunteers lacked basic tests to distinguish the curable from the incurable. Their lack of medical training encouraged potentially fatal errors. They failed to provide minimum comforts and did little pain management. They sometimes overmedicated to a dangerous level while missing opportunities to offer simple but effective treatments.[7]

Other visitors testified that Teresa's hospices were "unsafe" and provided "neither proper nursing nor loving compassion." Suggestions for improvement regularly went unheeded by Teresa. When one of her nuns was asked, "What do you do for [patients'] pain?" she replied, "We pray for them."[8]

On one occasion, when staff members asked Teresa to try saving a teenager on the verge of death, she blessed the boy and said, "Never mind, it's a lovely day to go to Heaven."[9] One young volunteer recalls that on the infrequent occasions when surgery actually was performed at the hospice, anesthesia was not provided, it being considered too costly. Instead attendants told patients, "Pain is Christ kissing you."[10]

When tending to her own ailments, however, Teresa preferred anesthetics over Christ's kisses. She checked into some of the costliest hospitals and recovery care units in the world for state-of-the-art treatment, including angioplasties, CT scans, pacemaker implants, a personally designed spinal brace, and lifesaving heart surgery.[11]

When a Union Carbide plant spewed lethal pesticides over Bhopal, India, in what was history's worst industrial accident, killing over twenty thousand (at last count) and seriously injuring an additional hundred thousand, Teresa made a brief media-saturated appearance, walking among those who suffered agonizing burns in their eyes and lungs, saying "forgive, forgive." The luckless victims and their families were being asked to harbor no ill feeling toward the criminally negligent corporation. Teresa then swiftly departed Bhopal, never sending in her order, the Missionaries of Charity, to assist.[12]

Teresa journeyed the globe to wage campaigns against divorce, abortion, and birth control. When visiting Egypt she urged housewives to "have lots and lots of children"—at a time when the Egyptian government was trying to promote family planning to counter the nation's population explosion. On numerous occasions she said she would never allow families that practiced contraception to adopt any children from her orphanages.[13] At her Nobel award ceremony in 1979, she announced that "the greatest destroyer of peace is abortion." And she once suggested that AIDS might be a just retribution for improper sexual conduct.[14]

Her concern for the unborn child was matched only by an indifference toward the living child. What social conditions caused hundreds of thousands of children to die of malnutrition and disease in Asia and elsewhere was a question that failed to win her attention.

BENDING THE BOOKS

Teresa gave no accounting of the many millions of dollars she gathered from donations across the world. One nun who handled funds in New York estimated that there must have been $50 million in one Manhattan bank account alone. Additional bank deposits were reportedly kept in London and the Vatican. The bulk of her money was believed not to be in India because Indian law required auditing of accounts.[15]

In 1993 the Co-Workers, an organization of lay helpers who raised substantial sums for her, were required as a registered charity in the United Kingdom to produce accounts of their finances. Teresa suddenly and swiftly closed down the entire organization and announced that all future donations were to be funneled directly to her Missionaries of Charity. This decision, she assured everyone, reflected "the will of God for the Co-Workers."[16]

Teresa produced a continual flow of promotional misinformation about herself. She claimed that her mission in Calcutta fed over a thousand people daily. On other occasions she jumped the number to four thousand, seven thousand, and nine thousand. Actually her soup kitchens fed not more than a hundred and fifty people, six days a week. She said her school in the Calcutta slum contained five thousand children when actually it enrolled fewer than one hundred.

As one of her devotees explained, "Mother Teresa is among those who least worry about statistics. She has repeatedly expressed that what matters is not how much work is accomplished but how much love is put into the work."[17] Was Teresa really unworried about statistics? Quite the contrary, she consistently produced numbers that inflated her accomplishments. All her statistical "errors" went in a direction favorable to her.

Teresa claimed to have 102 family assistance and nutritional centers in India, but longtime Calcutta resident Aroup Chatterjee, who did a highly critical investigation of her mission, could not find a single such center. Rather than building new hospitals, orphanages, and schools, or upgrading the ones she had, Teresa spent many millions on convents all over the world and on training priests for missionary work. According to Chatterjee, shiploads of clothing and food donated to Teresa from abroad were often expropriated by the nuns and their families in India or sold off to local merchants for income rather than distributed to the needy.[18]

Over the years there were numerous floods and cholera epidemics in or near Calcutta, with thousands perishing. Various relief agencies responded to these disasters, but Teresa and her Missionaries of Charity were nowhere in sight except briefly on one occasion.[19]

When someone asked Teresa how people without money or power can make the world a better place, she replied, "They should smile more." She herself was rarely seen smiling. During a press conference in Washington, DC, when asked, "Do you teach the poor to endure their lot?" she indicated that poverty was a soul-cleansing experience for the poor: "I think it is very beautiful for the poor to accept their lot, to share it with the passion [suffering] of Christ. I think the world is being much helped by the suffering of the poor people."[20]

Mother Teresa is a paramount example of a "saint" who supposedly assisted the poor but *without ever bothering to ask why they were forced to live as they do*. She caressed poverty rather than opposed it. The poor were her pets and her props.

She uttered not a critical word against social injustice or against those in power. One of her former nuns describes her as "colluding with wealth."[21]

Teresa spent as much as eight months a year traveling abroad, quartering at luxurious accommodations in Europe and the United States, jetting from Rome to London to New York in private planes.[22] While counseling victims to suffer patiently, she herself was known to have been impatient and unforgiving with her staff over petty matters. The two times I saw her on television, she sounded more like a crabby scold than a loving saint.

When Teresa died in 1997, the denizens of Calcutta did not turn out in any visible numbers to attend her funeral. Her burial procession rolled through empty streets. The impoverished population apparently felt they owed her nothing and most had never even heard of her.

After Teresa's demise Pope John Paul II waived the five-year waiting period usually observed before beginning the beatification process leading to sainthood. The five-year delay is intended to ensure a sober evaluation, after which any claims made on behalf of a candidate are subjected to critical challenge by an *advocatus diaboli*, a "devil's advocate." John Paul brushed aside this entire procedure. In 2003, in record time Teresa was beatified, the final step before canonization.

A few years later, her canonization hit a bump in the firmament when it was disclosed by Catholic authorities who investigated Teresa's diaries that she had been continually racked with disbelief: "I feel that God does not want me, that God is not God and that he does not really exist," she wrote. "People think my faith, my hope and my love are overflowing and that my intimacy with God will fill my heart. If only they knew." She goes on: "Heaven means nothing" and "I am told God loves me—and yet the reality of darkness and coldness and emptiness is so great that nothing touches my soul. . . . I have no Faith." Rome's popular daily newspaper, *Il Messaggero*, commented: "The real Mother Teresa was one who for one year had visions and who for the next fifty had doubts—up until her death."[23]

OTHER FAST-TRACK SAINTS

An earlier example of a fast track to sainthood occurred in 1992 when John Paul II swiftly beatified the reactionary Msgr. José María Escrivá de Balaguer, supporter of fascist regimes in Spain and elsewhere, and founder of Opus Dei, a powerful secretive reactionary movement "feared by many as a sinister sect within the Catholic Church."[24] Escrivá's beatification came only seventeen years after his death, a record fast-track run until Mother Teresa came along. In accordance with his own political agenda, the pope used a church institution, sainthood, to bestow special sanctity upon right-wingers such as Escrivá and Teresa.

Among the many reactionaries whom John Paul set up for sainthood was Pius IX, who reigned as pontiff from 1846 to 1878 and who referred to Jews as "dogs." John Paul also beatified Cardinal Aloysius Stepinac, the leading Croatian cleric who welcomed the Nazi and fascist Ustashi takeover of Croatia during World War II. Stepinac associated with top-ranking Nazis and unswervingly supported the Croatian fascist regime that exterminated hundreds of thousands of Serbs, Jews, and Romanys.[25]

Of the scoundrels whom John Paul canonized, mention should be made of Padre Pio, who died in 1968. In 1947, when John Paul was Father Karol Wojtyla (an obscure young priest), he had Padre Pio as his confessor on at least one occasion. Wojtyla went through much of his life convinced that Pio was a special agent of God's will. Pio certainly was a genius at self-promotion and today is a widely celebrated saint. He claimed a capacity to be in two places at the same time, although he never allowed that feat to be put to the test. By his own account he telepathically turned away an American bomber squadron that was intent upon destroying San Giovanni during World War II; and he engaged in knockdown wrestling bouts with the devil himself, who never succeeded in getting the better of Padre Pio.

Pio also said he had Jesus' crucifixion stigmata, nail holes in his hands and feet and a lance wound in his side. Given that his body and feet were hidden under his monk's robe and that he wore gloves at all times, no one ever saw the wounds. Nor did he permit medical examination of the stigmata, which he claimed bled continuously for fifty years, most profusely on Fridays. An examination of his body after his death revealed no trace of stigmata. His followers immediately claimed his wounds must have been miraculously healed.[26]

Confronted with all these wonders, John Paul joyfully canonized Pio in 2002. There were other things about Pio that the pope admired. The monk readily attacked liberals who advocated social betterment for the poor and understanding for women who had abortions. John Paul long urged priests to accept Pio as their role model. But not every pope had been convinced of Pio's saintliness. From 1931 to 1933, the Vatican banned the monk from hearing confessions and from all contact with worshipers. Pope John XXIII, elected in 1958, put him under surveillance. Pio was twice suspended and then reinstated on charges of faking mystical powers and engaging in sexual misconduct with women in the confessional.[27]

In John Paul's celestial pantheon, reactionary rapscallions had a better chance at canonization than compassionate reformers. Consider his treatment of Archbishop Oscar Romero, who spoke against the injustices suffered by the impoverished populace of El Salvador and for this was assassinated by a right-wing death squad. Romero was thought by many poor Salvadorans to be something of a saint, but John Paul attempted to ban any discussion of his beatification for fifty years. Popular pressure from El Salvador caused the Vatican to cut the delay to twenty-five years.[28] In any case, Romero was consigned to the slow track.

Continuing John Paul's policy of packing the sainthood roster with ultraconservatives, Pope Benedict XVI beatified 498 "martyrs," the largest beatification ceremony in church history, consisting almost entirely of priests and nuns killed in Spain during the 1936–39 civil war. All these newly anointed had actively supported Franco's fascist Falangists, in many cases helping to single out and round up Republican supporters for execution.[29] Benedict's action was viewed by many as a move against the liberal Spanish government that was waging a campaign to expose the atrocities of the Franco regime and pay reparations to Franco's victims.[30]

The beatification ceremony for the 498 clergy drew protests in Rome from socialist Italian youth groups who argued that those "who have killed, tortured and exploited cannot be beatified." The demonstrators were physically assaulted by members of the reactionary Opus Dei, who sang praises to Spain's former fascist dictatorship.[31]

One exceptional and genuinely laudable beatification by the Vatican was of Franz Jagerstatter, a devout Catholic who was beheaded by the Nazis in 1943 for refusing to fight in their war. The Roman Church even admits that Jagerstatter had not enjoyed the support of his priest and bishop in his heroic decision.[32]

COMING SOON: ST. JOHN PAUL II

In 2005, Benedict waived the five-year waiting period in order to put the recently deceased John Paul himself on a fast track to canonization, running neck and neck with Teresa. Reports of possible miracles attributed to him arose almost immediately. One such account came from Cardinal Francesco Marchisano, who, when lunching with the pope some years ago, indicated that because of an ailment he could not use his voice. John Paul "caressed my throat, like a brother, like the father that he was. After that I did seven months of therapy, and I was able to speak again." Marchisano thinks that the pope might have had a hand in his cure: "It could be," he said.[33] *Un miracolo! Viva il papa!*

9

CASHING IN ON HEAVEN

The silver is mine, and the gold is mine, saith the Lord of hosts.

—HAGGAI 2:8

Ideas can affect history when used by people to define reality and inspire social action. Ideas have an important feedback upon the very conditions that give birth to them. They acquire a material force when they trigger sentiments and galvanize minds. But adherents of *philosophical materialism* would argue that ideas do not arise of their own accord as disembodied self-generating entities divorced from human transmission and artifice.

Most religious believers reject this view. They hold that there do exist certain purely ideational forces, such as spirituality, the will of God, and the devil's machinations, and these act—independently of human imagination—directly from the ethereal realm onto the material world. As a famed philosophical materialist once remarked: For such believers "the products of the human brain appear as autonomous figures endowed with a life of their own."[1] The faithful accredit a heavenly origin to many of their own subjective thoughts, or a satanic origin if the mental images are experienced as iniquitous.

99

TURNING TO GOD IN THEIR TIME OF GREED

Aside from philosophical materialism, in more common parlance, the word "materialism" refers to consumerism and material acquisition, what has been variously called *acquisitive materialism* and *consumer materialism*. Many religious leaders who oppose philosophical materialism are heavily involved in the acquisitive variety. To their followers they preach "pie in the sky, bye and bye" while themselves living high off the hog here and now.

There are the televangelists who preside over lucrative megachurches and TV ministries, and who are often implicated in dubious financial finagling. Charges regarding monetary malfeasance have surfaced involving the Christian Anti-Communism Crusade, Rev. Billy Graham's Evangelistic Association, Reverend Moon's Unification Church, Children of God, the Universal Life Church, and various televangelists such as Jim and Tammy Bakker, Oral Roberts, and Jerry Falwell. In 1987 Falwell was charged with illegally transferring $6.7 million intended for his religious ministries to his political action committees, without the knowledge of contributors. He was found guilty and fined only $6,000.[2]

Billy Graham, a friend of presidents, who officiated at any number of nation-worshiping events, was asked to explain how his organization had accumulated a $23 million fund that most of his followers had not heard about. He never did explain.[3]

On one occasion, television preacher and self-proclaimed faith healer Oral Roberts said the Almighty would take his life unless his supporters came up with $8.3 million for "missionary scholarships." It seems God is a homicidal extortionist. In truth, Roberts did not need the money for scholarships, but to rescue his faltering financial empire. It was not God who was after him; it was the bankers.[4] In one television appearance Roberts claimed the *devil* was hunting him down: "When the money [viewer contributions] stopped coming in, Satan appeared." His wife, who was sharing the program with him, chimed in smartly: "Yes, but I said to Satan: 'You just get yourself away from my husband, Satan. Go on away.' And Satan, he ran away." The image of this plucky little lady, possibly with rolling pin in hand, routing the Prince of Darkness, moved the credulous audience to brainless applause.

Almost twenty years later, Oral Roberts's son, Richard, resigned as president of Oral Roberts University amid accusations of lavish personal spending of donors' funds and illegal involvement in a political campaign. Richard said he quit "because God insisted."[5]

There was the widely publicized case of Jim Bakker, who was charged with having illegally diverted millions of dollars from his telecasting ministry for his own personal use. He was convicted on twenty-four counts of fraud and conspiracy, and sentenced to eighteen years in prison, but served less than four.[6]

A notable case involved Ralph Reed, former director of the Christian Coalition and leader of the antiabortion campaign known as "Operation Rescue." Reed engaged in a multimillion-dollar swindling of Native American Indian casino operators that reaped him a huge payoff distributed through a dummy foundation.[7]

Rapacity exists at the parish level too. In Pittsburgh for many years, a Catholic priest skimmed at least $1.5 million from church donations.[8] The state of Illinois charged an evangelical Protestant bishop with diverting to his personal use $468,000 in state grants intended for care of the sick. A Baptist minister in Indiana used a $445,000 federal grant slated for a women's shelter to buy rental properties from which he profited handsomely. And a federal program in Washington, DC, was suspended because the religious group administering it was using it for realty speculations.[9]

Msgr. John Woolsey was convicted of stealing more than $800,000 from a Catholic church in New York City and using the money to pay for his vacations and luxury items. That same year, a Protestant minister from Charlotte, North Carolina, was charged with five counts of tax evasion involving hundreds of thousands of dollars.[10] In 2007 a Catholic priest in Darien, Connecticut, pleaded guilty to federal charges of defrauding his parishioners of at least $1.4 million, which he spent on parties, jewelry, and an ocean-view condominium.[11] Two priests in Delray Beach, Florida, were accused of stealing more than $8.6 million by skimming weekly church collections for years. They spent the money on luxury condominiums, girlfriends, travel, and other indulgences.[12]

A survey by Villanova University researchers found that 85 percent of Roman Church dioceses in the United States had been hit by embezzlements during the 2001–2006 period, some of them for more than $500,000. Only a small number of dioceses conducted internal audits of parishes.[13]

Protestant leaders of Overlake Christian Church in Redmond, Washington, admitted that they used disaster relief donations to cover their salaries and "personal expenses."[14] Protestant pastors in Ripon, California; Eugene, Oregon; and Cold Spring, Ohio, were caught spending large amounts of church funds on themselves and their gambling habits.[15] Protestant clergy in Illinois, California, and Florida were caught stealing what totaled to almost $8 million from their churches, to be spent on luxury homes, cars, jewelry, and girlfriends.[16] A preacher in Ohio was charged with defrauding the state of $2.2 million by running a charter school in which students sometimes went without heat or lunch and teachers sometimes without pay.[17]

On a still grander scale, both the president and the chief counsel of the Baptist Foundation of Arizona were convicted of defrauding eleven thousand investors, many of them congregants, of $585 million. They were ordered to pay only $159 million in restitution.[18]

One study found that religion-related investment fraud in the United States is increasing, with *billions* of dollars stolen in recent years. Devoted congregants are lured into investing their money in a variety of church-sponsored fraudulent business ventures. It is hard for many parishioners to believe that their clergy are swindling them out of their life savings. Law enforcement authorities often find victims to be in denial and unwilling to cooperate with investigators.[19]

The above examples could easily be multiplied many times over. *Every few days* around the country, a clergyman or some other religious leader is charged with or convicted of financial felony. In Matthew 6:24 we read, "No one can serve two masters. . . . Ye cannot serve God and Mammon." But there is no shortage of religionists who use both God and Mammon to serve themselves.

WONDERS FOR YOUR WALLET

Most televised god-peddlers no longer preach fire and brimstone as in days of yore. To be sure, the hard-core Bible-thumping fundamentalists still admonish their flocks to eschew "sinful" things like swearing, gambling, alcohol, abortion, adultery, pornography, fornication, and homosexuality. But the message today proffered by the slicker megachurch televangelists, described as *prosperity gospel* and *prosperity theology*, promises material affluence. To them God is not a forbidding mysterious force but a kind of genial and generous rich uncle. "We talked about God as a real person," said Tammy Faye Bakker, "not someone far away on high, but someone who is right there for you."[20]

God will tend to our monetary needs if we only *believe*. More than anything else, we must cast away our reasoned doubts and have unquestioning faith. How can followers best show that they believe? By materially supporting God's representative on earth, the preacher who appears in their church pulpit or on their television screen. By donating money to God's earthly ministry, the faithful will be rewarded many times over by God himself.

Prosperity televangelists like W. V. Grant and Robert Tilton collected tens of millions of dollars from poor, sick, and desperate viewers, while claiming to be supporting orphanages that did not exist. Meanwhile, both live in utter opulence. Tilton does not directly trust in God for financial miracles, preferring to get his money the old-fashioned way—from other people. In 1991 it was disclosed that he had pocketed over $80 million tax free from contributions sent by viewers of his television ministry, aptly titled "Success N Life." Tilton lived in a $4.5 million home, paid for in cash, had another house in Florida, a luxury boat, and an additional $60 million in bank deposits, treasury bonds, and real estate. He promised miracles to the needy—if they sent in their contributions: "If you want to get rid of that dump you live in, that car that breaks down, you have to have faith. I've been supernaturally blessed by God to help. . . . Yes, the Lord's ministry gets a portion of it [pointing to himself] but you get most of it." However, the prayer cards that sick and needy contributors sent in with their money—containing pleas for help that Tilton promised to meditate upon and transmit to heaven—were found untouched, in large trash bags in a Dumpster on his estate.[21]

In 2007, eight years after the scandalous disclosures concerning his immense wealth, Tilton was still in business, extracting funds from desperate viewers in exchange for the promise of divine intervention. On one telecast from Tallahassee, he claimed to have received that very day a message *directly from God* who said to him, "Bob, I do a little here and a little there." Not exactly a momentous or edifying communication considering its source.

Tilton then related the story of a couple plagued by financial worries until they started donating to his ministry, after which "God got them out of debt." The televangelist assured his listeners, "Faith is what makes things happen. I'm talking about what my God will supply." The viewer need only make a monthly pledge of "$100 or $25, whatever amount" to "enter that covenant with God, and you will get back twenty, thirty, or one hundred-fold. . . . I will administer to you. I love you."[22]

Purveyors of prosperity theology have been around for some

time. A century ago there was Billy Sunday and then Aimee Semple McPherson, both of whom pointed to their wealth as proof that God was rewarding them for their devotion. "If the rich were happy to hear that they too could be righteous, the righteous were even happier to hear that they too could be rich."[23]

There was Father Divine, who claimed to be not only a messenger of God but God himself; and Frederick Eikerenkoetter, known as Reverend Ike, who used to say, "The best thing you can do for the poor is not be one of them."

A leading exponent of prosperity theology is the aptly baptized Dr. Creflo A. Dollar, who as of 2009 presided over the World Changers Church with its annual budget of $80 million, and a network of churches and television shows that extended worldwide. Dollar (his actual family name) tells his listeners, "You are not going to be peaceful and happy in life if you are broke." Like Tilton, Dollar repeatedly reminds congregants that if they wish to receive, they first must learn to give. He urges them to give 10 percent of their income, for the Lord takes pleasure in the prosperity of his servant (Preacher Dollar) and looks disapprovingly upon those who skimp in their donations.

Dollar himself looms as living evidence of prosperity theology, appearing close to God and even closer to the money. "I can't preach prosperity to somebody if I can't demonstrate that the principles work in my own life," he explains.[24] His followers cannot fail to notice the hand of providence in his custom-tailored suits, alligator shoes, Rolls-Royces, and private airplanes. It seems not to have dawned on them that *they*—not God—are the source of his wealth.

Another booster of prosperity theology is the ever-smiling religious telecaster Joel Osteen. His widely broadcasted services bring in about $70 million a year. Worldly wealth, he declares, is God's way of rewarding us. "God wants you to be a winner, not a whiner." When congregants "give to the Lord" (that is, to Osteen), the Lord will give it back many times over. Osteen even claims to have successfully enlisted divine intervention when praying to make a winning shot while playing basketball with friends or finding a choice parking space. He never explains why God would service such trifling matters. Osteen seems aware that he is trafficking in the quiet desperation of his followers. In return for all the money he pockets, he tries, in his words, "to plant a seed of hope in people's hearts."[25]

To witness the televangelist's hokey snake-oil, money-grabbing act, watch Tilton doing his version of glossolalia. Closing his eyes and extending his hands upward, he babbles a gibberish that supposedly elicits profitable returns from the deity. Or watch televangelist Jimmy Swaggart pause in the middle of a frothy sermon, put his hand to his forehead, and say, "Hold on, God is telling me something," after which he conveys the celestial message to his audience, none of whom roll over laughing.

On television as in life itself, God communicates *silently* to the entitled individual, never audibly to entire audiences, and never on camera or on microphone. Oddly enough, he who wants so furiously to be believed in and worshiped manifests no willingness to have his utterances directly heard by multitudes. Instead, he remains completely invisible and soundless—except to a few self-selected, self-enriching preachers.[26]

THE GREATEST SELL ON EARTH

The religious hucksters sell not only God but also godly artifacts: crucifixes, plastic Jesus statuettes, saints pictures, hymn books, rosary beads, Sunday missals, holy medals, inspirational booklets, and photographs of religious leaders, in what amounts to a multimillion-dollar industry. Televangelist Kerney Thomas markets his own special brand of soap, which, he claims, has divine healing powers. Then there are the talking dolls of Jesus, Mary, Moses, and other holy figures who recite biblical verses thanks to a computerlike circuit chip installed in them. The dolls are sold online by Target and in hundreds of Wal-Mart stores. Their purpose, according to the manufacturer, is to "nourish children's souls."[27]

Along with prosperity theology, there is a more generalized *feel-good theology.* The megachurches are studiously nondenominational, run by CEOs and businesspeople who avoid Pentecostal riffs and sulfuric eschatology. Instead they market a feel-good Jesus. They preach to people's "felt needs" and personal problems, trying to be relevant to their lives, as might any self-help organization. They establish small affinity groups to boost self-esteem and foster a sense of belonging. They hold seminars on "God's Plan to Make You a Winner."

They minister—even if only in a passing way—to a broken marriage, substance abuse, or individual isolation. They understand that congregants want relief in the here and now, a warm haven with coffee and donuts and childcare, not a sin-flogging chamber or a demon-ridden theology. They want good news, not tormenting condemnation. The feel-good megachurches make some gesture at filling a void for the many afflicted souls who in this atomized free-market society are assailed by money problems while bereft of social services and support networks.[28]

No commodity compares to religion when it comes to marketing. There exists no worldly reformer, no revolutionary visionary, no captain of industry who can offer anything comparable to what the religious hucksters dangle before the fevered faces of the world. Consider the following:

Instead of the eternal darkness of death and nonexistence that is to come upon us all, there is the promise of everlasting life. And what a life it will be. The earthbound years of hardship and pain will be followed by an eternity of celestial bliss. Who can match that? Furthermore, good things are dished up not only in the hereafter but also in the here and now:

For the many who feel unloved, God loves them.

For the many who feel dispirited and aggrieved in this vale of tears, God shall make light their burdens, watch over them, and fill them with joy.

For the many whose lives seem empty of meaning, God shall implant purpose and direction in their hearts.

For the many who endure serious ill health, God shall

deliver them from all maladies. And if the miracle cures fail to materialize, then certainly in the next world where only the spirit endures, eternal bliss will replace physical suffering.

For the many who bear the terrible afflictions of material want and feel like losers, God shall bring prosperity and revamp them as winners.

In 2004, I heard a "New Life" radio preacher urge listeners to send money to subscribe to a "deep spiritual program" that helped them lose weight. God not only puts us in the money, he also puts us in shape.

We are all familiar with the *suffer-quietly-and-accept-your-misery* brand of religiosity marketed by Mother Teresa and other traditionalists. They tell us that when disaster strikes, don't complain, don't be a crybaby. God must have wanted it that way; he is testing us. When loved ones are torn from this life, it is because God wanted to clasp them to himself, bringing them to a better place.

Today's televangelists promise life improvements and happiness in *this* world as well as the next. Their god offers splendiferous fortune as is befitting a deity fashioned by money-driven preachers. They hardly ever mention heaven or hell or sin, so fixed are they on acquisitive materialism. So it has come to pass that a nondenominational loving God will make you forever so joyful, prosperous, and happy. All you have to do is *believe* in him and keep sending in those contributions.

God is a product marketed to beleaguered buyers, but with no guarantee, no warrantee, no refund for unanswered prayers, and in fact, no actually visible product of any discernible sort. All the boundless promises the hucksters make in God's name must be taken on faith. From the seller's point of view, there is no more fabulous item to vend than this, an invisible commodity, fashioned with words, that promises everything and ultimately is obliged to deliver nothing. And the customers who are disappointed have only themselves to blame for being of little faith.

10

MONEYED GURUS AND CULTS

Mammon is god of the world's leading religion.
—AMBROSE BIERCE

For centuries there has prevailed a strong link between secular and religious moneyed interests. Today major ministries hold billion-dollar investments in armaments, oil, banking, and just about every other large corporate enterprise. Behind the cross there stands the dollar. Behind the prelate there stands the plutocrat.

MASTERS FOR THE MONEY

First in mind when thinking of wealthy religionists might be the Roman Catholic "Holy Father," better known to us as the pope, bedecked in his gold-laced robes, padding about the Vatican's richly appointed chambers, presiding over mountains of treasure. The Roman Church is a worldwide organization that possesses more wealth in real estate, gold reserves, stocks, bonds, and art treasures than any other single institution or transnational corporation.[1]

Another example might be His Highness the Aga Khan, imam of the Ismaili Muslims, reportedly a direct descendant of the prophet Muhammad. This great holy leader owns six hundred race horses, several factories, and over forty "prayer and business centers." His personal worth is placed at £1.25 billion.[2]

One of the more mysteriously rich figures is the Reverend Sun Myung Moon, cult leader of the Unification Church (later renamed Family Federation for World Peace and Unification). Moon is seen by his followers as the Messiah who will lead the world to salvation. Moon owns an international empire of publications and properties, and is a generous contributor to right-wing causes. Most of the labor for his business enterprises is provided free by his devotees who, as in most any cult, work for mere subsistence and submit to a strict regimen. He has officiated at mass weddings in which hundreds of followers met their spouses-to-be only shortly before the actual ceremony, having been arbitrarily paired off by Moon himself.

Moon was subjected to a congressional investigation for financial misdeeds, including a scheme to siphon money from a front group disguised as a fund-raiser for sick children.[3] In 1982 he was convicted of conspiracy and filing false tax returns, and he spent thirteen months in federal prison. New evidence suggests that his organization is continuing its shady financial operations, laundering mysterious cash flows through church-connected firms. Moon reportedly has ties to overseas drug lords.[4]

A book by Moon's daughter-in-law provides a firsthand view of the family's lavish lifestyle, drug and alcohol abuse, domestic violence, antipathy between parents and children, and Moon's numerous infidelities, along with a glimpse of the venality and financial corruption of his entire organization. As the daughter-in-law writes, "The evil at the heart of the Unification Church is the hypocrisy and deceit of the Moons," a family with an "incredible level of dysfunction. To continue to promote the myth that the Moons are spiritually superior to the idealistic young people who are drawn to the church is a shameful deceit."[5]

Another religious organization that bears strong resemblance to a cult is the Mormon Church (officially the Church of Jesus Christ of Latter-day Saints), with its headquarters in Salt Lake City, Utah, and thirteen million members worldwide, growing at an impressive rate through the tireless efforts of its proselytizers. Many young Mormon men devote two years to missionary work spreading the word abroad.

And what a word it is. The Mormons believe that the early Christian church lost its way not long after the death of Jesus. But a great restoration took place in the 1820s when a certain Joseph Smith Jr. of Missouri experienced visitations from an angel named Moroni, as well as from illustrious biblical personages, including Jesus and God the Father. Guided by heavenly directives, Smith dug up a set of golden plates covered with a script in an unknown language, which he was able to decipher with the aid of a pair of magical spectacles.[6]

The plates revealed to Smith that Jackson County, Missouri, was the original location of the Garden of Eden and would be the future site of the New Jerusalem. Smith reported that Jesus already made a Second Coming in the New World centuries before Columbus arrived and had converted vast numbers of North American "Indians"—themselves descended from earlier Hebrew immigrants. Furthermore, Smith claimed Jesus would return again to rule the entire world from within the United States—probably Jackson County—bringing us a thousand years of peace, followed by the Last Judgment. Smith also taught that making money was a righteous pursuit. God smiled upon the rich, as well as those who aspired to become rich.[7]

Polygamy retained divine approval within the Mormon Church until 1890 when, according to Mormon elders, God changed his mind in time for a Mormon-dominated Utah to be allowed into the Union. In 1978 God belatedly revealed that African Americans could enjoy full membership in the Mormon Church. Homosexuals too, but they must refrain from their proclivities or risk excommunication. All Mormons must avoid premarital sex, masturbation, and sexual fantasy.

Another controversial organization of size and wealth is the Church of Scientology. Boasting devotees throughout North America and Europe, Scientology defines itself as an "applied religious philosophy" for human and social betterment. It teaches reincarnation and the existence of many deities. Scientologists roundly denounce the baneful effects of antidepressants and other "mood stabilizer" drugs pushed by the pharmaceutical industry and the psychiatric profession. Mental health and spiritual purity are to be achieved through Scientology's mind exercises and discipline, taught in guided sessions for substantial fees.[8] Some devotees claim that these sessions rescued them from addiction and helped reshape their lives.

In the 1980s, eleven top Scientologists were sent to prison for infiltrating, burglarizing, and wiretapping more than a hundred private and government agencies in attempts to block investigations into their often secret doings. In the following years, hundreds of adherents departed from Scientology, charging psychological and physical abuse and oppressive control by the leadership. Some sued and won substantial settlements. In various cases judges have declared the church to be "schizophrenic and paranoid" and "corrupt, sinister and dangerous."[9]

Recent decades have witnessed a proliferation of guru-dominated cults in the United States and elsewhere. An estimated two to four million Americans are involved in groups that market eclectic teachings lifted from established religions or a generalized "spirituality" that eschews traditional theism. While basking in the adoration of their followers, the cult "spiritual masters" often affect a humble pose, with disclaimers such as: "I am merely a channel for the higher knowledge." Pretending to an inner quietude and profound modesty, many are endowed with raging egos and immersed in nasty rivalries that are played out with a vehemence redolent of less spiritually advanced individuals.[10]

Devotees usually are expected to toil long hours without recompense in order to provide income for the cult's facilities and leadership. In many instances, they hand over their cars, property, savings, and inheritances to the organization. In return, they receive blessings from their masters and are assured that they are shoring up "good karma" or some other pie in the sky.[11]

Like so many other "spiritual" leaders, most gurus manifest an insatiable hunger for material acquisition. In this respect they resemble more traditional religious leaders down through the ages. Maharishi Mahesh Yogi, one of a number of "spiritual teachers" who journeyed to America to do good and ended up doing well, had this to say when interviewed by the *Washington Post*:

> Q: You're a multimillion-dollar corporation. You have property all over.
> A: But that is not yet enough. Want more and more. . . . Here I sit with all the possibilities. I need as much money as possible.
> Q: Why don't you raise money and distribute it to needy people? Would this not be a more effective way to bring about change?
> A: No, no, it's not the money that can make one happy.
> Q: How can Third World people think about their [spiritual] consciousness when they're hungry?
> A: If they use their brain properly . . . the infinitivity [*sic*] of nature will make them capable of not only earning their ordinary bread but very first-class bread.[12]

The Maharishi's message seems to be: Money cannot make you happy, so give it to me.

One former cult participant describes a common problem: the glaring discrepancy in worldly possessions between leader and followers. "I know of several people who had children who were living on less that $300 a month, and in some cases $7 a week. That disturbed me when I saw [the guru] with a fleet of Mercedes and Cadillacs and several homes."[13]

How do cult leaders justify their opulent lifestyle? One explained that he could live amid wealth without being corrupted because he was so much more advanced than his devotees. Furthermore, wealth naturally gravitated to him because of his elevated spiritual state. More accurately, wealth came his way because his followers worked long hours at his enterprises and lived in poverty so they might donate the better part of their earnings and life savings to their master.[14]

At a yoga retreat I attended, the Indian swami preached a daily sermon on how "spiritual things are everything, material things are nothing." One could not help notice that this pronouncedly celibate and self-denying holy man had an attractive young disciple who was always by his side and spent her nights with him. I could only speculate as to the exact nature of their relationship, but it appeared to be close. As for his indifference to material things: he resided in a large comfortable house while the paying guests made do with tents or cramped, leaky cabins. He owned a yacht, a private airplane, a munificent estate in Quebec and another on a Caribbean island. At one yoga session he exclaimed, "Nobody is perfect; only *I* am perfect." Despite his perfection, he had a sugar addiction that caused him to consume great quantities of candy bars and left him considerably overweight and suffering from diabetes. In addition, he was easily vexed, overcome with paroxysms of fury when things did not go his way, and showed neither love nor patience toward those less perfect than he.

HARMFUL HAVENS

Not all spiritual and meditative groups are cult-ridden. Many of them encourage egalitarian engagement and allow for casual, part-time participation. They are neither authoritarian nor exploitative. And their teachers are genuinely caring individuals with no aggrandizing agenda. Such groups are not the subject of this chapter. Our attention is on the totalistic, self-enriching, guru-worshiping cults, of which there are too many.

As the master is elevated, the followers are infantilized and diminished. Some devotees emerge from cults embittered by the experience. They relate how they learned to distrust their own judgment; how they gave their money, labor, uncritical obedience, and sometimes their bodies to the "spiritual master"; how they were separated from former friends and family, given new names and identities. As one ex-votary put it, "It's classic brainwashing. They make them so they cannot fit in with other parts of society."[15]

Individuals are usually lured into cults with flattering attention and promises of an elevated spiritual development. Some recruits are lonely, inexperienced, or having a hard time in life. Others are trusting and receptive to an idealistic cause. Most would-be followers do not go searching for a cult to join. More often it is the cult that sallies forth to snare members.[16] Proselytes usually have little awareness of what is in store for them when they join. Isolated from their families and the wider community, they are worked hard, often kept exhausted and confused, and subjected to constant groupthink. One leader of a Bible cult urged his acolytes to embrace childlike mental imagery: "Get your mind as it once was, the mind of a child, free and innocent, not a thought in your mind. Let me think for you."[17]

But even when their critical perceptions are dampened, cult members are not mental zombies. They are intellectually armed with well-honed explanations that enable them to parry skeptical thrusts. Every encounter with the unenlightened leaves them all the more fortified. In this sense they are not much different from the orthodox believers of major religions. Like some Pentecostal and evangelical churches, various cults promise a joyful path to God, with blissful enlightenment, and in some cases even communication with other-worldly entities.

Those who surrender their lives to a totalitarian cult are not necessarily morally weak. In many instances they are just morally hungry, longing for something better than the exigencies of diurnal existence.[18] Once harnessed by the appropriate huckster, their spiritual yearnings harden into glorious certitude.

Given such stakes, there is little tolerance for those within the cult who demur. Punishment measured out to recalcitrant or poor-performing votaries can be harsh, including food and sleep deprivation, forced confinement for prolonged periods, group humiliation, tongue lashings, and disciplinary assaults.

One of the most horrific examples of cult oppression centered around Rev. Jim Jones's Peoples Temple. Jones sexually abused both male and female followers. He got his devotees to live communally and sign over their property and possessions to his church. Many were held against their will. In 1977, subjected to critical publicity, Jones moved the bulk of his congregation to an outpost in Guyana. The following year he turned his religious cult into a death cult by presiding over mass suicides and executions of almost all his church members and their children, numbering upward of a thousand victims.[19]

The totalistic regimen that is the essence of cults invites many occasions for sexual abuse. Going back to Joseph Smith, the Mormon Church founder, he claimed that God gave him license to practice polygamy. Smith married thirty-three women, perhaps more. The youngest of his wives was just fourteen when he told her that God demanded that she wed him or face eternal damnation.[20] For years afterward, the Mormon Church (all-male) elders taught that women who refused to practice polygamy would be damned.

Today in remote corners of Utah and Arizona, there still exist whole townships dominated by self-styled "Fundamentalist Mormons," who practice polygamy in fortissimo style. One leader who called himself Uncle Rulon married an estimated seventy-five women, with whom he fathered platoons of children. Several of his wives were given to him when they were in their early teens and he in his eighties. His message is a familiar one: "I want to tell you that the greatest freedom you can enjoy is in obedience," and "Perfect obedience produces perfect faith." Uncle Rulon teaches his followers that "the penalty, under the law of God, is death on the spot" for anyone who indulges in homosexuality or sexual intercourse with someone of African blood.[21]

Regarding cultist sexual exploitation, the stories bruited about are remarkably similar. Trusting proselytes are seduced or otherwise sexually coerced into exploitative liaisons by "spiritual leaders" who assure the devotee that through joyful surrender she will reach a higher realm of godly enlightenment. In one instance, the cult leader of the Ananda Church of Self Realization, J. Donald Walters (also known as Swami Kriyananda), and another church official lost a $1.7 million judgment for having sexually exploited a devotee "under the guise of helping her to make spiritual advancement."[22]

In 2005, a young San Francisco woman charged that while a member of the Church of Scientology, she was used as a sex slave, to be raped and sodomized many times during the course of a year. She testified that she was ordered by her superiors to share a room with a man who had sexually assaulted her. He subsequently pleaded guilty to aggravated sexual battery and was sentenced to prison.[23]

One writer, favorably disposed toward "spiritual leaders," claims that "for every teacher who goes astray there are ten who never waiver."[24] Should we be reassured by this ratio? Given the number of vendors who crowd the guru market, one-in-ten going "astray" amounts to quite a few who indulge their abusive and soul-damaging impulses at immeasurable cost to others. Furthermore, for every cult leader who is caught there seems to be many more who are never held accountable.

SUFFER THE CHILDREN

The children of cult members usually lead a disheartening existence, subjected to a joyless regimen with little time for play or independent expression. They often witness bizarre punishments and stern mistreatment meted out to their own parents or other adults and children. Some are subjected to harsh beatings or worse. For example, five-year-old Luke Stice died of a broken neck in a survivalist cult in rural Nebraska. Luke was reportedly being punished because his father had escaped the cult, leaving his two sons behind. Before Luke's death, the leader made him spend most of his time in undershorts and forced him to wallow naked in mud and snow.

Then there was twelve-year-old John Yarbough, who died while in the House of Judah, a Michigan cult. He had been beaten for several days and could neither eat nor walk. The leader had tried to pick him up by the ears with pliers. Another boy in the House of Judah reported being burned on the face for punishment. Another had hot coals put in his mouth and on his hands.[25]

As clinical psychiatrist Margaret Thaler Singer and coauthor Janja Lalich observe in their book, *Cults in Our Midst,* some children who witness this kind of brutality eventually identify with and imitate the punitive leaders. Others sink into a terrorized docility to prevent such a fate befalling them. A former member of Moon's Unification Church observed, "It was very difficult to draw most of the children out of the consuming melancholy which engulfed them."[26]

Some cults *specialize* in the sexual abuse of children. The very worst among these is probably "The Family" and "The Family International" (originally known as the "Children of God"). Claiming members worldwide, The Family was founded by David Berg, a former Pentecostal minister who died in 1993. Berg maintained that good Christians were expressing God's love by practicing sexual promiscuity. "We have a sexy God and a sexy religion with a very sexy leader with an extremely sexy young following!" he gushed. "So if you don't like sex, you better get out while you can."[27]

But The Family's children had no opportunity to get out. The cult promoted a practice called "sharing," in which offspring as young as five years old were offered up as sexual partners to adult members, sometimes to their own parents. Numerous ex-members report witnessing cases of child-adult sex, or of being abused themselves.

The Family's leadership now claims that such incidents are no longer sanctioned. Still, the cult deploys its children and young women onto the streets to solicit money, lure sex customers, and recruit new members. A considerable number of the second generation born into the cult and abused since early childhood now suffer from emotional disturbances and drug and alcohol addiction. Some have committed suicide; others have attempted it. One offspring slit the throat of an ex-nanny (who had allegedly molested him as a child) and then killed himself in protest against the years of sexual abuse suffered by him and other children in the cult.[28]

Cultlike autocracy can assume many forms. Scattered about the Western Hemisphere are church-sponsored detention centers especially designed to discipline the children of those fundamentalist Christianist families that can afford two-thousand- to three-thousand-dollar monthly tuition per child. One such school for punishment is the Escuela Caribe in the Dominican Republic, described in harrowing detail by Julia Scheeres, who spent a portion of her childhood there. At Escuela Caribe, children are regularly threatened, deprived of food, and sometimes kept in protracted isolation. All children start at "zero level," obliged to request permission to sit, stand, walk, begin eating, or whatever—a crushing micromanagement designed to break their "rebellious" spirit and teach them slavish compliance. They earn back the limited "privileges" of movement by memorizing and reciting Bible verses and showing unswerving obedience toward authority figures. Those who give less than perfect performance to endlessly contrived commands are damned as sinners, subjected to forced exercises, grinding chores, and in some cases severe beatings.[29]

Some youths are sent to these faith-run camps because they show signs of independent thought or irreligious behavior. Many are victims of emotional or physical abuse within their families. At camp the children find themselves trapped in a joyless totalitarian order presided over by staffers who speak of love while practicing hate and who despise teenagers and seem to enjoy making them suffer. Indeed, suffer they do, sobbing themselves to sleep, racked by nightmares, and sometimes falling into acute depression.

The people who run Escuela Caribe claim to be instilling faith and virtuous character in the children. As one staff member said, "To succeed in The Program, you must trust our authority. Just as Jesus requires blind faith from his believers, we require blind faith from our students. We are here to help you. To save you."[30] Devoting herself to cruel martinets who demand blind faith was not Julia Scheeres's idea of salvation: "I still can't believe that a place like Escuela Caribe exists," she writes. "All I did was try to ring some happiness from life, a little fun and a little affection, and as a result I was banished to an island colony ruled by sadistic Jesus freaks."[31]

Another instance of fundamentalist cultlike autocracy is reported by Carrie Louise Nutt. In 1994, she was sent to a Baptist school for "troubled teens" at the foot of the Ozark Mountains, where the students were not allowed to discuss what they had done to deserve internment. They could not talk about sex, drugs, or their personal lives. They could not hug or have friends, nor express their unhappiness or keep journals. It was verboten to wear "worldly clothing" or pants, or even say the word "pants." All their incoming and outgoing mail was read. They were rarely let outside and had no windows in their dorms. There were no private stalls in the communal toilets, so they had not a moment's privacy even when trying to relieve themselves.

Girls at this Baptist school were called degrading names and subjected to various forms of public humiliation. They were punished if they failed to memorize three Bible verses a day. Many of them stopped ovulating. Others suffered from ongoing constipation or diarrhea and never received medical attention. Some tried to kill themselves.[32]

The most important lesson Carrie Louise Nutt learned was that "if you don't do exactly as they tell you, they will tear you apart . . . leaving only a shell of your former self. . . . I gained weight and grew to hate myself. They encouraged self loathing, as you are nothing without Christ." The school authorities forced one girl to give up her baby. A murder in 1996—

followed by an attempted cover-up by these law-abiding, God-fearing Christianists—led to a state investigation and closing of the school in 2003. This was only one of many fundamentalist-run institutions that employ "methods for breaking and remaking worldly teens in the image of God."[33]

Punitive schools aside, children in traditional religious families do worse than those in secular homes. Studies show that fundamentalist religious affiliation is "one of the greatest predictors of child abuse, more so than age, gender, social class, or size of residence."[34] As Scheeres warns, "Beneath the much-hyped 'family values' morality of the Bible Belt, you'll find child abuse, intolerance, and racism."[35]

Punishing and shaming small children for crying, talking back, and showing anger or any hint of independent opinion is standard practice in fundamentalist homes and has been for centuries. Playing a central role in the religionist child-rearing industry is James Dobson and his Focus on the Family. Dobson has reached millions with his stern parental advice. He advocates beating any children over fifteen *months* of age "with sufficient magnitude to cause the child to cry genuinely." But if they cry excessively in response, then they are to be treated to additional blows.[36]

Citing passages in the Bible that promote corporal punishment of children, fundamentalist childcare "experts" recommend whipping babies and older children with straps, paddles, and switches—without worrying about laying it on too heavily. Children are expected to obey their parents without question, in the same way that parents are expected to obey God.[37] Parental guidance devolves into parental mistreatment anchored in violence. "In a home headed by religious zealots," concludes writer Erica Etelson, "the line between discipline and abuse can get dangerously murky."[38]

WHEN CULT MEETS CHURCH

Women too often have a hard time in fundamentalist house-holds. Consigned to traditional roles as wives and mothers, they are seriously dependent on their husbands for support and thereby less able to take recourse against mistreatment. The conservative clergymen they consult advise them to suffer quietly like good wives as God ordained. Pastor Ted Haggard, when presiding over the National Association of Evangelicals, preached that God's dominion over man was replicated in man's dominion over his wife; so women must learn "total surrender."[39] Heartless cutbacks in welfare support make it all the more difficult for women with children to leave oppressive and potentially lethal relationships.[40] In short, the fundamentalist household can itself serve as a kind of mini-cult.

Consider the sexism endured by women in the Mormon Church. All Mormon men are ordained into a priesthood from which Mormon women are excluded. So men preside over the home with a priestly authority derived from their church membership. As in 1880, the official view today remains that woman's primary place is in the home; her highest purpose in life is to bear children and abide the counsel of her husband.[41] Gender roles are considered unchanging and eternal. At marriage, Mormon women are accorded secret names known to only their husbands, so that after death their spouses can usher them to the heavenly level. This is the only way women can reach heaven, by being ushered in by their deceased mates. Only men enter heaven on their own; a woman's subservience persists into the afterlife. For Mormon women to pursue divorce is to be untrue to the Lord's covenants. Women who have sought to modify the sexist roles have risked excommunication.[42] In most respects the Mormon Church remains something of an oppressive cult to women.

All this suggests that the line between cult and fundamentalist sect is sometimes a blurry one. Both indoctrinate their followers in sacred dictates that allow for no critical reasoning. Both engage in intensive campaigns to spread the word and multiply membership. Both extract ample material resources from followers, either through volunteer labor or monetary contributions or both. One might wonder if a sectarian church is just a cult that has been better established for a longer duration.

PART IV

HYPOCRITES, REACTIONARIES, AND VIPERS

11

GOD, LEFT AND RIGHT

> How odd . . . that a country as riddled with
> Christian faith as America has so little regard for
> its poor, sick, and imprisoned.
>
> —MATTHEW CHAPMAN

For all their claims to spirituality, religious institutions are deeply immersed in the politico-economic affairs of this world. Down through the ages, secular and spiritual authorities worked hand in hand to advance their privileged positions in the social order.

THE LORD'S LORDS

We need only think of the Middle Ages, when the higher circles of church and state together exploited the hapless peasants and artisans of Europe. While promising the common people everything in the next world, prince and bishop lived lavishly off their toil in this one.

Consider Martin Luther, known to us as the great rebel who sparked the Protestant Reformation. There is a lesser-known

Luther, the stern defender of the aristocracy, the darling of the German princes. In 1525, a few years after Luther's break with Rome, the German peasants, along with some townships, rebelled against the misery they had long endured under the nobility and higher clergy. They plundered castles and monasteries and set up political communities of their own. The rebels called for the election of pastors, an end to serfdom, and the restoration of hunting, fishing, and pasturage rights that were being abrogated by higher clergy and nobility. Even Frederick the Wise, Luther's own prince, allowed that "perhaps the peasants have been given a reason for such rebellion. . . . In many ways the poor have been wronged by us secular and spiritual rulers."[1]

Not so in Luther's eyes. On a few occasions he did gently chastise the nobility for the profligate way they lived off the backs of the peasantry, but Luther never thought to rally the poor. When peasant rebels quoted scripture to justify their struggle against ruinous rents and taxes, Luther considered it a "blasphemy." He drew passages from the Bible, including St. Paul's deadly syllogism drawn from Romans 13: All authority comes from God; the rebel is against authority; ergo, the rebel is pitted against God. Luther repeatedly urged everyone to "smite, slay, and stab [the insurgents] secretly or openly, remembering that nothing can be more poisonous, hurtful, or devilish than a rebel. It is just as when one must kill a mad dog." The princes were only too ready to oblige. Their armies butchered tens of thousands of luckless peasants.[2]

Throughout feudal times and into the modern era, church structure reflected the wider social order. The church hierarchy was recruited almost exclusively from the nobility, who drew lavish incomes from their ecclesiastical offices. Meanwhile the parish priest, who tended to the common people, generally lived in poverty and was himself of humble origin. The church oligarchs looked down on these priests as coarse and ignorant. Some of the lower clergy, in turn, seethed over the corrupt opulence of their superiors.[3]

The alliance between church and state continued into the

nineteenth and twentieth centuries. Protestant and Catholic religious leaders in Europe and North America denounced labor unions and condemned syndicalism, anarchism, communism, and socialism as the devil's work.[4] They defined sin in personal rather than social terms, as a failure to restrain pleasurable impulses, an infection of the soul arising from flawed spiritual development. Workers were to be taught the virtues of regular church attendance, hard work, sobriety, punctuality, and compliance to managerial authority. Occasionally Christianist leaders urged the rich to show more regard for the poor, but such chiding had little impact.

SOCIAL JUSTICE WITH JESUS

Privileged conservatives are not the only ones who mesh their sacred beliefs with their political agenda. Religionists of progressive bent, those of the *religious Left*, have waged campaigns against plutocrats, slaveholders, and empire builders. In the United States during the early part of the twentieth century, there was the *Social Gospel movement*, led by Protestant clergy and laypersons who believed that God's way could best be realized not only with prayer and piety but also with a collective commitment to building peace and economic justice.[5]

Down to our own day, members of various denominations, including many of an evangelical strain, have done battle with fundamentalists over various social issues including US military interventions, the ordination of female clergy, gay rights, and the environmental crisis. Groups such as Pastors for Peace, Pax Christi, the Catholic Worker movement, the American Friends Service Committee, Jewish Voice for Peace, and the Unitarian Universalists continue to promote a progressive agenda despite almost no attention from the major media.

In 2007 the somewhat conservative National Association of Evangelicals, an umbrella group representing more than 45,000 churches with 30 million members, endorsed a declaration condemning torture and any other degrading treatment of detainees. The association urged a government-wide embrace of the Geneva Conventions and the reversal of any US policy or practice that violated humanitarian moral standards.[6]

Regarding environmentalism, some Christianist leaders now talk about our responsibility to act as stewards of God's earth, including Pope Benedict XVI and the US Conference of Catholic Bishops. Ecumenical Patriarch Bartholomew, leader of the Greek Orthodox Church, declared environmental degradation a sin. One thousand mostly mainstream Protestant clergy and congregational lay leaders across the United States signed a statement expressing disagreement with the Bush administration's damaging policy on climate change.[7]

Liberal religionists have deplored the rise of a rightist "culture of Christianity that does not encourage thought" and shows "its pious aversion toward so-called secular culture."[8] In the words of Rev. Michael Livingston, president of the National Council of Churches of Christ, the religious Right is a media-driven "false religion, a political philosophy masquerading as gospel; an economic principle wrapped in religious rhetoric and painted red, white and blue."[9]

In April 2005, in the heart of the Bible Belt, hundreds of believers filled the Central Presbyterian Church "to condemn Republican Party efforts to hijack Christianity." One Baptist minister denounced the religio-political reactionaries for whining whenever they "hit an obstacle on their way to total domination."[10]

A dramatic instance of progressive religious activism has been *the theology of liberation*, a social movement that began in the 1960s in Latin America and later extended to the Philippines and to some areas of Africa, in part inspired by the Vatican II Council convened by Pope John XXIII in 1962. The pontiff's call for an aggiornamento brought to the fore the adherents of liberation theology, mostly Catholic clergy. They maintained that Christianity offered a doctrine of communal justice to be realized through struggle against oppressive oligarchs. As the church began to side openly with the poor, the makeup of its clergy changed. In countries like Brazil, seminarians who once were recruited from relatively privileged middle-class families now more likely came from militantly working-class backgrounds.[11]

SOCIAL INJUSTICE WITH JOHN PAUL II

By the late 1970s, liberation theology nurtured a real revolutionary potential. The Vatican, however, now under the rule of Pope John Paul II, threw its weight against the movement, berating it for dangerously insinuating the church into the temporal political world. In Latin America, the pope—himself deeply insinuated into the temporal political world—appointed a large number of conservative bishops to impoverished urban dioceses and transferred liberal ones to remote rural areas or gerrymandered their dioceses out of existence. He suppressed liberation theology curricula and silenced its theorists, imposed only Vatican-approved manuals in seminaries, and forbade liberal and radical clergy from holding public office, instructing them to avoid political activities.[12]

In 1980, in the midst of a US-funded counterinsurgency in El Salvador that the UN Truth Commission termed *genocidal*, Archbishop Oscar Romero sided with the downtrodden and called for international intervention to stop the carnage. For his efforts Romero was assassinated. Just weeks before his murder, high-ranking officials of the Arena party, the legal arm of the Salvadoran death squads, sent a well-received delegation to the Vatican to complain of Romero's public statements on behalf of the poor.[13] John Paul never denounced the killing or its perpetrators, calling it only "tragic." Hundreds of other priests and nuns were tortured and assassinated, but the pontiff seemed not to take notice of the terror raining down upon his more progressive-minded clergy.

By 1988, the death squad assassinations and US funding of

Latin American media and social science had taken their toll. The surviving adherents of liberation theology began focusing more on "issues of spirituality."[14] John Paul II continued to denounce political involvement by reform-minded clergy and laity, while he supported the political activities of his reactionary associates who operated in ultraconservative secretive organizations like Opus Dei.[15]

John Paul, that most political of all popes, remained up to his ears in counterrevolutionary politics in Latin America and elsewhere. He occasionally criticized neoliberal capitalism, "which subordinates the human person to blind market forces."[16] But such verbal slaps measured little against his ultraconservative stratagems and his close cooperation with political reactionaries such as US president Ronald Reagan. The pontiff directed no critical attacks against right-wing dictatorships, which he valued as bulwarks against communist revolution. He had the Vatican's secretary of state intervene on behalf of the erstwhile fascist dictator and free marketeer Augusto Pinochet when the latter was under house arrest in London, facing indictment by a Spanish court.[17] And John Paul played an active role in the overthrow of communism in Eastern Europe, encouraging the Polish clergy to involve itself in political action.

The pope opposed female clergy, married clergy, abortion, stem cell research, divorce, and same-sex marriage. He persistently condemned contraception as an "evil," regardless of the health risks involved in unprotected sex.[18] For the longest time, however, he refused to address the epidemic of pedophilia that plagued the Roman Church (see chapter 12).

John Paul appointed 231 new cardinals, stacking the College of Cardinals entirely with like-minded ultraconservatives. Upon his death, the College of Cardinals almost unanimously selected his second-in-command as the new pope, the hard-line conservative Cardinal Joseph Ratzinger, who had served as John Paul's enforcer in the suppression of liberation theology.

Church historian Father John O'Malley concluded that the "tolerant and open spirit" of Vatican II was "largely extinguished" by John Paul II. The pope "created a law-and-order, fear-driven, clerically controlled Church." Many diocesan priests left the church; others "agreed to be silent on issues of change," while some quietly continued to struggle for reform at the parish level.[19] More than ever, power was centered in the Holy Office in Rome, hampering those clergy who wished to pursue issues of social justice.

During John Paul's reign, economic ills through much of Latin America only worsened. In recent years there has been a quiet resurgence of grassroots liberation theology groups in Brazil and elsewhere. At the upper levels of the church hierarchy, however, liberation theology has been successfully tamped down. Bishops and cardinals who protected the movement in the 1970s and 1980s have either died or been pressed into retirement, replaced by carefully vetted appointees hostile to progressive reforms. In 1984, Cardinal Ratzinger, speaking for John Paul and himself, announced that "the theology of liberation is a singular heresy."[20]

MARKETING THE MESSAGE

It is no accident that we hear almost nothing about the religious Left and so much about the religious Right. Progressive dissidents usually are denied access to mass media audiences. As with politics, so with religion: there is no free market of ideas, no level playing field. Conservative religious organizations possess a vast constellation of publications, television and radio networks, and satellite and cable channels that gather millions of listeners and viewers. When the federal government began offering licenses for low-power radio stations in 2004, it was the well-financed religious Right that bought up the lion's share of the frequencies, thereby further extending its grip over the airwaves.[21]

The secular corporate-owned media also show a striking favoritism toward the religious Right. On the major television networks, cable news channels, and PBS, conservative religious leaders have been quoted, mentioned, or interviewed almost 400 percent more often than progressive ones, and over 250 percent more often in major newspapers.[22]

Backed by moneyed interests, the right-wing Christianist media propagate free-market corporatism, militarism, and super-patriotism. Christianist activists flood the postal mails with unsolicited pamphlets and the Internet with Jesus spam, in support of reactionary issues. The religious Right boasts richly financed lobbying groups, foundations, think tanks, mission schools, colleges, and law schools, recreational parks, summer camps, business directories, writers conferences, novels, poems, rock bands, and songs, along with training centers for future preachers dedicated to "spiritual warfare." Some of the wealthy fundamentalist megachurches recruit followers by offering employment clinics, childcare, English language classes, and loans.[23]

There are "Faith Nights" at professional sporting events that feature Christianist bands and statements from players and clergy about the need to connect with Jesus. Promoters give away thousands of Bibles and dolls depicting biblical heroes. The home team may sport jerseys with Bible verses printed on their backs. Churches are given stacks of discounted tickets "to family-friendly evenings of music and sports with a Christian theme." In return, the clergy mobilize their followers to fill the stadiums.[24]

At mass gatherings sponsored by groups like the Promise Keepers, thousands of men affirm their roles as protective leaders of their families and vow to "take back the nation for Christ."[25] The ultimate goal of all these activities is to generate an ever-expanding Christianist presence in secular society, until all the world belongs to Jesus, or to those who claim to act in his name.

Youth rallies are big sells. Thousands of evangelical teenagers gather in stadiums to pray, sing, and scream in "a mix of pep rally, rock concert, and church service," while Christianist comedians deliver standup routines with predictable digs at atheists and rock bands pound out songs filled with a Gospel message.[26]

A computer game produced by Left Behind Games and sold by Wal-Mart and other retailers brings the message home.

Players either join the "good side," which has license to slaughter nonbelievers, or join the Antichrist. The righteous team includes Gospel singers and missionaries. The evil team sports fictional rock stars and individuals with Arab-sounding names. As one liberal Presbyterian minister wryly commented, "So under the Christmas tree this year for little Johnny is this allegedly Christian video game teaching Johnny to hate and kill." A right-wing Christianist group, Focus on the Family, endorsed the game, calling it the kind that "Mom and Dad can actually play with Junior."[27]

FOR GOD AND CAPITALISM

Christianists worldwide are involved in a "renewalist" movement involving Pentecostals and charismatics who practice "the gifts of the Holy Spirit," such as glossolalia and prophesying. Renewalists generally concentrate on supernatural pursuits, but in recent times they have boosted conservative political leaders who promise to reverse the "moral decline" of modern society.[28]

Political involvement by the Roman Church hierarchy has centered on opposition to abortion, birth control, and gay rights. In the 2004 presidential election many leading Catholic bishops threatened their own congregants with excommunication if they voted for the liberal Democratic candidate John Kerry, who himself was a Catholic.[29] On this occasion, the Protestant fundamentalists discarded their age-old concerns about "papist influence" in American politics. The papists, after all, now shared the same reactionary agenda as the Protestant right-wingers. Politics is thicker than faith.

This was certainly true of televangelist Pat Robertson, a candidate for the Republican presidential nomination in 1988. In 2007 Robertson endorsed Rudy Giuliani for president, putting aside Giuliani's religion (Roman Catholic) and even his permissive position on abortion and gay rights, giving priority to his rightist politico-economic agenda. This same Robertson asserted that feminism "encourages women to leave their husbands, kill their children, practice witchcraft, destroy capitalism, and become lesbians."[30] He once praised the "enlightened leadership" of Guatemalan CIA-supported, military dictator General Efrain Rios Montt, notorious for his slaughter of tens of thousands of people.[31] In 2005 Robertson gave us another glimpse of his loving Christianist side when he called for the assassination of Venezuela's elected socialist-minded president Hugo Chavez: "If he thinks we're trying to assassinate him, I think that we really ought to go ahead and do it."[32]

A leading light of the religious Right and a kingmaker in the Republican Party was televangelist Jerry Falwell, who died in 2007, leaving a full trough of retrograde utterances from which his followers might feed. On the issue of segregation, Falwell pronounced as follows: "Facilities [for whites and blacks] should be separate. When God has drawn a line of distinction, we should not attempt to cross that line." Years later he determined that "AIDS is the wrath of a just God against homosexuals"; Jews could not enter heaven unless they converted to Christianity, "God doesn't listen to Jews"; and Americans who are not devout Christians are "foes."[33]

Supporting the 2003 US invasion of Iraq, Falwell determined that "God is pro-war." Like most other right-wing clergy, he paid little attention to actual Christian moral doctrine regarding just and unjust wars, preferring to rally around President Bush, whom he pictured as "a brother in Christ," who "has discerned that God's will is for our nation to be at war against Iraq."[34]

As for global warming, many far-right religionists agree with Falwell, who called it an issue "created to destroy America's free enterprise system and our economic stability." Fundamentalist reactionaries believe that concern for our planet's future is senseless because it has no future; we are on the eve of the Apocalypse when Jesus will make a grand reentry, and the righteous shall be elevated to heaven, while sinners and skeptics will roast in hell for all eternity. In the face of that breathtaking scenario, melting icecaps are of no great moment —if anything, they are welcomed as evidence of the impending Judgment Day "Rapture," the Second Coming of Jesus Christ.[35]

God mandates a neoliberal economic world order, according to erstwhile televangelist Ted Haggard, who described fundamentalist believers as "pro-free market; they're pro-private property. That's what evangelical stands for." Free-market globalization has made us free. Haggard also supported preemptive war, reminding us that "the Bible is bloody."[36]

Meanwhile, missionaries continue to impose upon the indigenous peoples of the world the competitive and selfish values of global industrial capitalism. "Where Protestant missionaries go, industrial capitalism follows."[37]

Today's right-wing religionists fashion a god wedded to their moralistic and *political* agendas. As already mentioned, their definitions of sin and virtue are seldom associated with the inequities of socioeconomic reality. Thus a worker who filches something from the business firm is a thief and has thereby sinned. But the corporate owners—who plunder the environment, market unsafe commodities, impose cuts in wages and benefits, and expropriate workers' pension funds—are not likely to be considered culpable by any luminaries of the religious Right.[38]

Truly egregious things such as wars of aggression, slavery, racism, sexism, pedophilia, exploitation of the many so that the few can accumulate still greater wealth, and various other inequities and iniquities that we might condemn as gravely hurtful to innocents, and therefore evil, do not seem to trouble the right-wing religionists. For them virtue is a matter of personal piety, unquestioning faith, and "clean living." It is not a call to advance the human condition through more equitable social reforms. Collective action is urged only when the goals are reactionary ones: abolition of human services, tax cuts for the super rich, and endless increases in military spending.

Both Catholic and Protestant fundamentalists denounce progressive activism as an untoward political intrusion upon faith, while linking ultraconservative political involvement with the practice of faith itself. In a word, those believers who move leftward are deemed guilty of politicizing Christianity, while those who move rightward are struggling to preserve the faith and are Christianizing political affairs by "putting God back into public life."

12

PIOUS PREDATORS

> The wicked are wicked no doubt, and they go
> astray and they fall and they come by their
> deserts; but who can tell the mischief which the
> very virtuous do?
>
> —WILLIAM MAKEPEACE THACKERAY

The fundamentalists tell us that sex is "a wondrous and beautiful gift from God," but one that we must not touch with our filthy hands and sordid minds. It is to be experienced only in a purified monogamous marital context propelled by the highest procreative intent. The holy hucksters preach this moralistic line, but in their personal behavior they are no better than the rest of us—and frequently far worse.

DEVILISH DIVERSIONS

How the religionists and their political counterparts wish to lead their private lives is their business, as long as they bring no harm to others. At issue here is the moral chasm between what is preached and what is practiced. Also at issue is their homophobia and—in the case of pedophiles and rapists—their criminal venality and the damage they inflict upon the innocent. Consider some of the more prominent cases.

As president for twenty-six years of Hillsdale College, a conservative Christian school in Michigan, George C. Roche III championed family values and railed against liberal government. He raised vast sums from wealthy donors who enjoyed the ultraconservative message he put forth in Hillsdale's widely circulated newsletters. Roche named a campus building after himself and showed no tolerance toward anyone who vented a critical word about his administration.[1]

Along with his godly crusades Roche found time to carry on a nineteen-year affair with his son's wife, Lissa Roche, who worked at Hillsdale. In 1999, Roche divorced his own cancer-afflicted wife of forty-four years, kicked her out of his spacious home, and prepared to marry another woman, a move that sorely distressed daughter-in-law Lissa. In the presence of Roche and his new bride, and her own husband (Roche's son), Lissa announced that she and daddy-in-law had been lovers for almost two decades. Roche's son reports, "I could tell by looking at him that she was telling the truth. I saw the look in his eyes. He was caught."[2] A few hours later, Lissa was found dead on campus, shot by a gun owned by her husband. Police treated it as a suicide. Two days afterward, Roche and his new bride whizzed off on their honeymoon.

For years the trustees had turned a deaf ear to reports about Roche's womanizing, including his affair with his daughter-in-law. Now they quickly accepted his resignation and instructed all Hillsdale employees never to address the issue. Roche was granted retirement payoffs amounting to $3 million. Six years later, Hillsdale officials paid tribute to him with a special dinner and an award. When he died in 2006, they published a laudatory obituary in the college's official publication.[3]

Lissa did not fare as well. Immediately after her death, Roche began describing her as mentally unbalanced and a pathological liar. As one observer remarked, "It appears that

Roche was unprepared to fight a living Lissa Roche but more than happy to smear a dead one."[4]

Another, more widely reported scandal involved Jimmy Swaggart, one of the television-pumped religionists who make great play at denouncing loose morality. In 1988 it came to light that Swaggart, married and a father of one, had been repeatedly disporting with a prostitute. The lady in question said he even requested a session with her nine-year-old daughter, an offer the mother rebuffed. Swaggart made a tearful ("I have sinned") confession on television and resigned his ministry.[5] A short time before, with boundless hypocrisy, he himself had unleashed fire and brimstone against rival televangelist Rev. Jim Bakker for having indulged in illicit sexual relations. Swaggart also helped defrock rival preacher Martin Gorman for having an affair with a parishioner. Gorman returned the favor by publicizing photos showing Swaggart visiting a motel with a prostitute.[6]

Some years after his downfall, Swaggart rose like a phoenix from the ashes, once more telecasting to millions of viewers. More recently he made the news again when stopped by police while riding with a prostitute. No doubt he was only trying to save the blemished woman from perdition.

A sex scandal of biblical proportions involved Archbishop Earl Paulk, leader of an independent megachurch in Georgia. He had fathered a child with his brother's wife thirty-four years earlier. Court-ordered test results showed that the nephew, now head pastor of the church, was really the archbishop's son. In 2007, Paulk also confessed to manipulating an employee into sexual relations for years, telling her it was her only path to salvation.[7]

Some religious leaders rail tirelessly against homosexuality. An Anglican archbishop in Kenya called for a break with the Episcopal Church USA for its consecration of a gay bishop. "The Devil has clearly entered our church," he cried. In Nigeria Anglicans warned that ordination of a gay bishop "comes directly from the pit of hell. It is an idea sponsored by Satan himself."[8] Of course, gay bishops are nothing new to Christianity. What is unprecedented is the emergence of an *openly* gay bishop.

Homophobia only drives the homosexual proclivities of certain fundamentalist leaders further underground, thereby intensifying their torment. A textbook case is Rev. Ted Haggard, who in 2006 was forced to resign as president of the National Association of Evangelicals and as pastor of the fourteen-thousand-member New Life Church. Haggard, married with five children, used his pulpit to denounce homosexuality—while himself regularly trysting with a male prostitute. Haggard was one of a coterie of influential right-wing religious leaders who met a number of times with President George W. Bush while enjoying regular entrée to the White House staff.[9]

In a letter to his church board, Haggard denounced his own "repulsive and dark" homosexual tendencies against which he had been warring "all my adult life." Several months later, however, he pronounced himself "completely heterosexual" thanks to three weeks of intensive therapy. Unwilling to accept this miracle, his church overseers advised him to seek employment in the secular sector.[10]

A similar fate descended upon Rev. Paul Barnes, senior pastor of a nondenominational megachurch in Denver, who regularly pronounced homosexuality to be "an abomination in God's eyes." Confronted with testimony about his own sexual relations with men, Barnes resigned his pulpit. Married with two children, he confessed to grappling with a hidden homosexual life since he was five-years-old.[11] Others have tripped the same primrose path: for instance, the Southern Baptist minister in Oklahoma City, who supported a church directive aimed at converting gays into heterosexuals and who himself was arrested after inviting a male undercover police officer to his hotel for sex.[12]

Among the most steadfastly homophobic institutions is the Roman Catholic Church, which judges homosexuality to be both a sin and a "personality disorder." Hence it is always of interest to discover closet-gay clergy—especially in the upper reaches of the Vatican itself. In October 2007, Monsignor Tommaso Stenico, who occupied a senior post at the Holy See in Rome, was forced to resign after being secretly filmed making advances on a young man while telling him that gay sex was not sinful. The monsignor also frequented online gay chat rooms and regularly met with gays, supposedly as part of his work as a psychoanalyst. As he explained, he only *pretended* to be gay in order to glean information about "those who damage the image of the Church with homosexual activity."[13]

With a firm hand Stenico ventured undercover to probe and penetrate the ranks of homosexuals, looking for openings to expose, getting close to gay men in order to erect a treatment that would rectify their ways. Judging from the ejaculations of innocence he repeatedly mouthed during press interviews, Monsignor Stenico must have found his undercover efforts distasteful and exhausting.

PRIESTLY PROCURERS

Shocking revelations of sex *crimes* perpetrated by Catholic clergy have made headlines for some time now. Reports released by the US Conference of Catholic Bishops documented the abuse committed by 4,392 priests against thousands of children between 1950 and 2002. One of every ten priests ordained in 1970 was charged as a pedophile by 2002, and those were only the ones reported.[14]

Pope John Paul II was quick to dismiss these crimes as an "American problem" (as if that would be sufficient reason to downplay them). But by the late 1990s pedophile scandals involving Catholic clergy had surfaced in about a dozen countries.[15]

In the United States, with cases ranging back over decades, many child rapists have been able to avoid prosecution because of the statute of limitations. Far from being isolated misfits, the pedophile priests often have been well positioned as administrators, vicars, and parochial school officials, allowed to remain in responsible posts sometimes even while involved in litigation.[16] At times, perpetrators have been repeatedly charged yet repeatedly promoted. There is the case of the Salesian priest who, though accused of molesting young boys for more than thirty years, was made a high school principal in Los Angeles. Years later, despite additional complaints, he was promoted to treasurer of the entire Salesian Society, a position held until he retired in 2005.[17]

A three-year grand jury investigation in Philadelphia found that Cardinals John Krol and Anthony Bevilacqua concealed child sex-abuse cases involving at least sixty-three clerics over a thirty-five-year period. The two cardinals transferred predator priests without alerting the police or the congregations to which they were rotated. Among them was a priest who raped and impregnated an eleven-year-old girl, then took her for an abortion. Another priest sexually violated a teenage girl while she was immobilized in traction after a car accident.[18] At the height of these revelations, Cardinal Bevilacqua denounced homosexuality as "a moral evil"—when homosexuality was not the issue.[19]

In 2002 it was revealed that Boston's Cardinal Bernard Law had knowingly covered up hundreds of pedophilic crimes from as early as 1977, "shielding child rapists and recklessly allowing them unfettered access to yet more victims."[20] When one of the worst perpetrators, Rev. John Geoghan, was forced into retirement after seventeen years and nearly two hundred victims, Law could still write him, "On behalf of those you have served well, in my own name, I would like to thank you. I understand yours is a painful situation."[21]

Responding to charges that one of his priests sexually assaulted a six-year-old boy, Cardinal Law asserted that "the boy and his parents contributed to the abuse by being negligent."[22] Law never went to jail as an accessory to these crimes. In 2004, Pope John Paul II appointed him to head one of Rome's major basilicas, where he lived in palatial luxury on a generous stipend, supervised by no one but a permissive pope.[23]

There is the case of Rev. Donald McGuire, Mother Teresa's

confessor and spiritual adviser, and spiritual director of her Missionaries of Charity. After McGuire's arrest in 2006, his superiors wrongly told prosecutors that the church possessed no information regarding his case. Documents made public in 2007, however, revealed that at least ten separate church officials had been aware of the priest's pedophilic crimes for decades—and had done nothing. McGuire was sentenced to seven years but remained free on appeal. Later he was again arrested and charged anew, then finally defrocked but was still not incarcerated.[24]

By July 2007, sexual abuse settlements had cost the Roman Church in the United States more than $2 billion spent on compensation to victims, legal fees, and counseling for priests.[25] In one instance among many, the church paid an out-of-court settlement to a Wisconsin woman who had been repeatedly raped by Rev. Bruce MacArthur, beginning when she was ten years old: "The abuse was severe and frequent," she testified. "Because he was a priest he was a God-like figure to me and could do no wrong in my Catholic world." Nine other people subsequently came forward with charges against MacArthur, who admitted to being a serial predator with at least twenty-five victims. Living in a church-run housing center for pedophile priests, he told police how church prelates kept shuttling him to different parishes instead of reporting him to the authorities.[26]

The church hierarchy has directed more fire at the media for publicizing the crimes than at the clergy for committing them. In 2002, Cardinal Oscar Rodriguez Maradiaga of Honduras compared the US media to Hitler and Stalin for reporting sex-abuse scandals. At the same time, Maradiaga himself helped find a safe haven in Honduras for a Costa Rican priest accused of pedophilia.[27]

Pope John Paul II remained sedulously unwilling to deal with the pedophilia plague within the Roman Church. When Archbishop Robert Sanchez of Santa Fe, New Mexico, resigned because of a *60 Minutes* TV exposé of his abuse of teenage girls, John Paul denounced the media for "sensationalizing" the issue.[28] For years, John Paul ignored the complaints targeting Rev. Marcial Maciel, founder of the cultlike order the Legion of Christ. Maciel was a particularly cruel and long-term predator, accused of having sexually assaulted about twenty seminarians and a large number of children. When eight former members of the Legion of Christ filed a canon-law case with detailed allegations against the priest, John Paul refused to acknowledge the charges, and the case was squelched. The pope continued to heap praise upon Maciel, publicly hailing him as an "efficacious guide to youth."[29] It must have been painful for the predator's victims to hear such utterances tumbling from the pontiff's lips. Facing revived charges, Maciel was allowed to retire unscathed in 2005. He died a few years later at the age of eighty-seven.

In 2002, John Paul ordered that charges against priests were to be reported secretly to the Vatican and hearings were to be held *in camera*. In 2004 a lay reform group, Voice of the Faithful, with chapters around the United States, submitted a petition with twenty-five thousand signatures asking that the pope meet with a group of abuse survivors. He ignored the request.

Consider how John Paul handled the case of Archbishop William Levada, who for years did nothing to weed out sexual predators in his clergy.[30] Instead of removing him from office, the pope assigned Levada the task of softening the measures initiated against pedophilia by the US Conference of Catholic Bishops. After John Paul's death, it was more of the same. Levada was appointed by the newly ensconced Pope Benedict XVI as head of the Congregation for the Doctrine of the Faith, an office considered to be the second-highest position in the church.[31] (It used to be the Office of the Inquisition but underwent a name change in 1965.)

When Benedict was still Cardinal Joseph Ratzinger and occupied the same important position to which he later appointed Levada, he did nothing about the church's pandemic pedophilia problem. Instead, like John Paul before him, he accused the media of conducting a "planned campaign" to cast the church in a bad light. He argued that the percentage of offending priests was no higher than for other professions, and perhaps even lower.[32]

A judge of the Holy Roman Rota, the church's highest court, wrote in a Vatican-approved article that bishops should *not* report sexual violations to civil authorities. Some bishops agreed, perhaps fearing that a thorough investigation of the lower ranks might lead upward into the hierarchy itself. Indeed, the John Jay College Survey commissioned by the US bishops found that among 5,450 complaints of clerical sexual abuse in the United States there were charges against at least sixteen bishops.[33]

OBSTRUCTING JUSTICE

The sexual abuse of children and others has been tolerated by the Catholic Church hierarchy for centuries.[34] Upon receiving a complaint, church officials either ignored it or responded with a denial. They seemed primarily concerned with avoiding lawsuits and bad publicity. They did not investigate to see if other children had been victimized by the same priest. They told parishioners not to talk to the authorities and offered no pastoral assistance to young victims and their shaken families. Some potential plaintiffs were threatened with excommunication or suspension from Catholic school. Church officials impugned their credibility, even going after them with countersuits.[35]

Sexual "misconduct" with children seemed to be considered "not that important, and certainly not serious enough to be worth compromising a priestly career."[36] Church leaders refrained from cooperating with law enforcement authorities, refusing to hand over abusers' records in both criminal and civil cases, claiming that the confidentiality of their files came under the same legal protection as privileged communications in the confessional—a view that has no basis in canon or secular law. Bishop James Quinn of Cleveland even urged church officials to send incriminating files of "brother priests" to the Vatican Embassy in Washington, DC, where diplomatic immunity would prevent the documents from being subpoenaed.[37] A good number among the hierarchy continued to abet criminal offenders, obstruct justice, and act as accessories to the crime.

For years church leaders clung to the "few bad apples" argument, treating the charges as hysterical exaggeration. Courageous priests who called for investigations of the problem sometimes had their careers blocked. Some church officials hid pedophilic fugitives from the law, arguing in court that criminal investigations of church affairs violated the free practice of religion as guaranteed by the US Constitution—as if pedophilia were a sacrosanct religious practice.[38] Church authorities tended to treat it as just a personal failing that needed healing through prayer and forgiveness. They were often quick to believe the pedophile's denials or his seemingly heartfelt vow that he would err no more.

The church hierarchy seems to have shown little regard for the sexual *victims* whose lives are so deeply scarred and who continue to pay a heavy price for the rest of their lives: years of depression, anger, alcoholism, drug addiction, eating disorders, nightmares, panic attacks, sexual dysfunction, broken marriages, mistreated offspring, and in some instances mental breakdown and suicide.[39] The parents in turn live with the pain of having their children raped by men whom the family had trusted and respected as ordained purveyors of the holy sacraments.

Church leaders act today as if the crisis has been resolved. But there still are pedophiles within the religious orders in this country and around the world who have yet to be brought to justice. Cover-ups by high-ranking clergy continue to come to light.[40] In 2007, for instance, Bishop Tod Brown of the Roman Catholic diocese of Orange, California, was charged with criminal contempt of court for sending a high-ranking church official to Canada for "medical treatment" before he could be fully deposed in a sexual abuse case.[41]

In 2009, a nine-year investigation in Ireland found that, for some sixty years, over thirty thousand Irish children had been sexually and physically abused by priests and nuns in what was described as a "sexual underground," a network of reformatories, orphanages, and "industrial schools" run mostly by the Christian Brothers, a religious order. Some children were institutionalized for petty crimes like stealing food, or for truancy, or merely for being born out of wedlock. In many cases their parents tried unsuccessfully to reclaim them. The commission found that Ireland's Department of Education and the Catholic Church "colluded in perpetuating an abusive system," and that sexual molestation and rape were "endemic" in boys' facilities, perpetrated by Christian Brothers. The girls, supervised by nuns, suffered much less sexual abuse but endured frequent assaults and humiliation designed to make them feel worthless.

The report noted that no steps were taken on behalf of the raped children. "At worst, the child was blamed and seen as corrupted by the sexual activity, and was punished severely." The commission concluded that church officials always shielded their pedophiles from arrest amid a culture of self-serving secrecy. The report could not be used for criminal prosecutions because the Christian Brothers successfully sued the commission to keep it from revealing the names of Christian Brothers, dead or alive, who were charged with pedophilia.[42]

On a visit to the United States in 2008, Pope Benedict XVI seemingly struck a new note, announcing that the priesthood was "absolutely incompatible" with the sexual abuse of minors; he "who is guilty of being a pedophile cannot be a priest." The pontiff added, "We are deeply ashamed. We will do what is possible so that this cannot happen again in the future."[43] But the man he assigned to investigate the problem was none other than the aforementioned Cardinal William Levada, who for years had done nothing about the pedophile priests in his archdiocese.

PEDOPHILIC PROTESTANTS

The presupposition that Catholic clergy are especially driven to pedophilia because they are deprived of marriage as an outlet is perhaps put to rest by the prevalence of sex offenders among Protestant clerics, all of whom are married or allowed to marry. A victims' advocate group recently turned its attention from the Roman Catholics to the Southern Baptists, charging America's largest Protestant denomination with failing to deal with child abusers. In the latter half of 2006, the advocate group received reports of about forty cases of sexual crimes by Southern Baptist ministers.[44]

In North Carolina, the pastor at New Life Christian Center was charged with repeatedly raping a twelve-year-old girl and fathering her child.[45] Ministers of a wide variety of Protestant churches in Illinois, Florida, Louisiana, Ohio, Missouri, and elsewhere were charged with raping numerous young girls and some boys.[46] Rev. Eugene Paul White, Baptist minister in Orangevale, California, was convicted of sexually abusing his four adopted foster daughters from 1999 to 2004. He was sharply criticized by the judge for blaming the girls, ages eight to twelve, for deliberately enticing him, and was sentenced to 180 years in prison.[47]

More often perpetrators escape prosecution because of the statute of limitations, or receive light sentences by judges who seem disinclined to treat child rape as a serious crime. One of the worst cases of leniency involves a Jehovah's Witnesses deacon, Michael Porter, convicted in Britain on twenty-five counts of committing "gross indecency" with thirteen children (including an eighteen-month-old baby), over a fourteen-year period. For this he was sentenced to three years of "community rehabilitation." Families of the victims were outraged.[48]

Topping any list of religious evil-doers would be Paul Schaefer, leader of Colonia Dignidad, a paramilitary religious cult of German émigrés established in a remote part of Chile in the early 1960s, later aligned with the Pinochet dictatorship. A former corporal in Hitler's army, Schaefer preached a fiery brand of apocalyptic fundamentalism heavily laced with anticommunism and anti-Semitism. For almost forty years Schaefer controlled the lives of hundreds of residents at Colonia Dignidad, deciding whom they could marry, often taking babies from their parents and raising them under his charge. He was captured in 2005 in Argentina and sentenced in Chile to twenty years for torturing minors and committing sodomy and pedophilia with at least twenty-six little children. He faced additional charges of murder, kidnapping, forced labor, and tax evasion.[49]

Every month, an atheist publication, *Freethought Today*, issues long lists of clergy of all denominations who are connected to a dismaying litany of pedophilic crimes: "felony rape of a child," "aggravated sexual assault of a minor," "rape and gross sexual imposition involving children," "oral copulation with a child," "impregnating a minor," and on and on. *Freethought Today*'s staggering lists of crimes by clergy also include voyeurism, indecent exposure, solicitation, theft, embezzlement, fraud, burglary, drug trafficking, felonious assault, and an occasional murder or attempted murder.

In 2006 the Church of Latter-day Saints (Mormons) and the Boy Scouts of America were sued by six men for perpetrating an "infestation of child abuse, stretching across the country, involving hundreds of predators and thousands of children." The plaintiffs further charged that both organizations knew about it but had failed to protect children. (The Mormons sponsored 28 percent of all Scout units nationally in 2006.) One of those charged, Timur Dykes, was a former Scout leader and Mormon Sunday school teacher who was convicted of child sex abuse several times and was serving probation until 2013 as a predatory sex offender. More than a dozen men have brought charges against the Mormon Church.[50]

Not all sexual victims are underage. Many grown women parishioners end up as victims of rape and sexual battery by clergy to whom they turn for support in times of personal distress. The pastor of a Protestant church in Fort Worth, Texas, was accused of raping a congregant under the guise of "casting out demons." She had gone to him for counseling.[51] A Hindu priest in New York was charged with sexually assaulting two underage sisters; he told one of them that he was cleansing her of "evil spirits."[52]

SUPPRESSING SECULAR SEXUALITY

While covering up pedophilia for many years, church leaders have uncompromisingly policed other forms of sexuality. Like John Paul II, Pope Benedict XVI focused on the "intrinsic moral evil" of homosexuality, gay marriage, divorce, birth control, masturbation, and fornication.

Consider birth control. The Vatican continued to uphold a 1968 encyclical prohibiting any action before, during, or after sexual intercourse intended to prevent procreation. One was not allowed to use condoms to avoid transmitting or contracting AIDS, syphilis, or any other sexually related disease. If a diseased husband could not remain abstinent, it was better to infect his wife rather than wear a condom, because the spiritual sacrament of marriage took precedence over the health and safety of one's spouse. Benedict also continued John Paul's opposition to in vitro fertilization and artificial insemination as an unnatural interference. In sum, there was to be no sex without potential pregnancy, and no pregnancy without sex.

In recent years Protestant fundamentalists have become just as preoccupied as any pope with suppressing human sexuality, even within the confines of heterosexual marriage. They oppose contraception because it allows for sex with impunity, thereby encouraging promiscuity. Once the risk of conception has been removed, they reason, there is greater license for premarital sex, adultery, and a tendency within marriage itself to separate the sex act from procreation, leaving people more inclined to get an abortion should an accidental pregnancy occur.[53]

While maintaining a suppressive stance against sexuality in

the secular world, Catholic and Protestant church leaders have not accorded sufficiently serious attention to the sexual abuse within their own religious world. This is more than just hypocrisy. The hypocrisy itself effects an immense betrayal and often is a cover for *criminal behavior* that is seriously injurious to innocent lives.

It is argued that predator transgressions are not an indictment against religion as such but are the doings of flawed individuals. But the cases discussed herein involve something more than flawed characters. We are all flawed in that we are all far less than perfect. These perpetrators and their organizations are corrupt and criminally hurtful of human life. They have operated with something close to impunity, using their sacred robes, elevated status, and moral authority to prey upon the vulnerable, while making the religious establishment their base of operation, a den for soul-damaging deeds.

13

POLITICOS AND OTHER PHARISEES

A Pharisee is a man who prays publicly and preys privately.

—DON MARQUIS

Standing close to the clerical hypocrites are their right-wing secular counterparts, the *politicos* who espouse an unflagging devotion to old-fashioned morality and family values. They inveigh against homosexuality, gay marriage, adultery, feminism, abortion, crime, secularism, modernity, and liberalism—all of which they tend to treat as different facets of the same evil decadence. They dilate on the need to "put God back into public life" and even claim to be guided by a godly mandate when governing. Their deeds, however, frequently betray their words.

BAD BOYS, NASTY BOYS: THE GOP IN ACTION

Consider this incomplete sampling of politically prominent "social conservatives" who preach the conventional virtues to their constituents while practicing something else after hours.

Representative Henry Hyde, Illinois Republican, played a key role in the impeachment campaign waged against the adulterous president Bill Clinton. In the midst of this, it was revealed that Hyde had carried on a six-year liaison with a young married mother of three children. The woman's former husband blamed Hyde for the divorce that followed and for the emotional damage inflicted on the children. Hyde dismissed the affair as "a youthful indiscretion"—it having ended when he was just a callow youngster of forty-three or so. In 1992, Hyde divorced his wife of forty-five years. Soon after the divorce she died and he quickly remarried.[1]

Representative Bob Livingston, Louisiana Republican, married with four children, resigned as House speaker-elect after his marital infidelities made the headlines in 1998.[2]

The three leading candidates for the Republican 2008 presidential nomination, Rudolph Giuliani, John McCain, and Newt Gingrich, had five divorces between them, all involving adultery. Years earlier, Speaker of the House Newt Gingrich led the charge against the philandering President Clinton; at the same time he was carrying on an affair with a congressional aide. Gingrich hastened a divorce action against his (second) wife while she was hospitalized with cancer in order that he might marry the aide. At one point his ailing ex-wife and children had to get assistance from their local church, having received insufficient support from Gingrich himself. In 2007, he claimed to have come to grips with his "personal failures" and sought God's forgiveness.[3]

Baptist minister Bill Randall, who had been aggressively touted by the Republican Party as a candidate for the House of Representatives, admitted to fathering an illegitimate child in the 1980s. After confirming the child's existence, he changed his story the next day during a press interview, now insisting that his teenage son was the father. Sensing that no one would run with that story, Randall again reversed course and admitted to paternity. He did everyone a favor by dropping out of the 1998 congressional race.[4]

Bob Barr was a Georgia Republican congressman until 2003, after which he became a conservative activist. While still married to wife #1, he was romancing the woman who would become wife #2. Barr was on record as a staunch right-to-lifer, but this did not prevent him from driving wife #2 to a clinic and paying the costs for her abortion. He soon took on a new mistress who became wife #3 shortly after he shed #2. While in Congress, with no sense of irony, Barr authored the "Defense of Marriage Act."[5]

In 2007, Senator David Vitter, a Louisiana Republican and family-values man, made the news for having patronized a prostitution ring in Washington, DC, for several years and having used the services of a New Orleans brothel over a five-month period. Vitter refused to resign, assuring everyone that "I asked for and received forgiveness from God and my wife."[6]

In 2008, Republican Congressman Vito Fossella of Staten Island, New York, was arrested for drunken driving outside Washington, DC. The woman who came to bail him out, it was discovered, was his mistress and the mother of his three-year-old daughter. In addition, Fossella had a wife and three children at home, and on certain days of the week he was a strong advocate of conservative family values.[7]

In June 2009, within days of each other, two Republican notables, Senator John Ensign of Nevada and Governor Mark Sanford of South Carolina (both considered potential GOP presidential candidates for 2012), were exposed as being involved in extramarital liaisons. Senator Ensign was an evangelical Christian church member who had a 100 percent voter approval record from the right-wing Christian Coalition. Married with three children, Ensign confessed to having an affair with a married woman who was a close family friend and an employee on his staff. Some fundamentalists would denounce Ensign's affair as sinful, adulterous fornication, but he himself referred to it as "inappropriate behavior."[8]

Scarcely a week later, Governor Sanford, married with four children and chair of the Republican Governors Association, was exposed as having an affair with an Argentinean woman. Years earlier, as a congressman, Sanford had voted to impeach Bill Clinton for violating his marital oath, an oath that should "be taken very, very seriously," in Sanford's words. For stalwart GOP moralists like Sanford, Ensign, and others becoming too numerous to mention, holy matrimony is a sacred bond between one man and one woman—and one or more hot cuties on the side.

To be sure, there have been Democrats who have wavered in their familial devotions, most notably Governor Eliot Spitzer of New York, who resigned in 2008 while under investigation for cavorting with expensive prostitutes, and former senator John Edwards, who admitted to an extramarital affair and possibly fathered a child out of wedlock. But substantially fewer Democrats than Republicans have been caught in compromising situations, and the errant ones have not had as pronounced a history of pretending to be sexual puritans and defenders of traditional sexual morality.

REPUBLICAN GAY BLADES

Along with the hypocritical Republican philanderers, there are the subterranean gay blades. Virginia GOP congressman Edward Schrock resigned from office in 2004, having been caught soliciting sex from a telephone service that specialized in gay liaisons.[9] In 2007, Bob Allen, Florida Republican state legislator, married with one child, was arrested in a public restroom after offering to perform oral sex on an undercover officer for a meager twenty dollars.[10]

Another restroom adventurer was Senator Larry Craig, Republican of Idaho, an outspoken opponent of gay marriage and gays in the military. Craig was famously arrested for directing sexual advances toward an undercover police officer in a men's toilet at Minneapolis–St. Paul International Airport. The police had been monitoring the restroom because of complaints about sexual activities there. Craig pleaded guilty to disorderly conduct. Other men, including one from Craig's college days, identified the senator as having engaged in sexual activity with them or having made overtures with that intent, including an encounter in the restrooms at Union Station in Washington, DC.[11]

Another GOP politico who consistently voted against gay rights, Washington State representative Richard Curtis, appears to have been caught with his pants down. According to police reports, while on a GOP retreat, Curtis allegedly met a man in a local erotic video store and went with him to a downtown hotel for a night of sex. Once the story broke, Curtis resigned from office.[12]

In 2002, a high-level defector from conservative ranks, and erstwhile closet gay, David Brock, revealed in his tell-all book that any number of moralistic, family-values Republicans with whom he was personally acquainted were engaging in infidelities, homosexual trysts, and other behavior that would be judged scandalous by GOP keepers of the faith.[13]

There are the three classic cases of ultraconservative antigay gays who go back half a century: FBI director J. Edgar Hoover, McCarthyite investigator and Washington lobbyist Roy Cohn, and Cardinal Francis Spellman of New York's Roman Catholic archdiocese. All three of these prominent right-wingers and keepers of American homophobic vigilance were themselves secretly full-blown homosexuals who sometimes partied together in the company of choice male escorts—back in the days when the press dared not touch such stories.[14]

What is deplorable is not only the obviously hypocritical inconsistency between professed beliefs and private behavior, but more important the professed beliefs themselves, beliefs that advocate discrimination against gays, brand prostitutes as criminals, equate abortion with murder, denounce divorce as a mortal threat to family and society, and treat sex between unmarried consenting adults (even of the heterosexual variety) as sinful fornication.

Consequently, a noticeable number of conservative politicos

face the daunting task of trying to submerge their lascivious desires in order to live up to their puritanical mouthings, trapped as they are in an unyielding cycle of surreptitious sin and furious public denunciation of those same sins.

PREYING WHILE PRAYING

In recent years, Republican ranks appeared to be riddled not only with sexual hypocrites but, far worse, sexual predators. There was the former Republican mayor of Waterbury, Connecticut, Philip Giordano, who is now serving a thirty-seven-year sentence for sexual abuse in 2001 of two girls, ages eight and ten.[15]

Republican activist and Christian Coalition leader Beverly Russell admitted to an abusive incestuous relationship with his stepdaughter that extended over a period of years right up to the time the distraught girl murdered her own children.[16]

Former chair of a Republican Party county organization and head of the Oregon Christian Coalition, Lou Beres had to resign his post after three female relatives accused him of sexually abusing them for a number of years when they were children. Not long after that, Beres confessed to molesting a thirteen-year-old girl.[17]

Ohio Republican county commissioner David Swartz pleaded guilty to molesting two girls under the age of eleven and was sentenced to eight years in prison in 2004.[18] Maine Republican county commissioner Merrill Robert Barter pleaded guilty to sexual assault on a teenage boy but received only a suspended sentence.[19]

Director of the Young Republican Federation in Bakersfield, California, Nicholas Elizondo molested his six-year-old daughter and was sentenced to six years in prison. Republican antigay activist Earl "Butch" Kimmerling of Anderson, Indiana, was sentenced to forty years in prison for raping an eight-year-old girl after he attempted to stop a gay couple from adopting her. Republican candidate Richard Gardner of Clark County, Nevada, admitted to having sex with his two daughters. Several other Republican politicos were arrested and convicted of possession of child pornography.[20]

Jim West, conservative Republican mayor of Spokane, Washington, backed a measure to prohibit gays and lesbians from teaching in public schools on the presumption that they might get too close to their pupils. Meanwhile, he purportedly was using his city hall computer to troll for sex with high school boys. Two men accused West of molesting them when they were Boy Scouts and he was a troop leader. He was ousted in a recall election in 2005.[21]

An Illinois Republican county board candidate, Brent Schepp, was charged with molesting a fourteen-year-old girl. Schepp killed himself three days later.[22] Meanwhile, Kentucky GOP leader Bobby Stumbo was arrested for raping a five-year-old boy.[23] And Republican antiabortion activist Howard Scott Heldreth was found to be a convicted child rapist and a registered sex offender in Florida and Illinois.[24]

A GOP congressman from Florida, Mark Foley, was caught sending sexually explicit e-mails to teenage boys who served as congressional pages. He invited one page to engage in oral sex with him; the boy refused.[25] Foley chaired the House Caucus on Missing and Exploited Children, which introduced stricter legislation for tracking sexual predators. Republican congressional leaders had received complaints about him from congressional pages, which they repeatedly failed to act upon. Foley resigned from Congress in 2006. At that time, allegations of improper interactions with congressional pages were leveled at another Republican congressman, Jim Kolbe of Arizona, who decided not to run for reelection.[26]

Florida Republican county commissioner Patrick Lee McGuire surrendered to police in 2007 after allegedly molesting girls between the ages of eight and thirteen.[27] That same year, J. D. Roy Atchison, a federal prosecutor appointed by the Bush administration, operating "one of the most conservative United

States attorney's offices in the country" dedicated to a hard-line law-and-order approach, was charged with traveling across state lines to engage in sex with a five-year-old girl. When arrested en route to his would-be rendezvous, Atchison was carrying a doll and petroleum jelly. While detained in a federal prison in Michigan, he committed suicide.[28]

One investigator catalogues over one hundred cases of sexual criminality and misconduct committed by Republican officials and supporters in recent years, including at least forty-four who have been involved in sex crimes against children.[29] In such instances, the most reprehensible thing is neither the hypocrisy nor the professed beliefs, but the behavior itself, involving the molestation and sexual assault of children and unwilling adults. The perpetrators are not merely hypocrites. They are criminals.

DEVOUT SWINDLERS

Right-wing moral hypocrisy and malfeasance is not confined to the sexual realm. House majority leader Tom DeLay, a Texas Republican and born-again Baptist who read from Holy Scripture at church services in Washington, DC, was indicted for criminal conspiracy and money laundering and was forced to resign in 2005.[30]

A close associate of DeLay and acquaintance of President George W. Bush was the religiously devout lobbyist Jack Abramoff, who pleaded guilty to having bilked Indian tribes of $20 million. He also lied to clients, evaded taxes, and bribed lawmakers.[31] Three nationally known conservative religious leaders closely allied to the Bush administration—Rev. Louis Sheldon, James Dobson, and Ralph Reed—were implicated in Abramoff's scheme to fleece Indian casino owners. In the past, all three of these men of God had denounced gambling as a sin. When running for lieutenant governor in Georgia, Reed pocketed $5 million from Abramoff's casino deals.[32]

Speaking of gambling, there was William Bennett, secretary of education in the Reagan administration, a devout Catholic who volunteered nagging preachments on every moral issue afoot. He especially held forth about how people must eschew liberal permissiveness and build stronger moral character and self-control. Bennett himself however suffered from an uncontrollable addiction, having gambled away $8 million in casinos over ten years.[33]

In both 2005 and 2006, Senate majority leader Bill Frist, a Republican from Tennessee, was singled out as one of the most "corrupt" members of Congress because of dubious stock sales, cover-ups, and alleged violations of campaign finance laws. A member of the National Presbyterian Church and champion of the religious Right, Frist decided not to run for reelection.[34]

Numbering among the holy hypocrites are religiously devout corporate plunderers like the Hunt brothers, oil billionaires from Texas and born-again Jesus worshipers who were convicted of conspiring to corner the silver market; and Charles Keating, who founded moralistic censorial groups such as Citizens for Decency through Law while looting his Lincoln Savings & Loans and bilking investors of $200 million. He served four years in prison.[35]

As a devout Christian, John Rigas, CEO of Adelphia Communications Corp., censored programming on his cable networks that he deemed unseemly. This self-appointed protector of public morals was sentenced to fifteen years for his role in a multibillion-dollar fraud that led to Adelphia's collapse.[36]

Enron's duplicitous duo, CEO Ken Lay and CFO Andrew Fastow, were both religious gentlemen. Lay proclaimed that God "does work all things for good for those who love the Lord."[37] Fastow was an active member of a Hebrew congregation. Both were found guilty of conspiracy and fraud, having bilked thousands of employees and small investors out of millions of dollars.

Another man of God was Bernie Ebbers, who wrote of his personal relationship with Jesus Christ. Ebbers was convicted of conspiracy and lying to investigators to cover up the $11 billion accounting fraud that he helped mastermind at WorldCom.[38]

The holy hypocrites, both lay and clerical, crow a devotion to traditional morality while pursuing material and emotional plunder more rapaciously than any of us ordinary infidels and libertines. Looking at the above cases, and the many others that one could add if space and patience allowed, we can conclude that religious profusion is no guarantee of moral behavior. If anything, the criminals use religion as a bludgeon to be brandished against liberal opponents and as a cover for their own crimes and sins.

PART V

THEOCRACY, PAST, PRESENT, AND FUTURE

14

CHURCH *IN* STATE

When fascism comes to America, it will be wrapped in the flag, carrying a cross.
—SINCLAIR LEWIS

Leaders of the religious Right repeatedly claim that the United States was founded on the Christian faith. During the presidential campaign of 1992, President George Bush, the elder, proclaimed that "America, as Christ ordained" is "a light unto the world." Various evangelical groups have repeatedly called for "restoring a Christian nation" and reviving "the biblical worldview of the Founding Fathers."[1] The 2006 platform of the Texas State Republican Party declares, "America is a Christian nation."[2] In 2007, while running for the Republican presidential nomination, Arizona senator John McCain asserted that "the Constitution established the United States of America as a Christian nation."[3]

A SECULAR STATE

In fact, the founders of this nation did not maintain that the Republic was beholden to Christianity or any other religion. As

James Madison wrote, "Religious bondage shackles and debilitates the mind, and unfits it for every noble enterprise, every expanded prospect."[4] Madison fought against a Virginia bill that would allocate state money for the training of religious teachers. In similar spirit, George Washington urged that all should be free to worship according to the dictates of their own conscience. While serving as president of the United States, he edited out any references to Jesus Christ in the government proclamations he signed.[5]

Another Founding Father, John Adams, vented his fears of a reappearing Calvinist theocracy. He was grateful that religious fanatics could not whip, burn, and mutilate people in the United States. He was sure that if they could they would. Adams felt strongly that "this would be the best of all possible worlds if there was no religion in it!"[6]

Benjamin Franklin did not see America as a Christian nation. Like many of the other founders, Franklin believed in one Creator but had serious doubts as to the divinity of Jesus Christ, "though it is a question I do not dogmatize upon, having never studied it."[7]

One of Thomas Jefferson's proudest accomplishments was the Virginia Statute for Religious Freedom. Passed into law by the Virginia legislature in 1786, it brought (in his words) "freedom for the Jew and the Gentile, the Christian and the Mohammeden, the Hindu and infidel of every denomination." Yes, even the *infidel* was to enjoy freedom of belief or disbelief without interference from state authorities. There was to be not only freedom *of* religion but freedom *from* state-promoted religion.[8]

The delegates to the Constitutional Convention in Philadelphia in 1787 (our "Founding Fathers") left the deity entirely out of the picture, even declining to open their daily sessions with a prayer for divine guidance.[9] At a time when some states still prohibited Catholics and Jews from holding public office, the newly minted Constitution made no mention of God or Jesus, and no claim that ours is a Christian nation. Article VI reads, "no religious Test shall ever be required as a Qualification to any Office or public Trust under the United States."

The First Amendment to the Constitution reads in part: "Congress shall make no law respecting an establishment of religion, or prohibiting the free exercise thereof." No religion is to be established as the nation's official church, supported by the public purse. At the same time, every religion is free to promote beliefs according to its own lights. The government can neither inhibit religious groups nor act as an agency in support of them; nor can it impose a credo on nonbelievers.

In 1797 the Treaty of Tripoli, negotiated by President Washington, ratified by the US Senate, and later signed into law by President John Adams, offered an assurance that the United States would not pursue a vengeful holy war in North Africa. Article 11 of the treaty read: "The Government of the United States is not in any sense founded on the Christian Religion." Here was an unequivocal statement of the founders' secular identity, in a treaty that stands as the law of the land.

As late as 1848, the French aristocrat Alexis de Tocqueville reported in his widely celebrated *Democracy in America* that everyone he met in his travels across the United States, lay and cleric, believed "that the main reason for the quiet sway of religion over their country was the complete separation of church and state." By staying free of the partisan vicissitudes and opportunistic interests that compose "the bitter passions of this world," religion prevails untainted, Tocqueville reported. Both lay and cleric believed that the less linkage between church and state, the less opportunity for state corruption and favoritism.[10]

In the century and a half since Tocqueville, however, the First Amendment's "establishment clause," keeping church and state separate, has been repeatedly compromised. As of 2009, religious qualifications for office still exist in a number of state constitutions. Maryland, North Carolina, South Carolina, and Texas still deny atheists the right to hold state office. The Arkansas Constitution also declares an atheist incompetent "to testify as a witness in any court." The Tennessee Constitution denies office to any person who does not believe in God and an afterlife ("a future state of rewards and punishments"). Atheist boys cannot be members of the Boy Scouts of America even though that organization receives government funds in many states.

While there is no state-established church in the United States, religion per se is so closely identified with state-sponsored events as to have become unofficially sanctioned. Convocations and public prayers by clergymen have been an essential prop for political party conventions, congressional sessions, and presidential inaugurations. "Under God" continues as an incantation in the Pledge of Allegiance. "In God we trust," embossed on US coinage, continues as our national motto under federal law. And in the last half century or more, just about every president has laid claim to a policy mandate from God when launching military attacks against people in smaller, weaker countries.

At the 1992 GOP national convention, various speakers averred that Republicans had higher moral standards and were closer to the Almighty than were Democrats.[11] This religious posturing was too much even for some religious groups. The National Council of Churches, for one, charged that it was blasphemy to make "partisan use of God's name" and "assert the moral superiority of one people over another or one political party over another." In like manner, the Baptist Joint Committee on Public Affairs announced, "We begin with the proposition that God is neither Democrat nor Republican nor, for that matter, American. God transcends all national and political affiliations."[12] One would think.

FAVORS FOR THE FAITHFUL

Seeking to undo the separation of church and state, President George W. Bush set up more Bible study groups in the White House than any previous president. He regularly entertained right-wing fundamentalist ministers who occupied a central place in the Republican Party.[13] Sounding much like an Old Testament prophet, he announced in June 2003, "I'm driven with a mission from God," and "God told me to strike at al Qaeda and I struck them, and then he instructed me to strike at Saddam, which I did."[14]

Bush claimed additional celestial mandates. On the night before his second inauguration, he told an audience of military officers in Washington, DC, that as Americans he and they had "a calling from beyond the stars to stand for freedom."[15] Who other than the deity calls from beyond the stars?

Bush put forth an executive order granting religious organizations monies—taken from the discretionary funds of various federal agencies—to administer human services with little or no government oversight. Critics pointed out that these *faith-based initiatives* eventually would replace government services for the needy without being sufficiently developed or reliably managed. Under such programs, seven federal agencies gave $2.1 billion to religious charities in fiscal 2005 alone.[16]

A Government Accountability Office investigation in 2006 found that some recipients of faith-based federal grants engaged in overtly religious activities, such as prayer sessions, while doling out government-funded social services.[17]

Religious organizations have been deep-dipping into the federal pork barrel for years. Catholic Charities USA, representing more than 130 Catholic social service agencies whose combined operating budgets total more than $2 billion, acknowledged that it received over 60 percent of its yearly income from the federal government. Publicly subsidized Catholic hospitals and clinics prohibit artificial fertilization, abortion, and birth control in all forms. Those hurt the most by such bans are rape victims denied access to the morning-after pill, and low-income women and young people dependent on hospitals for safe abortions and for contraceptive protection from pregnancy and sexually transmitted disease.[18]

The Salvation Army in New York received $50 million a year in government funds to conduct drug treatment programs, adoptions, and a range of other services, all of which were merged with the Salvation Army's evangelical work. Employees in the Salvation Army and other federally funded faith-based missions could be denied a job for not being a Christian, or the right kind of Christian. Some have been hounded by their bosses to reveal their religion and hand over the names and telephone numbers of their pastors.[19]

Some religious interests hire professional lobbyists to pursue legislative favors such as transferring parcels of federal land to individual churches and religious colleges, or winning multimillion-dollar contracts to administer largely unsupervised federal welfare grants.[20]

Church investments and properties enjoy tax-free status, obliging the rest of us to carry a still bigger portion of the tax burden amounting to billions of dollars each year. Ordained clergy can write off most of their housing expenses as federal tax exemptions. This supposedly is to assist poorly paid clergy who serve their communities. No such exemption is available to employees of secular nonprofit organizations or low-paid inner-city teachers and daycare workers who serve *their* communities. In addition, clergy of every faith are exempt from income tax withholding and can opt out of having to make Social Security payments.[21]

Tax exemptions go to religious organizations that are heavily engaged in lobbying efforts to criminalize abortion, support antigay legislation, and preserve their tax-exempt status. Bills pending in Congress are designed to grant religious denominations greater freedom to make partisan political endorsements without losing their tax-exempt status.[22]

President Bush appointed right-wing fundamentalists to scientific advisory councils and to administer health programs. He eliminated funds for organizations that offered abortion counseling and allocated millions of federal dollars to church groups that promoted sexual abstinence and (heterosexual) marriage. In 2006, Bush threatened to veto a bill that would expand federal funding for embryonic stem cell research, arguing that embryos are an inviolate form of human life.[23]

Under the Bush administration, larger numbers of Justice Department lawyers were recruited from conservative religious institutions to aggressively defend faith-based organizations. These organizations wanted to circulate religious literature in public schools, and they claimed a right to discriminate on religious grounds when hiring people to run federally funded programs. Meanwhile, the Justice Department significantly diminished its involvement in the traditional areas of voting rights, police abuse, and hate crimes.[24]

INFILTRATING THE MILITARY

Religionist incursions reached right into the US Air Force Academy. Years ago, the academy had six chaplains, consisting of three mainline Protestants, two priests, and a rabbi. By 2004, a dozen evangelical chaplains had been added to the roster, even as the cadet population decreased 25 percent. The evangelical chaplains persistently pressured cadets to attend chapel and receive religious instruction, warning that those "not born again" would "burn in the fires of hell." Monday night fundamentalist Bible studies were attended by at least half of the academy's cadets, with no priest, rabbi, or mainline Protestant chaplain participating.[25]

Some cadets accused the fundamentalists of harassment. Jewish cadets said they were blamed for the death of Jesus and subjected to anti-Semitic slurs. One cadet was refused permission to form a group for freethinkers and atheists because it was not "faith-based." On one occasion all the cadets were marched into a large hall and made to stand at attention and watch Mel Gibson's film *The Passion of the Christ*.[26]

Academy commandant Brig. Gen. Johnny Weida included biblical passages in official e-mails and correspondence to subordinates and cadets. In 2005, a Yale Divinity School team, initially investigating sexual harassment at the academy, could not help but report that nonconforming cadets were being subjected to coercive religious indoctrination by the fundamentalists on campus. When the academy's Lutheran chaplain signed the report, the air force transferred her to Asia.[27]

Academy faculty members introduced themselves to their classes as born-again Christians and urged their students to find Jesus. A "Christmas Greeting" published in the academy's newspaper, signed by three hundred academy personnel, declared that "Jesus Christ is the only real hope for the world" and there is "salvation in no one else." A banner hanging in the football team locker room announced, "I am a Christian first and last . . . I am a member of Team Jesus Christ." The academy's baseball coach, recruited from an evangelical college, required players to lead team prayer during practice.[28]

In a sterling example of doublespeak, Brig. Gen. Cecil R. Richardson, air force deputy chief of chaplains, said, "We will not proselytize, but we reserve the right to evangelize the un-churched."[29] Less circuitous was the academy luncheon attended by hundreds of air force officers who addressed the topic "Why We Cannot Let You Have Your God While We Have Ours."[30]

After being sued for proselytizing cadets, and amid calls for tolerance of religious belief, the US Air Force Academy rescinded an obviously unconstitutional code that had allowed chaplains to evangelize military personnel. Cadets and employees were informed that they could not use government e-mail to send religious messages, put up posters with religious themes, or use positions of authority to endorse a particular faith or coercively influence the religious views of subordi-nates.[31] The fundamentalist stranglehold was thereby loosened but not broken.

There are other hotbeds of religiosity in the military. Students and staff at West Point and the Naval Academy have com-plained about the institutional promotion of religion, including pressure to attend religious services and mandatory banquets involving prayer and Bible readings.[32] Army Brig. Gen. Robert Caslen, who once stated, "We are the aroma of Jesus Christ here in the Pentagon," served as commandant of army cadets at

West Point in 2007. When charged (along with several other generals) by the Pentagon's inspector general with violating rules by promoting a Jesus-worshiping group, Caslen acknowledged his "mistake" and unconvincingly recanted: "I fully believe in pluralism, tolerance and inclusion of all faiths, all ethnicity. . . . I would never use my position, my uniform or my rank to force my political or religious beliefs on anyone else."[33]

Meanwhile, at Fort Jackson Army Base in South Carolina, chaplains were teaching recruits that police and military were "God's Ministers," and they should "accept Jesus Christ as a personal savior." Evangelical proselytizing was occurring at many other military installations.[34] Throughout the military in the United States and abroad, there exist an Officers Christian Fellowship (for officers) and a Christian Military Fellowship (for enlisted ranks). Their openly stated goal is to establish a spiritually transformed US military, with "ambassadors for Christ in uniform" who are "empowered by the Holy Spirit."[35]

PASTORS AND PRISONS

A 2007 news story from CBS affiliate KSLA-TV of Shreveport, Louisiana, confirmed a whistle-blower's story that there exists a nationwide program, conducted by the Federal Emergency Management Agency (FEMA), to train "Clergy Response Teams," consisting of "pastors and other religious representatives to become secret police enforcers who teach their congregations to 'obey the government' in preparation for the implementation of martial law, property and firearm seizures, mass vaccination programs and forced relocation." Pastors are expected to preach subservience to the authorities in preparation for the government round-ups, telling their parishioners that it was all for their own good. Pastors were assured that they would be fully backed by law enforcement in controlling uncooperative individuals, including the use of SWAT teams to quell resistance.[36]

One of the key tools the clergy has in helping FEMA tamp down public agitation, KSLA-TV continued, "is the Bible itself, specifically Romans 13," Paul's proclamation that all terrestrial authority is derived from God; hence everyone must submit to the governing authorities. Behind this FEMA program looms the White House directive of May 9, 2007, which allows the president to bypass all other levels of government during a "catastrophic event."

The Clergy Response Teams already seem to be in place, judging from at least one Milwaukee sermon in 2008 that can be viewed on the Internet, in which the preacher tells his attentive but somewhat uneasy congregation that "there is too much talk about rights but not enough focus on the need to obey authority." "It is so easy to criticize," but we must learn to obey. "We are free to make ourselves slaves and must learn to submit accordingly. . . . Jesus submitted to the death sentence." He went on: "Christians should not be rebels. We must honor the king and be purveyors of his rule. . . . You are free to respect the government that God gives to you, free to submit to authority."[37]

Proselytizing has been going strong also in US prisons. Government-funded projects have been set up to rehabilitate prison inmates by immersing them in religious programs. Inmates whose "spiritual progress" satisfies their evangelical supervisors receive significant benefits, including better living accommodations, special food menus, and opportunities to see loved ones in surroundings more congenial than the typical visiting room. Inmates are taught "how God can heal them permanently, if they turned from their sinful past."[38] No secular organizations are allowed to conduct such rehabilitative programs.

The religious atmosphere of these prison projects, in the words of one federal judge, "is not simply an overlay or secondary effect of the program—it is the program." It amounted to an unconstitutional use of taxpayer money for religious indoctrination, he ruled.[39] Nevertheless, the programs continue to flourish, involving tens of thousands of inmates around the country. The fundamentalist Protestant managers often discourage Catholics, Jews, and Muslims from joining the program. Those who do are required to participate in born-again Jesus-worshiping services that are likely to offend their own religious beliefs. One Roman Catholic inmate left the program after a year, feeling that its staff was hostile toward his faith.[40]

In sum, the government has established within its penal institutions evangelical proselytizers with authority over the lives of thousands of inmates, without benefit of safeguards or oversight—all at taxpayer expense. Just as the nation's founders had feared: when the separation of church and state is violated, so is our freedom of conscience. When disestablishmentarianism is undermined in order to advantage one particular denomination, the rights of other believers and nonbelievers are compromised.

HOLY HOLIDAY

Religious conservatives rail against the secular state even as they pilfer its resources and advocate an expansion of its police and military powers. They want government scientific research and the public healthcare system to be tailored along obscurantist biblical precepts. They demand that their children—and eventually everyone else's—pray together in public schools, study only religiously vetted subjects, and make religious pledges of allegiance ("under God") to secular state symbols like the flag, in support of a nation they imagine was founded by Jesus Christ or some of his latter-day worshipers.

They want nativity scenes of the baby Jesus and replicas of the Ten Commandments displayed in public schools, town halls, court houses, and public libraries. Which variation of the Ten Commandments is to be featured is never made clear. There are three versions in the King James Bible: Exodus 20:2–17, Exodus 34:12–26, and Deuteronomy 5:6–21, with additional variants in Catholic and Hebrew Bibles.

The religionists are, of course, free to display any of their religious symbols, icons, and commandments in front of their own churches, private clubs, recreational centers, Christian-owned businesses, and on their many millions of lawns, front doors, house windows, cars, T-shirts, and lapels. But that is not enough; they want the entire public domain.

Ultraconservative believers complain that their religious freedom is being jeopardized by those who defend the separation of church and state and resist the religious tide. For televangelist Pat Robertson, the threat to the United States from "activist judges [is] probably more serious than a few bearded terrorists who fly into buildings."[41] State judges have been the targets of well-financed recall campaigns, electoral challenges, impeachment attempts, hate mail, and death threats. "Conservatives are having a large and increasing impact on the judicial selection process," mourns one law professor.[42]

Fundamentalist Jesus worshipers also have convinced themselves that there is, in the words of Rev. Jerry Falwell, "a concerted effort to steal Christmas." They mobilize their troops to fight this nonexistent war, watching out for the wicked, insidious shopkeepers and media hosts who wish you "happy holidays" and "seasons greetings" (phrases that have been in circulation for the better part of a century), or "Happy Kwanzaa" and "Happy Hanukkah" instead of "Merry Christmas." Most right-wing Christians say nothing about the crass corporate commercialization of Christmas; instead they direct their ire only at those who try to inject a more ecumenical, nonsectarian tone.

Some of the more enterprising religionists have made millions of dollars selling Christmas buttons, magnets, greeting cards, bracelets, tree ornaments, and lapel pins—all bravely promoting the defiant message that Christmas is for Jesus and his worshipful shoppers. So profitable have these campaigns become that the religious Right began branching out to fight against the imaginary "war on Easter." Their goal is to keep a close watch for stores that promote spring baskets and bonnets instead of celebrating Christ's resurrection.[43] Easter Bunny beware.

There is a lesser contingent of believers who reject the Christmas holiday because it has no basis in scripture and is freighted with secular features and pagan origins. They point out that the word "Christmas" does not appear in the Bible, nor does any date for the nativity. Jesus never commanded anyone to celebrate his birthday.[44] December 25 was originally a pagan holiday, the birthday of various deities and prophets such as the Persian god Mithra, whose arrival was reportedly witnessed by shepherds and Magi bearing gifts long before Jesus' birth. Most of the Christmas story seems to have been lifted from earlier pagan sources. The Bible makes no mention of Christmas trees, wreaths, lights, lavish dinners, or the exchange of gifts. If anything, God warns his people (Jeremiah 10:2–4) to avoid the vain customs of the heathens, such as cutting a tree out of the forest, decking it with silver and gold, and fastening it to the ground.

Most fundamentalists are undeterred by such considerations. As we shall see, they lay claim not only to Christmas but also to the entire nation—indeed, the whole world.

15

THE RETURN OF
TOTALITARIAN THEOCRACY

> One is often told that it is a very wrong thing to
> attack religion because religion makes men vir-
> tuous. So I am told; I have not noticed it.
> —BERTRAND RUSSELL

Many of us fear living under the rule of theocrats whose tolerance for diversity and dissent only lessens as their own power grows. Looking at history we have good reason to tremble.

THEOCRACY REMEMBERED

In the fourth century AD, the Christianists—backed by affluent converts and the emperor's sword and purse—managed to make Christianity an officially recognized religion of Rome, enjoying state support. Once so established, they strove to make their religion not merely the dominant one but the *only* one. By AD 395, they succeeded in getting paganism banished from public life. Those who continued to practice pagan rites or who failed to report such doings were subjected to severe sanctions.[1]

The theocracy that emerged exercised a deadening grip on Western civilization for centuries. Depicted as an oasis of scholarship amid the brutish ignorance of the Dark Ages, the church actually was a major purveyor of that ignorance, a suppressive force in such fields as literature, philosophy, art, theater, science, medicine, anatomy, astronomy, and commerce.[2] To give one example: Pope Alexander III (ca. 1100–1181) forbade monks to study medicine, his belief being that all ill health was rooted in demonic possession; hence, the only proper and effective remedy for sickness was prayer and exorcism.

The Christianist totalitarian theocracy demolished the great Greco-Roman tradition of rational inquiry and secular learning. Luciano Canfora refers to the relentless war waged against classical culture and its sanctuaries, "which meant, against the libraries. . . . The burning of books was part of the advent and imposition of Christianity."[3] In pagan times, Rome had more than twenty public libraries, some with up to 500,000 volumes. But by the end of the fifth century, with Christianity triumphant, the libraries were reduced to melancholy tombs. The profession of copyist disappeared, as did most secular writings, including the rich literature from Greek and Roman antiquity. All that remained were the church's meager monastic collections rarely numbering more than a few hundred volumes, mostly religious in content. For the next six hundred years hardly a book of note in secular learning was published in Christendom.[4]

THEOCRACY NOW

The theocratic extremists within Christianity, Islam, and various other religions today sing much the same refrain as did the absolutists of yore. It goes something like this:

> We embrace our religion because we *know* in our hearts and minds it is true. Were it not true, we would not hold to it. Since ours is the one true faith, it follows that all other faiths are false.

False beliefs about the most important questions of one's life and one's soul are not only wrong but wrongful, an offense to God. Therefore, inflicting sanctions upon recalcitrant heretics and infidels is a laudable service to the Almighty.

In addition, as St. Paul warns, those of little faith are most likely to succumb to degrading immoral passions. The nonbelievers and false believers are the fornicators, adulterers, self-abusers, and the "effeminate ones" given over to "vile affections."[5]

Today's reactionary theocrats are unmoved by dire socioeconomic ills. If they do charity work among the poor, it is principally with an eye to winning converts. They care not a whit about economic injustice, environmental devastation, and war. Rather they fix upon what they consider to be the *real* evils that plague America and the world: fornication, gay marriage, the teaching of evolution, sexual scenes on television, the lack of religion in civil society, and the like.

Their theocracy would be a vessel of politico-economic reactionism. Civil rights, labor unions, and public schools would be abolished. As Rev. Jerry Falwell made clear: "I hope to see the day when, as in the early days of our country, we don't have public schools. The churches will have taken them over and Christians will be running them."[6] Police and military forces (public and private) would be expanded still further than today, but human services would be abolished, including unemployment benefits, Social Security, and environmental protections. The destitute and disabled would have to rely on their families or private charity. Giant corporations will be free of all taxes and regulations. Women would be obliged to remain domiciled under the dominion of their men, who in turn would surrender themselves to a totalitarian church and state.[7]

In the mind of the theocrats, "religious freedom" means the right to roll back secular culture and impose a monochromatic belief system upon everyone. Right-wing fundamentalist leader Randall Terry told an audience of the like-minded faithful: "I want you to just let a wave of intolerance wash over you. . . .

Our goal is a Christian nation. . . . We are called by God to conquer this country. We don't want equal time. We don't want pluralism."[8]

The objective is to take over the US government and replace civil law with biblical law. This would mean extending the death penalty to blasphemers, gays, and women who commit adultery.[9] (Male adulterers are not mentioned in the Bible, hence they need not worry.) Referring to doctors who perform abortions, Terry warns: "When I or people like me are running the country, you'd better flee because we will find you, we will try you and we'll execute you. . . . I will make it part of my mission to see to it that you are tried and executed."[10]

Gary North, a leading "Reconstructionist" theocrat, looks forward to the day when only Christians will have the right to vote and those who refuse to "submit publicly" to religious rule will be denied citizenship. North and his theocrats are working to construct "a Bible-based social, political, and religious order which finally denies the religious liberty of the enemies of God."[11]

Fundamentalist minister James Kennedy, who hosts monthly luncheons for members of Congress, sums it up: "Our job is to reclaim America for Christ, whatever the cost. As the vice regents of God, we are to exercise godly dominion and influence over our neighborhoods, our schools, our government, our literature and arts, our sports arenas, our entertainment media, our news media, our scientific endeavors—in short, over every aspect and institution of human society."[12]

To achieve their goals, the theocrats infiltrate the armed forces (see previous chapter) and wage electoral campaigns to take over everything from local school boards to the White House itself. They claim the support of numerous members of the US Congress. And as of 2006, Christian fundamentalists reportedly held a majority of seats in eighteen of fifty state legislatures.[13]

Moderate Christians insist that reactionary theocrats are not "real Christians" and do not represent the Christianist majority. But as noted earlier, the moderates are not easily heard over the money-driven din and big-tent mobilizations produced by the religious Right. During the Middle Ages, when Christianity was in its glory days, the moderates were burned at the stake. Today they are simply outspent and marginalized.

ISLAM WITH A VENGEANCE

Islam too is inhabited mostly by moderates who adhere to a doctrine of peace, love, and mutual tolerance. But like their Christianist counterparts, the Islamist moderates are crowded out from public discourse or, worse still, intimidated into silence by militant theocrats.[14]

Islam's Allah resembles Yahweh and Jesus in his insistence on being treated as the one true god, to be obeyed and defended by his faithful flock. The Koran—gathered from various and sometimes conflicting versions of the prophet Muhammad's teachings, and compiled over twenty years after his death—is regarded as the word of God for Muslims. In it we read: "Allah is the enemy of all who deny him," and "Warn [everyone] that there is no god except Me; so do your duty unto Me."[15] Like Yahweh, Allah assists his warriors in the killing of infidels: "[E]ven if the enemy should rush here upon you in hot haste, your Lord will help you with five thousand angels making a terrific onslaught."[16] And in the manner of various biblical personages, the prophet Muhammad reportedly busied himself with war, plunder, assassinations, and multiple wives, including a nine-year-old bride in his later years.[17]

Like the Bible, the Koran contains heartening verses that emphasize peace, charity, and tolerance. But it also denounces Christians, Jews, and pagans for their failure to embrace Islam. "God's curse be on them: how they are deluded away from the Truth!" And "ye who believe! Take not the Jews and Christians for your friends and protectors. . . . Verily God guideth not a people unjust."[18]

Like most other religions, Islam was repeatedly racked by violent schisms. Yet within a century after Muhammad's death,

Muslim armies conquered the Persian Empire and defeated the Byzantines and the Visigoth kingdom in Spain. By the early Middle Ages, an Islamic military caste had extended its domain from Aquitaine down through Spain, across North Africa to the Middle East, and into India, ruling over millions of Christians, Jews, pagans, Hindus, and others. Non-Muslims who refused to convert to Islam were left pretty much alone in matters of worship. They had only to pay a modest and mostly symbolic poll tax.[19] In conjunction with this tolerant mode of governance, there existed secular studies and intellectual activity in the Islamic world that were far more advanced than anything found in medieval Christendom.[20]

Today's Islamist reactionaries, however, bear a closer resemblance to today's Christian reactionaries in their intolerance toward secularism and their conviction that both heaven and earth are their exclusive province. But unlike the Christianists who await their return to state power, the Islamists can already boast of existing bona fide theocracies such as Saudi Arabia, Iran, Afghanistan (under the Taliban), and Kuwait. In addition, in Pakistan, Indonesia, Nigeria, Egypt, Lebanon, Somalia, Algeria, Jordan, Turkey, Yemen, and elsewhere, the Islamic theocrats are a major force, able in many instances to impose *sharia*, the Islamic legal rules that regulate all public and private aspects of life. What follows are examples of Islamic reactionism in action.

In Afghanistan in 2006, senior Muslim clerics demanded the execution of an Afghani man on trial for converting from Islam to Christianity. Apostasy is punishable by death. The clerics warned that if the man, a medical aid worker, were released, they would call on the people "to pull him into pieces so there's nothing left." Cleric Abdul Raoulf (considered a "moderate" by some) declared, "Rejecting Islam is insulting God. We will not allow God to be humiliated. This man must die."[21]

Also in Afghanistan, in 2008 a twenty-three-year-old journalism student distributed an article taken from the Internet that questioned why men were allowed to have multiple spouses but women were not. Brought before a court, he was convicted of "humiliating Islam" and sentenced to death.[22] The Afghani government prohibited media coverage that offended "traditional values and the Islamic faith."[23]

When the Taliban seized power in 1996 they tortured, castrated, and then murdered Afghanistan's former revolutionary president Najibullah. They closed all girls' schools and required women to remain completely shrouded from head to toe. Women could neither work outside the home nor pursue an education. Nor could they appear in public unless accompanied by a close male relative. The windows of their homes were painted so they might not be seen by outsiders. Females without male support either starved to death or begged in the streets, even if they had earned advanced degrees during the previous revolutionary regime. They could not be treated by male doctors, which meant that many serious illnesses went unattended. Depression, madness, and suicide among women increased significantly under Taliban rule.[24]

The Taliban also banned secular writings, movies, television, dancing, singing, music, photography, chess, kite flying, shaving, and all social mingling between men and women who were not close family relatives. By early 2008, the once vanquished Taliban, surging forth against the NATO occupation, had succeeded in destroying or shutting down 590 schools in Afghanistan, killing almost 200 teachers and students and wounding some 250 others.[25]

In Iraq too, Islamic reactionism was gaining strength in response to the US invasion and occupation. In 2007, Muslim militia killed some forty women in Basra alone for being insufficiently covered or for other perceived transgressions such as attending school. The bodies of some showed signs of rape and torture. The situation in Baghdad was not much different. Many fearful families stopped sending their daughters to school. A Shiite cleric in Baghdad defended the killings by saying, "We are an Islamic country and we must commit to the restrictions of our religion. We must not allow corruption to invade our families under the flag of freedom and such nonsense."[26]

Muslim insurgents in Iraq spilled at least as much blood in sectarian massacres as in resisting the US occupation. The killings included suicide bombings of marketplaces, funerals, hospitals, and schools. The war was not only Sunni against Shiite but Shiite factions against each other. In some instances, splinter groups—convinced that they alone possessed the one true word of Islam—felt free to kill anyone who was not of their chosen circle, including other Islamists. During this same period, sectarian massacres of innocent civilians were carried out also in Lebanon, Palestine, and several other countries.

In Nigeria and Iran, under reactionary Muslim codes, scores of people have been flogged for drinking alcohol, stoned to death for adultery and sodomy, or have had a hand or foot (or both) amputated for theft. A Nigerian girl believed to be seventeen or younger received one hundred lashes administered at the Higher Sharia Court in front of her neighbors. She was charged with having sexual relations outside marriage and falsely accusing three men of raping her. The men—innocent lambs all three—claimed she was the eager instigator.[27]

Sharia was applied with coarsened rectitude in the Muslim region of Nigeria, where a man's leg was amputated as punishment for stealing a bicycle; another man's arm was chopped off because he stole a cow; motor-bike taxi drivers were severely lashed for carrying female passengers; and an unmarried pregnant girl was publicly lashed 180 times (after she delivered the baby).[28]

In Iran, when a newspaper ran photographs of peasant women harvesting wheat, a judge revoked its license, ruling that sharia prohibits publishing pictures of women.[29] In 2001, authorities shut down a prostitution ring of runaway girls who were pimped by a mullah who served as head of the sharia court in Qom. Prostitutes in Islamic societies are usually widowed or abandoned women who have no other means of feeding their children and themselves, or girls who have fled their homes to escape poverty, forced marriage, or the fear of dishonor that comes with having been raped or seduced.[30]

In Saudi Arabia a nineteen-year-old girl and her male companion were both savagely gang-raped. Professing to operate under Islamic principles, the Saudi court sentenced the girl to ninety lashes for being in the company of a man who was not a close relative. When she challenged the decision, an appeals court increased the punishment to two hundred lashes and a six-month jail term, and revoked her lawyer's license.[31] Only a sustained international outcry induced the Saudi government to suspend the sentence. The rapists went unpunished.

In Saudi Arabia a man can divorce his wife with a simple enunciation, but any woman seeking divorce faces a daunting legal labyrinth. As of 2009, Saudi women were still prohibited from operating motor vehicles because of the sinful temptations female drivers might create. As one cleric put it, "Can you imagine what it would be like if her car broke down? She would have to seek help from men."[32]

Like any genuine theocracy, Saudi Arabia restricts other faiths. Bibles and crucifixes are banned. Schoolchildren are taught that "every religion other than Islam is false," including all other Muslims who do not ascribe to the kingdom's severely orthodox Wahhabi teaching of Islam.[33] Under Wahhabi rule, in 2002 alone, seven people had their right hands amputated. Four men were executed on drug charges, while three others were given 1,500 lashes each and fifteen years' imprisonment. Two teachers, arrested following protest demonstrations, were sentenced to 1,500 lashes, carried out in front of their families, students, and other teachers. An Egyptian convicted of robbery was sentenced to 4,000 lashes administered 50 at a time, every two weeks. Over a twenty-year period there were at least ninety cases of amputations in the Saudi kingdom.[34]

A Saudi woman who was raped by her sister's husband received 65 lashes and six months' imprisonment for "adultery." The man was sentenced to 4,700 lashes and six years' imprisonment.[35] Usually the rapist skips free since (under some interpretations of sharia) the victim must produce four Muslim male eyewitnesses who will verify her story. In various Muslim countries, women who go to the police to report being raped or having been held in a brothel can be arrested for adultery because they have admitted to illicit sex but cannot provide the requisite four male witnesses to prove it was nonconsensual.[36]

In 2006, an Islamic court in Bulo Burto, Somalia, announced that residents who did not pray to Allah five times a day would be beheaded, "according to Islamic law." Shopkeepers who failed to close their shops and teahouses during prayer time would also be decapitated.[37]

In Yemen and some other countries, girls not older than nine or ten are pulled out of school and forced into marriage. Many end up having children before their bodies are sufficiently matured, sometimes resulting in serious health problems for both mother and infant. The belief is that a child-bride can be better molded into a dutiful wife than can an older female. Hard-line Islamic reactionaries in Yemen defend child wedlock, pointing to the prophet Muhammad's marriage to a nine-year-old.[38]

In one year, Pakistani Islamic extremists bombed four girls schools and threatened the students with death if they continued their education. Many girls stopped attending classes, ensuring that Pakistan would continue to have one of the lowest rates of female literacy.[39]

Militants in Egypt undertook the enforcement of sharia by demanding that women completely cover themselves. The extremists trashed music recitals, cinemas, video stores, and liquor stores, and rampaged against Egypt's Christian Coptic Orthodox minority, bombing its churches. Then they attacked a state security headquarters, decapitating its commander and "killing a large number of policemen."[40]

Bangladeshi author and self-proclaimed atheist Taslima Nasrin had to flee her country. Her "blasphemous" opposition to male oppression and religious intolerance sent mullahs raging through the streets demanding her death. Fifteen years later, on a visit to India, she was assaulted by Islamist extremists during a news conference.[41] Other notable female authors and journalists have been subjected to death threats and verbal attacks.[42]

Egyptian writer Nawal El Saadawi was driven from her government job and imprisoned after she spoke out against the oppression of women. A number of Iranian women produced memoirs about the arrests and assassinations perpetrated by the Iranian theocracy.[43] Iranian-born Canadian photojournalist Zahra Kazemi made headlines after she was arrested while visiting Iran then raped and tortured to death during interrogation.[44]

Pirate radio stations in the Middle East and central Asia feature radical clerics who denounce movies and female education, while heaping praise upon suicide bombers. The "Western onslaught" against Islamic values, they warn, must be met with holy war.[45] They teach that peace with infidels is tantamount to abject surrender, while those who support jihad, especially those who achieve martyrdom, will be rewarded in heaven.

SHARIA GOES WEST

Islamic reactionaries have targeted prominent figures in the Western world. In 1989, Ayatollah Khomeini issued a fatwa (death decree) against the noted author Salmon Rushdie, a British citizen, for penning a novel that "offended Islam." Fearing for his life, Rushdie lived for years under the protection of armed guards.

In 2005, a Danish newspaper published twelve cartoons depicting the prophet Muhammad, some of them unflattering. Images of the Prophet are forbidden under Islamic law. Furious mobs torched Danish embassies in Iran, Syria, and Lebanon. Riots in Nigeria, Afghanistan, and Pakistan brought the deaths of more than one hundred people. "We are angry, very, very, very angry," a Palestinian legislator said at the time. "No one can say a bad word about our prophet."[46] The publisher of a Muslim newspaper in California chimed in: "To tarnish, humiliate and degrade a prophet of God under the guise of 'freedom of speech' is the highest degree of immorality."[47]

The twelve cartoonists went into hiding. In 2008, Aman

Zawahiri, second in command of al Qaeda, urged followers to continue striking at Danish targets. Soon after, the Danish Embassy in Pakistan was car bombed, killing at least six people and wounding dozens more.[48]

When demonstrating in London, Islamists reactionaries imposed no boundaries on their own free speech, carrying signs that read, "Kill those who insult Islam," and "Slay," "Annihilate," "Massacre," and "Exterminate" ". . . those who insult Islam," and "Be prepared for the *real* Holocaust!" "Europe is the cancer, Islam is the answer," "Freedom go to hell," and "Europe you will pay, yes 9/11 is on its way."[49]

For producing an eleven-minute documentary about the subjugation of Muslim women, Dutch filmmaker Theo van Gogh was shot eight times and his throat was slashed. As the assassin explained at his trial, Islamic law compelled him to kill "anyone who insults Allah and the Prophet."[50]

In France, novelist Michel Houellebecq was charged with a hate crime for describing Islam as "the most stupid religion." He managed to win acquittal.[51] Buckling to the campaign waged by the Organization of Islamic Countries, the UN Human Rights Council adopted a resolution calling on all governments to "take action" against writers, journalists, artists, and others who defame religion.[52]

In 2006, during an address in Germany, Pope Benedict XVI quoted a fourteenth-century Byzantine emperor as saying that Muhammad brought into the world "things only evil and inhuman, such as his command to spread by the sword the faith he preached." The pontiff offered no rebuttal of the emperor's words (and said nothing about how his own Roman Church had used the sword). In quick time, riots erupted across the Muslim world. An Islamist movement leader in Palestine cried out: "It is our holy duty to fight all those who support the pope. . . . The green flag of Allah and Muhammad will be raised over the Vatican." In Europe, angry Muslim crowds called for the pope's death, waving placards that read "Islam will conquer Rome" and "Jesus is the slave of Allah."[53]

Islamic orthodoxy clashes with Western practices in other ways. Muslim women training in Britain at several hospitals refused to roll up their arm coverings during surgery or while washing their hands because under sharia that would be immodest. The Islamic Medical Association declared that no female Muslim doctor, nurse, medical student, or patient should be required to bare and wash any portion of her body, hygienic considerations notwithstanding.[54]

Young females living in Muslim communities in Britain have suffered severe beatings from their families for "acting Western." They have been subjected to genital mutilation, forced marriages, domestic abuse, rape, and an estimated ten to twelve "honor killings" every year.[55]

Some leaders of Muslim communities in Canada advocate rule by sharia, including the stoning to death of all married adulterers. Unmarried adulterers would get one hundred lashes. As one imam explains, "This is not extremism; this is Islam." Threats have been lodged against moderate, antiviolent Muslims in various Western countries, including parts of the United States. Muslim spokespersons and journalists, critical of extremism, have been the targets of assassination attempts, some of which have succeeded.[56]

MAN'S DESPERATION IS GOD'S OPPORTUNITY

Among those recruited for jihad in the West are young men who are frustrated with their marginalized social life and alienated by the "Western decadence and modernity" that purportedly besieges Islam. They are perennially worried that their women folk might slip out of control. In some instances, militant jihadists are highly educated professionals who, along with their less educated comrades, are furious at the humiliations and violence delivered upon Islamic populations by Western imperialism— including the bombings and invasions of Iraq and Afghanistan.[57]

In many Middle East countries human services for the poor

have been neglected or defunded by corrupt officials. Natural resources and markets are increasingly expropriated by foreign investors. Secular laws favor the superrich who increase their wealth while the poor increase only their numbers. In the midst of all this come the Islamist religious parties performing minor charities for the poor while preaching a message of reclamation, redemption, and revenge. Sharia is put forth as the one source of social justice for both the desperate down-and-outs and the ruffled professionals. Meanwhile, jihadist Web sites and bloggers preach holy war on the Internet. They discuss why the killing of infidels is a virtue and the killing of innocent bystanders is not a sin, and why jihad is mandatory for all Muslims.[58]

As with Islam, so with the Christianist Pentecostals: church membership surged as poverty deepened in Latin America, Africa, and elsewhere. Greater concentrations of land and natural resources are in the hands of transnational corporations; a dumping of "free trade" foreign goods undermines local markets and local production; add to this, ecological devastation, military attack, and deracinated populations. Enter the missionaries who inform the people that the old false gods are the cause of their present misery; they must embrace the new Christianist god of promised prosperity.

Just about every Middle Eastern, Latin American, African, and Asian country has had a secular political movement with economic democracy as its goal. Almost all were destroyed or short-circuited by Western counterinsurgency and economic strangulation. Denied a material means of betterment, many people turn to the "spiritual." The Christianist missionaries—or the mullahs and the imams—explain to victims why bad things happen to good people: They were not that good; they believed in false gods and evil material solutions such as leftist social revolution. Their suffering on earth is punishment for their sins.

Once their worldly struggles against colonizers and rulers are thwarted, the people "lapse into obscurantism and misdirected otherworldly supplications" that make "oppression more bearable and the ruling class more secure."[59]

16

FOR LORDS AND LAMAS

> The Buddha was amiable and enlightened; on his
> deathbed he laughed at his disciples for sup-
> posing that he was immortal. But the Buddhist
> priesthood—as it exists, for example, in Tibet—
> has been obscurantist, tyrannous and cruel in the
> highest degree.
>
> —BERTRAND RUSSELL

A long with the blood-drenched landscape of sectarian
conflict there is the inner peace and solace that every religion sometimes delivers, none more so than Buddhism.
Standing in marked contrast to the savage intolerance of other
faiths, Buddhism is neither violent nor dogmatic—so say its
adherents. For many practitioners, Buddhism is less a theology
and more a meditative discipline intended to promote an inner
harmony while guiding us along a path of enlightened living.
The spiritual focus is not only on oneself but also on the welfare
of others. One tries to put aside egoistic pursuits and gain a
deeper understanding of one's connection to all people and all
things.

In resemblance to Protestantism's Social Gospel movement

and Catholicism's liberation theology, *socially engaged Buddhism* tries to blend individual liberation with responsible social action in order to build a humane and equitable society. A glance at history, however, reveals that not all the many varying forms of Buddhism have been free of the violence, avarice, and doctrinal fanaticism emblematic of religion in general.

BELLIGERENT BUDDHISTS

Putting aside the legendary battles waged by Buddhist kings of yore, today's Buddhists have clashed violently with each other and with non-Buddhists in Burma, Korea, Japan, India, and elsewhere. In Sri Lanka, for some twenty-five years armed battles between Buddhist Sinhalese and Hindu Tamils took many lives on both sides. In 2007 Buddhist and Muslim armed groups continued a protracted conflict in Thailand's southern Muslim provinces. In 1998 the US State Department listed thirty of the world's most dangerous extremist groups. Over half of them were religious, including Muslim and Buddhist.[1]

In South Korea in 1998, thousands of monks of the Chogye Buddhist order fought each other with clubs, rocks, and firebombs in pitched battles that went on for weeks. They were vying for control of the order, the largest in South Korea, with its annual budget of $9.2 million, immense property holdings, and the privilege of appointing 1,700 monks to various offices. The brawls damaged the main Buddhist sanctuaries and left dozens of monks injured, some seriously. The Korean public appeared disdainful of both factions, feeling that no matter which side took control, "it would use worshipers' donations for luxurious houses and expensive cars."[2]

Other Buddhist denominations have known discord and violence in their history. But what of *Tibetan* Buddhism? Is it not an exception to this sort of strife? Many Buddhists maintain that, before the Chinese crackdown in 1959, old Tibet was a spiritually oriented kingdom free from the corrupting lifestyles and egoistic materialism that beset modern industrialized society. News media and Hollywood films have portrayed the Tibetan theocracy as a veritable Shangri-la. The Dalai Lama himself stated that "the pervasive influence of Buddhism" in Tibet, "amid the wide open spaces of an unspoiled environment resulted in a society dedicated to peace and harmony. We enjoyed freedom and contentment."[3]

Not everyone concurs with that depiction. "Religious conflict was commonplace in old Tibet," writes one Western Buddhist practitioner. "History belies the Shangri-la image of Tibetan lamas and their followers living together in mutual tolerance and nonviolent goodwill. Indeed, the situation was quite different. Old Tibet was much more like Europe during the religious wars of the Counter-Reformation."[4]

In the thirteenth century, Emperor Kublai Khan created the First Grand Lama, who was to preside over all other lamas. Several centuries later, the emperor of China sent an army into Tibet to support the Grand Lama, an ambitious twenty-five-year-old man who subsequently gave himself the title of Dalai (Ocean) Lama, ruler of all Tibet. This Dalai Lama seized monasteries that did not belong to his sect and is believed to have destroyed Buddhist writings that conflicted with his claim to divinity. The Dalai Lama who succeeded him pursued a sybaritic life, enjoying many mistresses, partying with friends, and acting in other ways deemed unfitting for an incarnate deity. For these transgressions he was murdered by his priests. Within 170 years, despite their recognized divine status, five dalai lamas were assassinated by their high priests or other courtiers for one reason or another. The thirteenth Dalai Lama, predecessor to the current one, narrowly escaped an assassination attempt allegedly perpetrated by his own regent.[5]

For hundreds of years competing Tibetan Buddhist sects engaged in violent clashes and summary killings. The Dalai Lama of 1660 was faced with a rebellion in Tsang province, the stronghold of the rival Kagyu sect with its high lama known as the Karmapa. The Dalai Lama called for harsh retribution against the Kagyu rebels, directing the Mongol army to obliterate the male and female lines, and the offspring too "like eggs smashed against rocks. . . . In short, annihilate any traces of them, even their names."[6]

In 1792, many Kagyu monasteries were confiscated and their monks were forcibly converted to the Gelug sect (the Dalai Lama's denomination). The Gelug school, known also as the "Yellow Hats," had this to say in one of their traditional prayers:

> Praise to you, violent god of the Yellow Hat teachings
> who reduces to particles of dust
> great beings, high officials and ordinary people
> who pollute and corrupt the Gelug doctrine.[7]

AN "INTOLERABLE TYRANNY OF MONKS"

Religions have an age-long relationship not only with violence but also with economic exploitation. Indeed, it is often the economic exploitation that necessitates the violence. Such was the case with the Tibetan theocracy. Until 1959, when the Dalai Lama last presided over Tibet, most of the arable land was still organized into manorial estates worked by serfs and owned by monasteries and secular landlords. Even a writer sympathetic to the old order allows that "a great deal of real estate belonged to the monasteries, and most of them amassed great riches." Much of the wealth was accumulated "through active participation in trade, commerce, and money lending."[8]

Drepung monastery was one of the biggest landholders in the world, with its 185 manors, 25,000 serfs, 300 great pastures, and 16,000 herdsmen. The wealth of the monasteries rested in the hands of high-ranking lamas. Most ordinary monks lived modestly and had no access to great wealth. The Dalai Lama himself lived richly in the thousand-room, fourteen-story Potala Palace, the largest monumental structure in Tibet.

Secular leaders also did well. The commander in chief of the Tibetan army, a member of the Dalai Lama's lay Cabinet, owned 4,000 square kilometers of land and 3,500 serfs.[9] Old Tibet has been misrepresented by some of its admirers as "a nation that required no police force because its people voluntarily observed the laws of karma."[10] In fact, it had a professional army, albeit a small one, that served mainly as a gendarmerie for the landlords to keep order and hunt down runaway serfs.

Young Tibetan boys were regularly taken from their families and brought into the monasteries to be trained as monks. Once there, they were bonded for life. Tashì-Tsering, a monk, reports that it was common for peasant boys to be sexually mistreated in the monasteries. He himself was a victim of repeated rape, beginning at age nine.[11] The monastic estates also conscripted children for lifelong servitude as domestics, dance performers, and soldiers.

In old Tibet there were small numbers of independent farmers who subsisted as a kind of free peasantry, and thousands of people who composed a "middle class" of merchants, shopkeepers, artisans, and tradesmen. There also were slaves, usually domestic servants, and beggars who owned nothing. A slave's offspring were born into slavery.[12] The majority of the rural population were serfs bonded for life to work the land owned by lord or monastery—without benefit of schooling or pay. They were expected to perform additional services such as repairing the lord's houses and providing transportation on demand.[13] Their masters told them what crops to grow and what animals to raise. They could not get married without the consent of their lord or lama. And they might easily be separated from their families should their owners lease them out to work at a distant location.[14]

One twenty-two-year-old woman, herself a runaway serf, reports: "Pretty serf girls were usually taken by the owner as house servants and used as he wished."[15] Fugitive serfs who fled were hunted down by the landlord's men and beaten mercilessly.[16] Serfs were taxed upon getting married and taxed for every birth and death in the family. They were taxed for planting a tree in their yard and for keeping animals, taxed for religious festivals and for public dancing, and taxed for being sent to prison and upon being released. Those who could not find work were taxed for being unemployed, and if they traveled to another village in search of work, they paid a passage tax. When people could not pay, the monasteries lent them money at 20 to 50 percent interest. Some debts were handed down from father to son to grandson.[17]

The poor were taught that they had brought their troubles upon themselves because of their wicked ways in previous lives. They had to accept the misery of their present existence as a karmic atonement and in anticipation that their lot would improve in their next lifetime. Conversely, the rich and powerful treated their good fortune as a reward for, and tangible evidence of, virtue in past and present lives.

In feudal Tibet, torture and mutilation—including eye gouging, the pulling out of tongues, hamstringing, and amputation—were favored punishments inflicted upon troublesome serfs. Journeying through Tibet in the 1960s, an American couple interviewed a former serf, Tsereh Wang Tuei, who had stolen two sheep belonging to a monastery. For this he had both his eyes gouged out and his hand mutilated beyond use. He explained that he no longer was a Buddhist: "When a holy lama told them to blind me I thought there was no good in religion."[18] Since it was against Buddhist teachings to take human life, some offenders were severely lashed and then "left to God" in the freezing night to die. "The parallels between Tibet and medieval Europe are striking," concludes historian Tom Grunfeld in his book on Tibet.[19]

In 1959, journalist Anna Louise Strong visited an exhibition of torture equipment that had been used by the Tibetan overlords. There were handcuffs, including small ones for children, and instruments for cutting off noses and ears, gouging out eyes, breaking off hands, and hamstringing legs, along with hot brands and whips. The exhibition also presented photographs and testimonies of victims.[20]

Earlier visitors to Tibet inveighed against the theocratic despotism. In 1895, an Englishman, Dr. A. L. Waddell, wrote that the populace was under the "intolerable tyranny of monks" and the devil superstitions they had fashioned to terrorize the people. In 1937, another visitor, Spencer Chapman, wrote, "The Lamaist monk does not spend his time in ministering to the people or educating them. . . . The beggar beside the road is nothing to the monk. Knowledge is the jealously guarded prerogative of the monasteries and is used to increase their influence and wealth."[21]

As much as we might wish otherwise, feudal theocratic Tibet was a far cry from the pastoral communalism so enthusiastically imagined by Buddhism's Western proselytes.

DISMANTLING THE FEUDAL THEOCRACY

What happened to Tibet after the Chinese Communists moved into the country in 1951 is another story. The treaty of that year provided for ostensible self-governance under the Dalai Lama's rule but gave Beijing control over the military and exclusive right to conduct foreign relations. The Chinese were also granted a direct role in internal administration "to promote social reforms." Among the earliest changes they wrought was to reduce usurious interest rates and build a few hospitals and roads. At first, they moved slowly, relying mostly on persuasion in an attempt to effect reconstruction. No aristocratic or monastic property was confiscated, and feudal lords continued to reign over their hereditarily bound peasants.

Over the centuries the Tibetan lords and lamas had seen Chinese come and go. They had enjoyed good relations with Generalissimo Chiang Kai-shek and his reactionary Kuomintang Party in China.[22] When the present fourteenth Dalai Lama was installed in Lhasa, it was with an armed escort of Chinese troops and an attending Chinese minister, in accordance with centuries-old tradition. What upset the Tibetan lords and lamas in the early 1950s was that these latest Chinese were *Communists*. It would be only a matter of time, they feared, before the Communists started imposing their collectivist egalitarian schemes on Tibet.

The issue was joined in 1956–57, when armed Tibetan bands ambushed convoys of the Chinese Peoples Liberation Army. The uprising received extensive assistance from the US Central Intelligence Agency (CIA).[23] Meanwhile in the United States, the Dalai Lama's eldest brother, Thubten Norbu, played an active role in the American Society for a Free Asia, a CIA-financed front that publicized the cause of Tibetan independence. The Dalai Lama's second-eldest brother, Gyalo Thondup, established an intelligence operation with the CIA as early as 1951, later upgraded into a CIA-trained guerrilla unit whose recruits parachuted back into Tibet.[24]

Many Tibetan commandos and agents whom the CIA dropped into the country were chiefs of aristocratic clans or the sons of chiefs. Ninety percent of them were never heard from again, according to a report from the CIA itself, meaning they were most likely captured and killed.[25] "Many lamas and lay members of the elite and much of the Tibetan army joined the uprising, but in the main the populace did not, assuring its failure," writes East Asia scholar Hugh Deane.[26] In their book on Tibet, George Ginsburg and Michael Mathos reach a similar conclusion: "As far as can be ascertained, the great bulk of the common people of Lhasa and the adjoining countryside failed to join in the fighting against the Chinese both when it first began and as it progressed."[27] Before long the resistance crumbled.

Whatever wrongs and new oppressions introduced by the Chinese after 1959, they did abolish slavery and the Tibetan serfdom system of unpaid labor. They eliminated the landlords' crushing taxes, started work projects, and greatly reduced unemployment and beggary. They established health clinics and secular schools and constructed running water and electrical systems in Lhasa.[28] Since 1950 the Tibetan population has doubled and its life span has risen from thirty-six years to the present average of sixty-five years.[29]

By 1961, Chinese occupation authorities had expropriated the landed estates owned by lords and lamas. They distributed many thousands of acres to tenant farmers and former serfs, reorganizing them into hundreds of communes. Herds owned by the nobility were turned over to collectives of poor shepherds. Changes were introduced in the breeding of livestock and in the farming of new varieties of vegetables, wheat, and barley, along with irrigation improvements.[30]

Heinrich Harrer (later revealed to have been a sergeant in Hitler's SS) wrote a bestseller about his experiences in Tibet that was made into a popular Hollywood movie. He reported that the Tibetans who resisted the Chinese "were predominantly nobles, semi-nobles and lamas; they were punished by being made to perform the lowliest tasks, such as laboring on roads and bridges. They were further humiliated by being made to clean up the city before the tourists arrived." They also had to live in a camp originally reserved for beggars and vagrants.[31]

Many peasants remained as religious as ever, giving alms to the clergy. But monks who had been conscripted as children into the religious orders were now free to renounce the monastic life, and thousands did, especially the younger ones. The remaining clergy lived on modest government stipends and extra income earned by officiating at prayer services, weddings, and funerals.[32]

Both the Dalai Lama and his advisor and youngest brother, Tendzin Choegyal, claimed that "more than 1.2 million Tibetans are dead as a result of the Chinese occupation."[33] The official 1953 census—six years before the Chinese crackdown—recorded the entire population residing in Tibet proper at 1,274,000.[34] Other census counts put the population within Tibet at about 2 million. If the Chinese killed 1.2 million in the early 1960s, then almost all of Tibet would have been depopulated, transformed into a killing field dotted with death camps and mass graves, of which there seems to be no evidence.[35] What is difficult to procure is hard data on the number of Tibetans who might have perished because of the Chinese occupation.

Chinese authorities claim to have put an end to floggings, mutilations, and amputations as a mode of criminal punishment. They themselves, however, have been charged with acts of brutality by exiled Tibetans. The authorities do admit to "mistakes," particularly during the 1966–76 Cultural Revolution when the persecution of religious beliefs reached a high tide in both China and Tibet. During the Great Leap Forward, forced collectivization and grain farming were imposed on the Tibetan peasantry, sometimes with disastrous effects and considerable misery.

In the late 1970s, China began relaxing controls "and tried to undo some of the damage wrought during the previous two decades."[36] In 1980, the Chinese government initiated reforms allowing Tibetans to cultivate private plots, sell their harvest surpluses, decide for themselves what crops to grow, and raise their own yaks and sheep.[37]

As of 2008, Buddhism was still practiced widely in Tibet. Religious pilgrimages and other standard forms of worship were allowed, but monks and nuns had to sign a loyalty pledge that they would not use their religious position to foment secession or dissent. And displaying photos of the Dalai Lama remained illegal.[38]

The ethnic Han, who are said to compose over 95 percent of China's immense population, are moving into Tibet in substantial numbers. On the streets of Lhasa and Shigatse, signs of Han influx have become readily visible. Actually "Han" is a catch-all label covering a population that is more diverse in physical makeup and languages than is often recognized. China is a multiethnic society containing some fifty-six minority groups. Intermarriage and the tendency to designate minorities as Han because they have lived in predominantly Han provinces for a couple of generations leads to underestimations of ethnic diversity. Millions of ethnics reside outside their original settlement areas, including Tibetans, tens of thousands of whom live in China's other western and northern provinces.

In Tibet today, Chinese of various ethnic backgrounds run the factories and many of the shops and vending stalls. Tall office buildings and large shopping centers have been built with funds that might have been better spent on water treatment plants and housing. Chinese cadres in Tibet too often view their Tibetan neighbors as backward and lazy, in need of economic development and "patriotic education." Tibetan government employees suspected of harboring nationalist sympathies have been purged from office. Individual Tibetans reportedly have been subjected to arrest, imprisonment, and forced labor for carrying out separatist activities and engaging in "political subversion," with some held in administrative detention without adequate food, water, and blankets, subjected to beatings and other mistreatment.[39]

Tibetan subjects are slighted in the state schools. Teaching materials, though translated into Tibetan, focus mainly on Chinese history and culture. Chinese family planning regulations allow a three-child limit for Tibetan families. (There is a more severe one-child limit for Han families throughout China, and a two-child limit for rural Han families whose first child is a girl.) If a Tibetan couple goes over the three-child limit, the excess children can be denied subsidized daycare, healthcare, housing, and education. These penalties have been enforced irregularly and vary by district.[40]

According to reports in the Western press, some Tibetans resented the proliferation of Chinese businesses. Others complained of being discriminated against in wages and hiring. Over a period of several weeks in 2008, riots and demonstrations for Tibetan independence erupted within Tibet and in neighboring locales that contained Tibetan populations. Tibet has been undergoing many dramatic transitions for better or worse, sometimes both.

17

GOOD-BYE, SHANGRI-LA

Can there be bliss when all that lives must suffer?
Shalt thou be saved and hear the whole world cry?
—*The Book of the Golden Precepts*
(ancient Buddhist writing)

According to the Shangri-la scenario, the people of old Tibet lived in contented symbiosis with their monastic and secular lords, mutually sustained by the balm of a spiritual and pacific culture. As we have seen, that is not a reliable accounting.

THE MYTH DIES HARD

One is reminded of the idealized image of feudal Europe presented by latter-day conservative Catholics like G. K. Chesterton and Hilaire Belloc. For them, medieval Christendom was a world of contented peasants living in the tranquil embrace of their church, under the benign protection of their lords.[1] That pastoral image bears no more resemblance to historic actuality than does the one of old Tibet.

In an earlier book, I argued that culture is seldom neutral. Those who profit most from the ongoing social order will propagate an idealized image of the dominant culture, passing over its murky aspects. Culture often operates as a cover for a host of grim realities and grave injustices, benefiting a privileged portion of society.[2] In feudal Tibet, ruling theocratic interests manipulated the traditional culture to their own advantage. They equated rebellious thought and action with satanic influence. The rich were represented as deserving their good life, and the lowly poor as deserving their mean existence. It was all karmic residue accumulated from past lives.

Were the more affluent lamas just hypocrites who preached one thing and secretly believed another? More likely they genuinely attached themselves to those beliefs that brought such good results for them. That their theology so perfectly supported their material privileges only strengthened the sincerity with which it was embraced.

It is said that we denizens of the modern secular world cannot grasp the customary equations of happiness and pain that characterize more traditionally "spiritual" societies. This is probably true, and it may explain why some of us idealize such societies. But still, a gouged eye is a gouged eye, a flogging is a flogging, a raped child is a raped child, and the grinding exploitation of serfs and slaves is a brutal injustice whatever its legitimating cultural wrapping. There is a difference between a human bond and human bondage.

Many ordinary Tibetans want the Dalai Lama back in their country, but it appears that relatively few want a return to the social order he represented. A 1999 story in the *Washington Post* notes that the Dalai Lama continues to be revered in Tibet, but

> few Tibetans would welcome a return of the corrupt aristocratic clans that fled with him in 1959 and that comprise the bulk of his advisers. Many Tibetan farmers, for example, have no interest in surrendering the land they gained during China's land reform to the clans. Tibet's former slaves say

they, too, don't want their former masters to return to power. "I've already lived that life once before," said Wangchuk, a 67-year-old former slave who was wearing his best clothes for his yearly pilgrimage to Shigatse, one of the holiest sites of Tibetan Buddhism. He said he worshipped the Dalai Lama, but added, "I may not be free under Chinese communism, but I am better off than when I was a slave."³

THE DALAI LAMA GOES WEST

For the religious and secular aristocracy of old Tibet, the Communist intervention was an unmitigated calamity. Most of them fled abroad, as did the Dalai Lama, who was assisted in his flight by the CIA. Some discovered to their horror that they would have to work for a living. Many, however, escaped that fate. Throughout the 1960s, much of the Tibetan exile community was secretly supported by the CIA, according to documents released by the US State Department in 1998. The Dalai Lama's organization itself eventually admitted that it had received millions of dollars from the CIA during the 1960s. As reported in the *Los Angeles Times*, the Dalai Lama's annual payment from the CIA was $186,000. Indian intelligence also financed both him and other Tibetan exiles. The Dalai Lama himself has refused to say whether he or his brothers worked for the CIA. The agency also has declined to comment.⁴

Into the twenty-first century, the US Congress continued to allocate funds to the Tibetan exile community via the National Endowment for Democracy and other conduits that are more respectable sounding than the CIA. In addition, the Dalai Lama received money from financier George Soros.⁵

The Dalai Lama really cannot be blamed for the abuses of Tibet's ancien regime, having been but twenty-four years old when he fled into exile. In a 1994 interview, he went on record as favoring the building of schools and roads in his country. He said the corvée (forced unpaid serf labor) and certain taxes imposed on the peasants were "extremely bad." And he disliked the way people were saddled with old debts passed down from generation to generation.[6]

During a half century of living in the Western world, he came to embrace concepts such as human rights and religious freedom. He even proposed democracy for Tibet, featuring a written constitution and representative assembly.[7] However, in April 1999, along with Margaret Thatcher, Pope John Paul II, and the first George Bush, the Dalai Lama called upon the British government to release Augusto Pinochet, the former fascist dictator of Chile and a longtime CIA client who was visiting England. He urged that Pinochet not be forced to go to Spain, where he was wanted to stand trial for crimes against humanity.

In the area of personal morals, the Dalai Lama, like some other celibate spiritual leaders, offers curious bedroom guidance to the multitude. "Sexual misconduct for men and women consists of oral and anal sex," he warns. "Using one's hand, that is sexual misconduct." On the other hand, having "sexual relations with a prostitute paid by you and not a third person does not constitute improper behavior."[8]

In 1996, he issued a statement that must have had an unsettling effect on the exile community. It read in part: "Marxism is founded on moral principles, while capitalism is concerned only with gain and profitability." Marxism fosters "the equitable utilization of the means of production" and cares about "the fate of the working classes" and "the victims of . . . exploitation. For those reasons the system appeals to me, and . . . I think of myself as half-Marxist, half-Buddhist."[9]

But he also sent a reassuringly un-Marxist message to "those who live in abundance": "It is a good thing to be rich. . . . Those are the fruits for deserving actions, the proof that they have been generous in the past." And to the poor he offers this cheery advice: "There is no good reason to become bitter and rebel against those who have property and fortune. . . . It is better to develop a positive attitude."[10]

In 2005, to his credit, the Dalai Lama signed a widely advertised statement along with ten other Nobel laureates supporting the "inalienable and fundamental human right" of working people to form labor unions to protect their interests, in accordance with the Universal Declaration of Human Rights. In many countries this right "is poorly protected . . . or brutally suppressed," the statement read. Even in the United States "millions of U.S. workers lack any legal protection to form unions."[11]

The Dalai Lama also supported efforts to remove the traditional obstacles that kept Tibetan nuns from receiving an education. In Tibet the nuns had devoted themselves to daylong periods of prayer and chants. Upon arriving in exile in northern India, they began reading Buddhist philosophy and engaging in theological study and debate, activities that in old Tibet had been open to only monks.[12]

The Dalai Lama is no pacifist. Speaking at Stanford University in 2005, he argued that violent actions committed "to reduce future suffering" are not to be condemned. He cited World War II as an example of a worthy effort to protect democracy. What of the years of carnage and destruction wrought by US forces in Iraq, a war condemned by most of the world—even by a conservative pope? The Dalai Lama was undecided: "The Iraq war—it's too early to say, right or wrong."[13] Earlier he had voiced support for the US/NATO military intervention and seventy-eight days' bombing of Yugoslavia, and the destruction of that viable social democracy. He also supported the US/NATO military intervention into Afghanistan.[14]

SECTARIAN RIVALRY AMONG THE ENLIGHTENED

Though the Dalai Lama is referred to as the "spiritual leader of Tibet," many Tibetan Buddhists see this title as little more than a formality. It does not give him authority over the four religious schools of Tibet other than his own, "just as calling the U.S. president the 'leader of the free world' gives him no role in governing France or Germany."[15]

The Dalai Lama is not the only highly placed lama chosen in childhood as a reincarnation. One or another reincarnate lama or *tulku*—a spiritual teacher of special purity elected to be reborn again and again—can be found presiding over most major Tibetan monasteries. The *tulku* system is unique to Tibetan Buddhism. Scores of lamas of the several Buddhist denominations claim to be reincarnate *tulkus*.

The historic rise of the Gelug sect headed by the Dalai Lama led to a politico-religious rivalry with the Karma Kagyu sect in particular that has lasted centuries, continuing to play itself out within the Tibetan exile community today. That the Kagyu has prospered, opening some six hundred new centers around the world in the last thirty-five years, has not helped the situation.

A difference arose over the selection of the seventeenth Karmapa, head *tulku* of the Kagyu, with the Dalai Lama and others supporting one candidate and most of the Kagyu monks supporting another, firing a dozen years of conflict, punctuated by intermittent riots and the looting of the Karmapa's monastery in Rumtek, India, by supporters of the Gelug faction.[16]

The Dalai Lama manifests a less than perfect tolerance for other religious denominations. He banned the worship of certain old masters and deities, claiming that such devotions cause Tibetan Buddhism to degenerate into idolatry. Many Tibetans living in India who venerate the Dorje Shugden deity testified to being subjected to threats and severe beatings. Their homes and crops were burned and their herds taken away by self-identified supporters of the Dalai Lama. While claiming to have not heard of these violent incidents, the Dalai Lama did opine that "if the goal is good then the method, even if apparently of the violent kind, is permissible."[17]

Not all Tibetan exiles are enamored of old Tibet. Kim Lewis, who studied healing methods with a Buddhist monk in Berkeley, California, had occasion to talk at length with more than a dozen Tibetan women who lived in the monks' building. When she asked how they felt about returning to their homeland, the sentiment was unanimously negative. They said they were extremely grateful "not to have to marry 4 or 5 men, be pregnant almost all the time," or deal with sexually transmitted diseases contacted from a straying husband. The younger women "were delighted to be getting an education, wanted absolutely nothing to do with any religion, and wondered why Americans were so naïve [about Tibet]."[18]

The women recounted stories of their grandmothers' ordeals with monks who used them as "wisdom consorts." By sleeping with the monks, the grandmothers were told, they gained "the means to enlightenment"—after all, the Buddha himself had to be with a woman to reach enlightenment. The women also mentioned the "rampant" sex that the supposedly abstemious monks practiced with each other in the Dalai Lama's Gelugpa sect. Some older women spoke bitterly about the monastery's confiscation of their young boys.

The monks who were granted political asylum in California applied for public assistance. Lewis, herself a devotee for a time, assisted with the paperwork. She observes that they continue to receive monthly government checks along with Medicare. In addition, the monks reside rent free in nicely furnished apartments. "They pay no utilities, have free access to the Internet on computers provided for them, along with fax machines, free cell and home phones and cable TV."

They also receive a monthly payment from their order, along with contributions and dues from their American followers. Some of the American devotees carry out chores for the monks, including grocery shopping and cleaning their apartments and toilets. These same holy men, Lewis remarks, "have no problem criticizing Americans for their 'obsession with material things.'"[19]

THE CHINA MODEL?

One common complaint among Buddhist followers in the West is that Tibet's religious culture is being undermined by the Chinese occupation. To a large extent this does seem to be the case.

A number of the monasteries are closed, and much of the theocracy has passed into history.

But other aspects of Tibetan culture have flourished. In old Tibet, only a few fine literary epics had been passed down through the centuries. Today with universal schooling, new writers—such as Jamppel Gyatso, Tashi Dawa, and Dondru Wangbum—are producing literature of considerable quality. For centuries, art in Tibet consisted of little more than repetitious religious designs for temples. Now there are many talented artists who explore a variety of themes. Tibet also has more than thirty professional song and dance ensembles, opera groups, and other theatrical troupes, according to China expert Foster Stockwell, who argues that "Tibetan culture is not dead; it is flourishing as never before."[20]

Whether Chinese rule has brought betterment or disaster is not the central issue here. The question I have tried to address is, what kind of country was old Tibet? We can advocate religious freedom for a new Tibet without having to embrace the mythology about old Tibet. Tibetan feudalism was cloaked in Buddhism, but the two are not to be equated. Old Tibet was a retrograde repressive theocracy of extreme privilege and poverty.

To welcome the end of feudalism in Tibet is not to applaud everything about Chinese rule in that country. This point is seldom understood by today's champions of a "Free Tibet." Tibet's future seems to be positioned somewhere within China's emerging free-market society. The dazzling economic growth throughout China has also brought heartless land grabs, widespread corruption, population dislocation, environmental devastation, harsh political controls, a rapacious superrich class, and a sharp deterioration of work conditions in some areas, especially in the corporate-dominated "business zones." If China's speedy free-market development is to be the model for Tibet's future, then there certainly is legitimate cause for concern. But to oppose the repressive aspects of Chinese policy does not mean we have to refrain from criticizing the feudal régime of old Tibet.

18

SECULAR TOLERANCE RISING?

If any religion allows the persecution of the
people of different faiths, if any religion keeps
women in slavery, if any religion keeps people in
ignorance, then I can't accept that religion.

—TASLIMA NASRIN, BANGLADESHI AUTHOR

Whatever our thoughts regarding the supernatural, most of us would welcome a world of people who tolerate the beliefs of others and who do not use religion as an instrument of political reactionism, material exploitation, and sexual and emotional abuse.

GOD'S CREATORS

Religion, Karl Marx famously wrote, "is the opium of the people." By this he meant that the masses (who could not afford real opium, a legal recreational drug of his time) used religion as a means of easing the pain of an oppressive existence. In that same passage just before his reference to opium, Marx wrote: "Religious suffering is at the same time an expression of real suffering and a protest against real suffering. Religion is the sigh of the oppressed creature, the sentiment of a heartless world, and the soul of a soulless condition."[1]

Marx notwithstanding, religion is sometimes more than just a balm for miserable social conditions. There are individuals who testify that their creed is a source of emotional stability and inner peace. Religion can be a wellspring of merciful charity and kindly devotion, bringing out the best in some people.

In such rough places as US prisons and on the mean streets of inner-city communities, Islam has sometimes emerged as a positive force, propagating self-discipline, a freeing from anger, and the promise of a clean start. Prison inmates report that their Muslim commitment provides a sense of community and offers protection from threatening conditions. Some individuals claim that Islam has helped them become better parents and better people.[2]

Still, as we have seen, organized religion too often serves as a demonic tool. Those who brim with the lower impulses represent a brutish sort of religious dynamic, with its violent intolerance for other faiths and its hatred of secular values. Throughout history and across the world such religionists fashion gods in their own ugly image. They have used armed force and state power to gain hegemony over other denominations. They have colluded with propertied interests and big-moneyed donors, gathering worldly wealth unto themselves. They have displayed a gaping disconnect between virtuous preachment on the one hand and subterranean concupiscence and moral corruption on the other.

While they promise us peace and unity within the One True Faith, religionists have given us centuries of factional enmity, a deafening cacophony of clashing orthodoxies. Early Christianity, for instance, from its inception paraded a bewildering array of local mystical cults, cosmic philosophers, faith healers, Jews and Gentiles, all claiming to be the chosen paladins of Jesus.[3] Nor have the competing disharmonies grown less clamorous or less violent in modern times.

To win our unswerving devotion why doesn't God communicate with us directly? The holy writings of the Hebrew, Christian, and Muslim faiths reveal that God is obsessed with getting us to *believe* in him. Why then does he do so little to make his presence known? How can we believe in his existence unless we have evidence of it? The "evidence" we do have comes from only the select few to whom he purportedly speaks: prophets, preachers, priests, pastors, popes, and patriarchs. He, who has a matchless capacity to transmit his message instantaneously and simultaneously to everyone in the world, has chosen a sadly piecemeal and unsure mode of communication.

Religious commentator Adrian Reddy notes,

> In addition to being extremely slow and inefficient, the use of prophets suffers from the drawback that each prophet has to establish his own credibility. In ancient times, as now, there [has been] no way . . . for a person to distinguish reliably between a real prophet and a false one and, as a result, false prophets confuse the picture even more. So the question is: why would God risk the rejection of His words by choosing a method of revelation which lacks credibility because it is so obviously open to fakery and self-delusion?[4]

The method of prophetic revelation is so unreliable that it has created *many* One True Faiths. The believers glean God's message from tattered scrolls of dubious ancient origin and from celestial communications transmitted only to self-selected champions who spread the faith with sword and fire, warring against false prophets and false gods. In the face of fruitless confusion and murderous discord, the Almighty never tells us which of the many proselytes is the one we should believe and follow. Why does an omnipotent, omniscient, omnipresent deity have such trouble—and *cause* such trouble—when getting his message across? Why does the Great Communicator pick such muddled and incompetent ways of communicating?

As much of this book suggests, perhaps we should not blame God for the endless religious turmoil but his *creators*, those self-appointed holy hucksters who deign to speak on his behalf. God himself is remote, removed, invisible, inaudible, and unknowable. He does nothing to us, nothing for or against us, because he probably does not exist, neither in the way he has been fashioned by his shills nor in any way that allows us to comprehend him (or her or it).

GLIMMERS OF LIGHT

Religionists frequently refer to their *deeply* held beliefs. So sacred and *deep* are these beliefs that they must never be subjected to critical discernment. When aspersions are cast their way, they become "*deeply* offended." Little recognition is given to how they themselves regularly give offense to the deeply held convictions of freethinkers. The absolutists and theocrats of various religions operate under this double standard. With perfect aplomb they can disrespect the heartfelt ideals and lifestyles of those outside their faith. But *their* tenets must be treated as being above any kind of negative locution. All of us must pay them mindful heed, while they owe us nothing but scornful disparagement and in some countries incarceration and death.

In recent years, signs of resistance have emerged within the United States and elsewhere against the suffocating impositions of theocratic orthodoxy. A number of atheists have written books denouncing religion that unexpectedly became national bestsellers. And the authors have drawn large and sympathetic audiences when making speaking appearances.[5] Atheists, agnostics, skeptics, apostates, and whatever other variety of freethinker there be, seem to be finding each other.

As of 2008, one in four adults in the eighteen to twenty-nine age bracket claimed no affiliation with a religious institution. Almost one in five men of all ages had no formal affiliation, the same for 13 percent of all women. According to a study by the Pew Forum on Religion and Public Life, over 16 percent of Americans (approximately 48 million people) reported having no religious affiliation. A 2009 survey found that the *nonaffili-*

ated are the fastest-growing minority in the country. Those who claim "no religion" are the only demographic group that increased in all fifty states over the last two decades, their numbers having doubled since 1990.[6]

We hear that America is a deeply religious nation, but many apparent believers seem to have only a hazy grasp of religious credo and are less than certain about what they actually believe. Religious affiliation for millions of people is little more than nominal. Respondents are telling the pollsters that they go to church in far greater numbers than they actually do. "There aren't enough churches in the country to hold the hoards who boast of attending," ventures Christopher Hitchens.[7]

A major Pew Forum survey in 2008 of more than 35,000 Americans found that most Americans do *not* promote a dogmatic approach to theological beliefs. Some 70 percent of those who claim to be affiliated with an organized religion do not believe their faith is the only path to salvation. And almost the same number believe that there is more than one true way to interpret the teachings of their religion. Even 79 percent of Roman Catholics and 57 percent of evangelical Protestants take a tolerant pluralistic view. Only among Mormons (57 percent) and Jehovah's Witnesses (80 percent) do majorities insist that their religion is the one and only faith leading to eternal life.[8]

In a 2007 survey conducted by a University of Connecticut research center, 68 percent of respondents said that they "don't like it when politicians rely on their religion in forming their policy." The Secular Coalition for America, consisting of ten national organizations of freethinkers, has joined with liberal religious groups to lobby in Washington for separation of church and state.[9] A 2005 conference on "Spiritual Activism," held at the University of California, Berkeley, and attended by 1,200 people, called for turning society away from materialism and selfishness and exposing the manipulative and opportunistic use of religion by political conservatives. "There is a silent majority out there—progressives and moderates—who saw how religion was used in the last election, and they're saying, 'Hey, I'm a person of faith, and that's not what I believe,'" commented one liberal evangelist.[10]

Interfaith groups are flourishing and becoming increasingly active. In 2008, a conference of such groups, including more than 150 religious leaders, met in San Francisco to promote peace and tolerance. In the words of one United Church of Christ minister: "We're trying to get people to stop killing each other in the name of God."[11]

Pat Robertson's once powerful Christian Coalition has drastically declined in membership and funds. Leading right-wing fundamentalists such as Ralph Reed and Ted Haggard have fallen into disrepute. James Dobson, founder of Focus on the Family, wondered aloud if the conservative church would be able to sustain itself in the years ahead. A Christian polling firm reported that 40 percent of all born-again "values voters" who intended to vote in the November 2008 presidential election said they would choose a Democratic candidate; only 29 percent supported a Republican. Various commentators noted that people were giving less attention to issues pumped by the religious Right and more attention to economic recession, ecological survival, and peace.[12]

Similar developments have been noted in the Muslim world. Some militant Islamist factions have come to realize that the indiscriminate violence perpetrated by their jihadist groups has wrung no real reforms from their respective governments and has only alienated Muslim populations. Rather than being hailed as heroes, the fanatics often find themselves isolated and loathed. After carrying out suicide bombings that killed hundreds of innocents, al Qaeda's popularity declined noticeably in Pakistan and elsewhere. Some al Qaeda members admit as much. As one cleric and former jihadist remarked, "There is nothing that invokes the anger of God and His wrath like the unwarranted spilling of blood and wrecking of property." And a Saudi Muslim insisted, "Muslims are supposed to be an example to the world in tolerance and lofty goals, not to become a gang whose only concern is revenge."[13]

AWAY WITH THE DEMONS

Let us end this book with a salute to two sixteenth-century thinkers: first, the heretical Dominican monk Giordano Bruno, who insisted that people of different religious persuasions should respect each others' freedom of conscience. Bruno himself rejected the divinity of Christ and the virginity of Mary. He not only adhered to the heliocentric theories of Copernicus but also posited the infinity of the heavens. He envisioned a vast cosmos of perhaps countless heliocentric worlds, a universe of unimaginable magnitude that could never be fully comprehended. He also maintained that God—whom the church trumpeted as an entity distinctly apart from the material world— inhered within the very elements of the biosphere.[14]

For such heresies, he was seized by the Inquisition and burned at the stake in 1600. Roberto Bellarmino, the Jesuit cardinal who conducted Bruno's trial, also presided over Galileo's trial years later. Hailed by the Vatican as a defender of the faith, Bellarmino was made a saint in 1930.

In 2000, to mark the four-hundredth anniversary of Bruno's death, hundreds of rationalists, agnostics, atheists, and pantheists gathered before his statue in Rome's Campo dei Fiori—the site of his execution—to lay flowers.[15] They demonstrated that deep conviction and strong historical memory are as much, if not more, the province of those who believe in freedom of conscience as of those who salivate for orthodoxy.

One of Bruno's contemporaries, although they did not know each other, was the conservative monarchist and devout Roman Catholic Michel de Montaigne, who penned these beautiful sentiments circa 1580: "I do not suffer from that common failing of judging another man by me. I can easily believe that others have qualities quite distinct from my own. . . . I can conceive and believe that there are thousands of different ways of living." Montaigne goes on, declaring himself, "contrary to most men," ready to contemplate another human being "simply as he is, free from comparisons. . . . My one desire is that each of us should be judged apart and that conclusions about me [or anyone else] should not be drawn from routine *exempla*."[16]

Being a devout conservative Catholic, Montaigne hardly qualifies as a secular humanist. Yet we might think of him as a *sacred pluralist*, if I may coin such a term: one who sees the hand of God not in the punitive monochrome imposed by theocratic authorities but in the richly diverse blossoming of human beings (so long as they do not harm others), in the "thousands of different ways of living," an orthodoxy that transcends itself, inviting us to live alongside it rather than under it.

For Montaigne the differences between people are a manifestation of the universe's God-given diversity. Individuality should be respected, not suppressed. Sanctity and virtue are not achieved by emptying people of all that is happily human in order to stuff them with a furious intolerance of anything different.

In the years to come, millions of people will continue to turn to religion for solace and inner peace, for transcendence and expanded consciousness, and for promised protection against the terrors of death and life. For many souls, religion will ever remain a haven in a heartless world.

The very best we can do—and all that we should want to do—is roll back the theocratic aggrandizement while strengthening our right to entertain our beliefs and disbeliefs openly and with impunity. Only secular strength and organized democratic activism on our part will counter the sectarian intolerance and state-assisted tyranny of reactionary theocrats.

Will the future ever arrive? We used to think so. Whatever the pessimism now afloat, we must maintain an optimism of the will. We must not only hope but also struggle for that time when "the better angels of our nature" shall prevail and God's demons are put to rest.

ACKNOWLEDGMENTS

For assistance rendered in researching this book, I wish to thank Elizabeth Valente, Tina Kimmel, Sophie Lee, Gary Aguilar, Erica Etelson, Peter Livingston, Gerry Foley, Justin O'Hagan, Richard Wiebe, Christian Parenti, James Petras, Jennifer Tayloe, Eric Dynamic, Tom Saltsman, Heather Cottin, Barry Lituchy, Julia Scheeres, and Rick Garves. In addition, a word of appreciation goes to Linda Regan of Prometheus Books for her careful editing of the manuscript and her encouraging words, and also to Christine Kramer for her expert cooperation. And thanks to my agent, Andy Ross, for his efforts and steadfast support.

NOTES

CHAPTER 1: UP FROM HEAVEN

1. For a discussion of Einstein's views, see Walter Isaacson, *Einstein, His Life and Universe* (New York: Simon & Schuster, 2007), p. 384.

2. Stephen Hawking, *God Created the Integers* (Philadelphia: Running Press, 2007).

3. See G. W. F. Hegel, "Realization of Spirit in History," in *Lectures on the Philosophy of World History* (Cambridge: Cambridge University Press, 1975), p. 47.

CHAPTER 2: THE GREAT EXTERMINATOR

1. See Thomas Frank, *What's the Matter with Kansas? How Conservatives Won the Heart of America* (New York: Henry Holt, 2004).

2. Samuel Butler, *The Way of All Flesh* (1903; New York: New American Library, 1960), p. 23.

3. Gene Lyons, "The Apocalypse Will Be Televised," *Harper's*, November 2004.

4. Falwell quoted by Brian Bolton in *Freethought Today*, December 2006.

5. See Bart D. Ehrman, *Misquoting Jesus: The Story behind Who Changed the Bible and Why* (New York: HarperCollins, 2005).

6. Ibid., pp. 7, 11, 90, passim.

7. On the story of the King James Bible, see Benson Bobrick, *Wide as the Waters* (New York: Penguin, 2002).

8. Bertrand Russell, *Why I Am Not a Christian* (New York: Simon & Schuster, 1957), p. 29.

9. Genesis 6:5–13. Several of the biblical instances discussed in this chapter and the next two were originally published in an article I wrote—"God's Fundamentalist Politics"—for *New Political Science* (September 2005). Several passages in Richard Dawkins's *The God Delusion* (Boston: Houghton Mifflin, 2006), published a year after my article appeared, bear a close resemblance to my treatment.

10. Genesis 9:11–15.

11. Genesis 19:24–25.

12. 1 Samuel 6:19.

13. 2 Kings 19:35.

14. Amos 1:1–14; 2:1–4; 9:10.

15. Deuteronomy 20:4.

16. Deuteronomy 20:11–14.

17. Numbers 31:17–18.

18. Deuteronomy 20:16–17.

19. Numbers 21:33 and Deuteronomy 3:3–6.

20. Deuteronomy 2:32–35.

21. Judges 20:48.

22. Psalms 2:8–9.

23. 1 Samuel 15:3, 15:18, and 18:27.

24. 1 Samuel 27:8–9,11; 1 Chronicles 20:3.

25. Joshua 6:21–24.

26. Proverbs 10:4.

27. Numbers 16:1–35.

28. 1 Kings 18:40.

29. Exodus 15:3.

CHAPTER 3: THE GREAT ABOMINATOR

1. For instance, Genesis 3:14; 7:21, 23; Leviticus 11:46–47.

2. Ezekiel 15:21 and 5:17, and Revelation 6:8.

3. Leviticus 26:22.

4. Genesis 22:1–12. My rendition of this incident was originally published in my article "God's Fundamentalist Politics," *New Political Science* (September 2005). A year later, a close version of it appeared in Dawkins's *The God Delusion*.

5. Genesis 19:26.

6. Malachi 2:2–3.

7. Amos 8:10.

8. Deuteronomy 21:18–21.

9. Proverbs 23:13–14; 29:15.

10. 2 Samuel 11:2–17, 27; 12:15–18.

11. Judges 11:1, 31–33, 38–39.

12. Job 1:1–5.

13. Job 1:11.

14. Job 1:14–22.

15. Ivor H. Evans, *Brewer's Dictionary of Phrase and Fable*, 14th ed. (New York: Harper & Row, 1989), p. 870.

16. Job 2:3–7; 3:2–16.

17. Job 10:1–3.

18. Job 42:11–13.

19. Leviticus 24:11–14.

20. Numbers 15:32–36.

21. For an incomplete listing, see Deuteronomy 13:13–15; see also Exodus 20:4–5, 23; Deuteronomy 4:16–18, 23, 28; Jeremiah 10:3–5; 2 Isaiah 40:18–20, 41:7, 44:9–20.

22. Deuteronomy 13:6–10.

23. Malachi 1:14.

24. Leviticus 25:44.

25. Zechariah 14:18–19.

26. Genesis 3:16–19.

27. Exodus 15:26.

28. Deuteronomy 22:22.

29. Genesis 20:1–7.

30. Leviticus 20:13.

31. Genesis 19:1–11. My treatment of this incident was originally published in my article "God's Fundamentalist Politics," *New Political Science* (September 2005). A close resemblance of it then appeared in Dawkins's *The God Delusion*, published the following year.

32. William Wright, *Harvard's Secret Court* (New York: St. Martin's Press, 2005), pp. 248–49.

33. Deuteronomy 22:5.

34. Genesis 38:10.

35. Leviticus 21:9.

36. Deuteronomy 22:23–24.

37. See the discussion in Michael Parenti, *The Culture Struggle* (New York: Seven Stories Press, 2006), pp. 65–78.

38. Leviticus 20:14.

39. Numbers 31:17–18.

40. Deuteronomy 21:10–14.

41. Exodus 21:7–9.

42. Leviticus 19:20.

43. Genesis 17:10–12.

44. NOCIRC Annual Newsletter, 2005 (publication of National Organization of Circumcision Information Resource Center). There is the notorious case of David Reimer, who was raised as a "girl" after a botched circumcision destroyed his penis. He took his life in 2004. See John Colapinto, *As Nature Made Him* (New York: Harper-Collins, 2000).

45. Leonard B. Glick, *Marked in Your Flesh: Circumcision from Ancient Judea to Modern America* (Oxford: Oxford University Press, 2005), pp. 179–281; Paul Fleiss and Frederick Hodges, *What Your Doctor May Not Tell You about Circumcision* (New York: Warner Books, 2002), pp. 124–30.

46. Leviticus 15:19–24.

47. Deuteronomy 15:1–2, 12–14; 23:19; Exodus 22:25; Leviticus 25:36–37; Nehemiah 5:10.

48. Betty Clermont, "What Annual Fee Would Jesus Charge?" *Atlanta Progressive News*, February 19, 2006.

49. Robert Scheer, "A Lesson in Greed," *San Francisco Chronicle*, March 16, 2005.

50. For instance, Ecclesiastes 2:24, 3:13; Isaiah 22:13; and Nehemiah 8:12.

51. Leviticus 19:34.

52. Isaiah 1:17; 3:14–15; 10:1–2.

CHAPTER 4: THE OTHER FACE OF OUR SWEET SAVIOR

1. Matthew 5:1–11, 39, 44; 6:24; 19:19; 22:39; 7:1.
2. John 3:18; 9:5; 12:31.
3. John 1:51.
4. John 6:35; 14:6; 12:26.
5. John 10:30, 36. See also Matthew 16:13–19.
6. Mark 13:5–6, 21–22; Matthew 7:15.
7. Matthew 12:41–42.
8. Matthew 28:18–20.
9. Luke 19:27.
10. Matthew 10:14–15; 11:21–24; Luke 10:13.
11. Respectively, Matthew 5:22; 10:28; 13:42, 50; 18:8–9; 23:33; Mark 9:43–48; Luke 16:23–28; Matthew 5:30.
12. Respectively, Matthew 23:33; John 8:43–44; Matthew 25:41; John 15:6.
13. Mark 11:13–14, 20–21.
14. Matthew 7:13–14.
15. Matthew 20:16.
16. John 8:44; Luke 8:30–33; Matthew 8:31–32.
17. Luke 8:2.
18. Matthew 10:8; 17:18–20.
19. See, for instance, Matthew 22:2–14.
20. Matthew 13:10–13.
21. John 3:16, 18.
22. Mark 13:7–8, with a similar passage in Matthew 24:7.
23. Matthew 3:2; 4:17; 24:30–34.
24. Mark 16:16–18.
25. Matthew 17:20; 21:21–22.
26. Mark 8:38.
27. John 8:3–11.
28. Matthew 5:32; 19:9.
29. Matthew 19:12.
30. Matthew 10:35–37; Luke 12:53.
31. Luke 18:28–30; Matthew 19:29.
32. Mark 13:12 and a nearly identical passage in Matthew 10:21.
33. Luke 14:26.

34. Matthew 12:46–50; the story is found also in Mark 3:32–35.

35. John 2:1–4.

36. Luke 7:44–47; see also John 12:3.

37. Matthew 19:23–24.

38. Matthew 21:12–13.

39. John 2:14–16.

40. Luke 3:14.

41. John 13:16.

42. Luke 12:47–48.

43. Matthew 24:45–47.

44. Luke 14:8.

45. Mark 14:3–7.

46. For instance, Mark 1:32–34; Matthew 4:23–24; 19:2.

47. Matthew 11:5.

48. Michael Parenti, *History as Mystery* (San Francisco: City Lights, 1999), pp. 60–65, and sources cited therein.

49. Romans 13:1–7; 1 Peter 2:13–14, 17.

50. 1 Timothy 6:1.

51. Ephesians 6:5–7.

52. 1 Peter 2:18.

53. Matthew 1:18; Luke 1:35.

54. Revelation 21:8; see also 14:10–11 and passim.

55. For an incomplete listing, see Acts 7:43; 15:20; 17:16, 29; Romans 1:23; 1 Corinthians 5:1 and 6:9; Revelation 2:14, 20–21 and 17:2–5; 1 Peter 2:11; Romans 1:26–27; 1 Timothy 1:9–10.

56. 1 Corinthians 11:3, 9; 14:34, 35; 1 Timothy 2:9, 11–12 and 5:13; Luke 7:45–46; John 12:3.

57. Luke 10:30–37.

58. John 4:6–22.

59. Matthew 10:5–6.

60. Matthew 15:22–28.

61. See Bart D. Ehrman, *Misquoting Jesus: The Story behind Who Changed the Bible and Why* (New York: HarperCollins, 2005), and the brief discussion in chapter 2 of this book.

CHAPTER 5: WHO KILLED JESUS AND
ALL THOSE OTHER JEWS?

1. Mark 11:18, 12:12; with similar passages in Matthew 21:46 and Luke 19:47–48.

2. See Hyam Maccoby, *The Mythmaker: Paul and the Invention of Christianity* (New York: HarperCollins, 1987); Gerd Lüdemann, *The Great Deception: And What Jesus Really Said and Did*, rev. ed. (Amherst, NY: Prometheus Books, 1999); David Wenham, *Paul: Follower of Jesus or Founder of Christianity?* (Grand Rapids, MI: Eerdmans, 1995).

3. Titus 1:10–11.

4. 1 Thessalonians 2:14–15.

5. See John 5:10, 16–18; 7:1, 11–13; 10:31–33; 18:29–40; 19:6–7.

6. John 19:8.

7. John Dominic Crossan, *Who Killed Jesus?* (San Francisco: HarperSanFrancisco, 1996), p. 111.

8. Bart D. Ehrman, *Misquoting Jesus* (New York: HarperCollins, 2005), p. 188; Crossan, *Who Killed Jesus?* p. 86.

9. Dagobert Runes, *The War against the Jews* (New York: Philosophical Library, 1968), p. 113.

10. St. Augustine, *The City of God* 18:46.

11. Runes, *The War against the Jews*, p. 96.

12. Edward H. Flannery, *The Anguish of the Jews: Twenty-three Centuries of Antisemitism* (New York: Macmillan, 1965), p. 95.

13. Malcolm Hay, *Europe and the Jews* (Biddeford, ME: Beacon Press, 1950), pp. 166–67; Yehuda Bauer, *A History of the Holocaust* (Danbury, CT: Franklin Watts, 1982), p. 22.

14. Archeological findings reported by Eric Meyers, cited in Rodney Stark, *The Rise of Christianity: A Sociologist Reconsiders History* (Princeton, NJ: Princeton University Press, 1996), p. 68.

15. Joshua Trachtenberg, *The Devil and the Jews* (New Haven, CT: Yale University Press, 1943), pp. 159–60.

16. Ibid., p. 162.

17. Jules Michelet, *Satanism and Witchcraft* (New York: Citadel Press, 1962).

18. John Kelly, *The Great Mortality* (New York: Harper Perennial, 2006).

19. Hay, *Europe and the Jews*, pp. 35, 86–87.

20. Bauer, *A History of the Holocaust*, p. 10.

21. Runes, *The War against the Jews*, p. 144; Norman Cohn, *Warrant for Genocide* (New York: Harper & Row, 1966), p. 39.

22. De Rosa quoted in James Haught, *Holy Horrors* (Amherst, NY: Prometheus Books, 1990), pp. 157–65.

23. *New York Times*, February 6, 2008.

24. James Carroll, *Constantine's Sword: The Church and the Jews* (Boston: Houghton Mifflin, 2001), pp. 380, 382.

25. Ibid., p. 44.

26. I. F. Stone, *In a Time of Torment* (New York: Random House, 1967), p. 432.

27. *Los Angeles Times*, March 13, 2000; also the earlier statement, *Memory and Reconciliation: The Church and the Faults of the Past*, issued from the Vatican in December 1999.

28. Robert Lee Wolff, *The Balkans in Our Time*, rev. ed. (New York: Norton, 1978), p. 205; John Cornwell, *Hitler's Pope: The Secret History of Pius XII* (New York: Penguin, 1999), pp. 248–60; Vladimir Dedijer, *The Yugoslav Auschwitz and the Vatican* (Amherst, NY: Prometheus Books, 1992), pp. 268–83, passim; Emond Paris, *Genocide in Satellite Croatia, 1941–1945* (Chicago: American Institute for Balkan Affairs, 1961); Daniel Jonah Goldhagen, *Hitler's Willing Executioners: Ordinary Germans and the Holocaust* (New York: Vintage, 1997), pp. 109–10, 453–54, 517, n. 119, passim.

29. Vatican Bank Claims, http://www.vaticanbankclaims.com. On the return of Ustashi Nazi sympathizers to power in Croatia after the breakup of Yugoslavia, see Michael Parenti, *To Kill a Nation: The Attack on Yugoslavia* (London: Verso, 2000), chap. 5.

30. Robert P. Ericksen, *Theologians under Hitler* (New Haven, CT: Yale University Press, 1985), pp. 84–87, 143, passim.

CHAPTER 6: WORKING HIS BLUNDERS
IN MYSTERIOUS WAYS

1. Proverbs 3:5–6.

2. Associated Press, January 13, 2006; Mecca statistics are from *New York Times*, January 13, 2006.

3. Evening news, ABC-TV, October 9, 2005.

4. *New York Times*, February 14, 2003.

5. "Soldiers Stories," *New Yorker*, June 12, 2006.

6. Nathaniel Philbrick, *Mayflower: A Story of Courage, Community, and War* (New York: Penguin, 2007).

7. *New York Times*, September 14, 2001.

8. *Wall Street Journal*, September 9, 2005.

9. *New York Times*, September 9, 2005.

10. Robert Scheer, column in *San Francisco Chronicle*, March 26, 2008.

11. On Hagee, see Dan Savage's comments, *East Bay Express*, June 18–24, 2008.

12. Mark 16:17–18.

13. *New York Times*, March 31, 2006.

14. Brian Bolton, "Does God Answer Prayer?" *Freethought Today*, April 2006; Richard P. Sloan, *Blind Faith: The Unholy Alliance of Religion and Medicine* (New York: St. Martin's Press, 2006); Sloan's comments in *Freethought Today*, January/February 2007.

15. Mitchell W. Krucoff et al., "From Efficacy to Safety Concerns: A STEP Forward or a Step Back for Clinical Research and Intercessory Prayer? The Study of Therapeutic Effects of Intercessory Prayer (STEP)," *American Heart Journal* 151, no. 4 (April 2006).

16. "Biggest Study: Prayer Harmful to Patients," *Freethought Today*, January/February 2007.

17. Sam Harris, *Letter to a Christian Nation* (New York: Knopf, 2006), p. 78n.

18. John 11:43–44.

19. On Moses Maimonides, see *The Guide for the Perplexed*, large portions of which are available online: http://books.google.com/books?id=kqvilagHvPcC&printsec=frontcover&dq=inauthor:Moses+inauthor:Maimonides&sig=keiJMMrHrGmpPLT. Be forewarned that Maimonides' enlightenment has its limitations; he manifests a hatred of Gentiles, especially nonwhites.

20. Michel de Montaigne, "Judgments on God's Ordinances Must Be Embarked Upon with Prudence," in *The Complete Essays* (New York: Penguin, 2003), pp. 242–43.

21. Michel de Montaigne, "On Judging Someone Else's Death," in *The Complete Essays*, p. 686.

22. James A. Haught, *Holy Horrors* (Amherst, NY: Prometheus Books, 1990), p. 14.

23. For an overview, see Arthur Frederick Ide, *Defending the Faith: Violence and War in Ancient Judaism, Christianity, and Islam* (Garland, TX: Tangelwuld Press, 2004).

24. All quotations in that paragraph are from Haught, *Holy Horrors*, pp. 25–26.

25. BBC News, November 9, 2005.

26. Haught, *Holy Horrors*, pp. 141–47.

27. http://www.religionnewsblog.com and *Los Angeles Times*, August 16, 2007.

28. Henry Chu, *Los Angeles Times*, February 25, 2007.

29. Mark Juergensmeyer, *Terror in the Mind of God* (Berkeley: University of California Press, 2000), pp. 20–26.

CHAPTER 7: JIFFY CREATION, DUBIOUS DESIGN

1. Edward J. Larson, *Summer for the Gods: The Scopes Trial and America's Continuing Debate over Science and Religion* (New York: Basic Books, 2006), pp. 229–67.

2. "GOP Doubts Evolution," *Freethought Today*, June/July 2007; also *New York Times*, September 27 and October 2, 2005; *Washington Post*, November 9, 2005; Matthew Chapman, "God or Gorilla," *Harper's*, February 2006.

3. See Richard Fausset, *Los Angeles Times*, May 31, 2007; also George Monbiot, "A Life with No Purpose," *ZNet Commentary*, September 13, 2005.

4. Mike Weiss, "War of Ideas Fought in a Small-Town Courtroom," *San Francisco Chronicle*, November 6, 2005.

5. John Paul's comment was in a 1996 address to the Pontifical Academy of Sciences.

6. Melissa Eddy, Associate Press, April 12, 2007.

7. Associated Press, November 19, 2005, and *Freethought Today*, October 2006.

8. Carl Zimmer, "Evolution in a Petri Dish," *Yale Alumni Magazine*, May/June 2006.

9. As one ID proponent put it, referring to evolution, "a theory is only speculation," letter to *USA Today*, November 16, 2005.

10. Scientist quoted in Weiss, "War of Ideas Fought in a Small-Town Courtroom."

11. H. Allen Orr, "Devolution," *New Yorker*, May 30, 2005.

12. The ID assertion is by Thomas Dawson, "Intelligent Design and Evolution," *American Chronicle*, August 10, 2005, cited in Monbiot, "A Life with No Purpose."

13. For a more detailed exposition and critique of intelligent design, see Mark Perakh, *Unintelligent Design* (Amherst, NY: Prometheus Books, 2003).

14. Monbiot, "A Life with No Purpose."

15. Keith Lockitch, "'Designer' Another Name for 'the Big G,'" *San Francisco Chronicle*, August 4, 2005.

16. "The Wedge Strategy" is available at www.texscience.org/files/wedge.htm; see also Owen Williamson, "War against Reason," *Political Affairs*, January 25, 2006.

17. Lisa Fullam, "Of God and the Case for Unintelligent Design," *San Francisco Chronicle*, August 4, 2005.

18. Ibid.

19. Sam Harris, *Letter to a Christian Nation* (New York: Knopf, 2006), p. 77.

20. Ibid., p. 78.

21. Francis Darwin, ed., *Life and Letters of Charles Darwin*, vol. 2 (1896; Whitefish, MT: Kessinger, 2007), p. 105.

22. Harris, *Letter to a Christian Nation*, p. 75.

CHAPTER 8: MOTHER TERESA, JOHN PAUL, AND THE FAST-TRACK SAINTS

1. Christopher Hitchens, *The Missionary Position: Mother Teresa in Theory and Practice* (London/New York: Verso, 1995), pp. 64–71.

2. Christopher Hitchens, "Teresa, Bright and Dark," *Newsweek*, August 29, 2007.

3. For a sharply critical view of Teresa's hospitals, see Aroup Chatterjee, *Mother Teresa: The Final Verdict* (Kolkata, India: Meteor Books, 2003), pp. 196–97, 224, and passim.

4. Anne Sebba, *Mother Teresa: Beyond the Image* (London: Weidenfeld & Nicolson, 1997), pp. 59–61.

5. Both the volunteer and the doctor are quoted in Chatterjee, *Mother Teresa*, pp. 188–97.

6. Sebba, *Mother Teresa*, p. 142.

7. Ibid., pp. 127, 135–36.

8. Ibid., pp. 141–42, 148, 152.

9. *Observer* (UK), August 26, 1990.

10. The remark of the student, Ajanta Ghosh, was reported to me by the writer Heather Cottin, October 30, 2007.

11. Chatterjee, *Mother Teresa*, pp. 189, 209, 385.

12. *Washington Post*, December 11, 1984; Deepak Goyal, "Bhopal: 20 Years Later, the Misery Continues," *Siliconeer*, December 2004.

13. Sebba, *Mother Teresa*, pp. 111, 200.

14. Mother Teresa, Nobel Lecture, December 11, 1979, http://www.nobel.se/peace/laureates/1979/teresa-lecture.html, and Hitchens, *The Missionary Position*, pp. 88–89.

15. Sebba, *Mother Teresa*, pp. 227, 231.

16. Ibid., pp. 106–107.

17. Chatterjee, *Mother Teresa*, pp. 19–22.

18. All the information in the above paragraph is from Chatterjee, *Mother Teresa*, pp. 23, 32–33, 92, 106–107, 157, 170, 179–80.

19. Ibid., pp. 332–33.

20. Hitchens, *The Missionary Position*, pp. 11, 95.

21. Sebba, *Mother Teresa*, p. 218.

22. Chatterjee, *Mother Teresa*, pp. 2–14, 95.

23. Serena Sartini, "The Night of Silence," *Inside the Vatican*, November 2007; Bruce Johnston, "Mother Teresa's Diary Reveals Her Crisis of Faith," http://www.telegraph.co.uk/news/main.jhtml?xml=/news/2002/11/29/wteres29.xml; and Hitchens, "Teresa, Bright and Dark."

24. http://www.odan.org/escriva_to_franco.htm, and Curtis Bill Pepper, "Opus Dei, Advocatus Papae," *Nation*, August 3–10, 1992.

25. Edmond Paris, *Genocide in Satellite Croatia, 1941–1945* (Chicago: American Institute for Balkan Affairs, 1961), pp. 201–205, passim; also *How the Catholic Church United with Local Nazis to Run Croatia during World War II: The Case of Archbishop Stepinac* (Washington, DC: Embassy of the Federal Peoples Republic of Yugoslavia, 1947), posted August 2, 2004, http://emperors-clothes.com/croatia/stepinac1.htm#11.

26. Eamonn McCann, "The Other Side of Miraculous Monk Padre Pio," *Belfast Telegraph*, October 25, 2007.

27. Ibid.

28. Barry Healy, "Pope John Paul II, a Reactionary in Shepherd's Clothing," *Green Left Weekly*, April 6, 2005.

29. As reported to me, October 29, 2007, by political scientist James Petras, who interviewed civil war survivors.

30. Tracy Wilkinson, *Los Angeles Times*, October 29, 2007.

31. RAI report, "Rissa a Roma tra giovani dei centri sociale e fedeli dell'Opus Dei," October 28, 2007.

32. Gordon Zahn, *In Solitary Witness, the Life & Death of Franz Jagerstatter* (Austin: Holt, Rinehart & Winston, 1964).

33. *New York Times*, May 14, 2005.

CHAPTER 9: CASHING IN ON HEAVEN

1. Karl Marx, *Capital*, vol. 1 (Harmondsworth, Middlesex, England: Penguin, 1976), p. 165.

2. *New York Times*, August 23 and October 8, 1987.

3. For these various instances, see *New York Times*, September 25, 26, and 30, 1977; October 9, 16, and 28, 1977; September 5 and 26, 1986; August 23 and October 8, 1987; March 21, April 19 and 30, May 16 and 30, June 6 and 14, 1988; October 6 and 25, 1989.

4. *New York Times*, February 8 and April 2, 1987; September 14, 1989.

5. Associated Press, December 7, 2007; CBS News, October 17, 2007.

6. Jim Bakker biography, http://atheism.about.com/library/glossary/western/bldef_bakkerjim.htm.

7. Reported by Bill Moyers, *Now*, PBS-KQED, November 19, 2004.

8. *San Francisco Chronicle*, August 12, 1998.

9. The Illinois, Indiana, and Washington cases are reported in "Faith-Based Initiative—In God We Trust?" *Nation*, January 6, 2003.

10. These two cases are found in *New York Sun*, May 27–28, 2006, and news14.com, May 22, 2006, respectively.

11. *New York Times*, September 13, 2007.

12. *Florida Sun-Sentinel*, September 29, 2006. Some of these examples were originally cited and summarized in *Freethought Today*, various issues.

13. *New York Times*, January 5, 2007.

14. *Seattle Times*, February 22, 2007.

15. "Pastor Reaches Plea Deal after Selling Church," January 26, 2006, http://www.kcra.com/news/6475822/detail.html?rss=sac&psp =new; *Register-Guard* (Eugene, OR), March 28, 2007, and *Cincinnati Enquirer*, October 21, 2005.

16. *Chicago Tribune*, August 31, 2005; *San Francisco Chronicle*, August 17, 2007; *Yahoo!News*, April 5, 2007.

17. *Cleveland Plain Dealer*, September 16, 2006.

18. *Washington Post*, October 1, 2006.

19. Associated Press, August 13, 2006.

20. Bakker NPR interview (replay), July 21, 2007.

21. See the investigative report "Televangelism," ABC's *Primetime Live*, November 21, 1991; also "Success N Life" telecasted show with Rev. Robert Tilton, February 5, 1991, and various other dates.

22. "Success N Life" telecasted show with Rev. Robert Tilton, February 21, 2007.

23. Kelefa Sanneh, "Pray and Grow Rich," *New Yorker*, October 11, 2004.

24. See Sanneh, "Pray and Grow Rich," and Leslie Fulbright, "Singing the Praises of God and Prosperity," *San Francisco Chronicle*, September 23, 2006.

25. *New York Times*, March 30, 2006.

26. The televangelists' opulent lifestyles drew the attention of a few US senators who in December 2007 attempted without success to ascertain how these media-based ministries were using their enormous tax-free funds: *Freethought Today*, December 2007.

27. Jenni Mintz, Scripps Howard News Service, December 14, 2007.

28. For a description of a feel-good megachurch, see Frances FitzGerald, "Come One, Come All," *New Yorker*, December 3, 2007.

CHAPTER 10: MONEYED GURUS AND CULTS

1. See Nino Lo Bello, *Vatican, U.S.A.* (New York: Pocket Books, 1973).

2. Peter Robbins, *Filthy Rich* (London: Zed, 2007).

3. Robert Boettcher, *Gifts of Deceit: Sun Myung Moon,*

Tongsun Park, and the Korean Scandal (New York: Holt, Rinehart and Winston, 1980).

4. "Dark Side of Rev. Moon," consortiumnews.com, September 8, 1997, and "Mysterious Republican Money," consortiumnews.com, September 7, 2004.

5. Nansook Hong, *In the Shadow of the Moons: My Life in the Reverend Sun Myung Moon's Family* (Boston: Little, Brown, 1998).

6. On Smith's beliefs, see Fawn M. Brodie, *No Man Knows My History: The Life of Joseph Smith*, 2nd rev. ed. (New York: Vintage, 1995); Ed Decker and Dave Hunt, *The God Makers* (Eugene: Harvest House, 1997); and Charles L. Wood, *The Mormon Conspiracy* (Mosheim, TN: Black Forest Press, 2004).

7. Jon Krakauer, *Under the Banner of Heaven* (New York: Doubleday, 2003), pp. 112–13.

8. Dana Goodyear, "Château Scientology," *New Yorker*, January 14, 2008.

9. "The Thriving Cult of Greed and Power," *Time*, May 6, 1991, http://www.cs.cmu.edu/~dst/Fishman/time-behar.html; Mitch Stacy, Associated Press, September 24, 2007; and Stephen A. Kent, "Scientology and the European Human Rights Debate," *Marburg Journal of Religion* (September 2003).

10. See Margaret Thaler Singer and Janja Lalich, *Cults in Our Midst* (San Francisco: Jossey-Bass, 1996).

11. Ibid., p. 48.

12. *Washington Post*, January 22, 1984.

13. Quoted in Nancy Duvergne Smith, "Spiritual Despotism," *New Age*, March 1978.

14. Peggy Karp, "Life with the Guru," unpublished manuscript, 1992.

15. Smith, "Spiritual Despotism."

16. Singer and Lalich, *Cults in Our Midst*, pp. xxiii and 19.

17. Ibid., pp. 158, 277–79.

18. See Theodore Roszak, "The Case for Cults: Skeptics and True Believers," *Nation*, February 10, 1979.

19. David Chidester, *Salvation and Suicide: Jim Jones, the People's Temple and Jonestown*, rev. ed. (Bloomington: Indiana University Press, 2003); and the forthcoming book by Julia Scheeres, whose comments to me inform the above paragraph.

20. Krakauer, *Under the Banner of Heaven*, pp. 5–6.

21. Ibid.

22. Ron Russell, "Sign of the Cult-Buster," *San Francisco Weekly*, October 5, 2005.

23. Ibid. For other examples of sexual abuse within cults, see Timothy Egan, "Polygamous Settlement Defies State Crackdown," *New York Times*, October 25, 2005, and Krakauer, *Under the Banner of Heaven*.

24. John Kain, *A Rare and Precious Thing: The Possibilities and Pitfalls of Working with a Spiritual Teacher* (New York: Harmony/Bell Tower, 2006).

25. All the examples in the above paragraph are from Singer and Lalich, *Cults in Our Midst*, p. 250.

26. Ibid., p. 253.

27. Don Lattin, *Jesus Freaks: A True Story of Murder and Madness on the Evangelical Edge* (New York: HarperOne, 2007); Bill Hewitt and Maureen Harrington, "Was the Family Doing God's Work—Or Unspeakable Harm?" *People*, July 18, 2005.

28. Lattin, *Jesus Freaks*; Hewitt and Harrington, "Was the Family Doing God's Work?; http://www.excult.org/vital.html.

29. Julia Scheeres, *Jesus Land: A Memoir* (Cambridge, MA: Counterpoint, 2005), pp. 169–337.

30. Ibid., pp. 181–82.

31. Ibid., pp. 248, 308.

32. Carrie Louise Nutt, "Christian Schools for the Damned," *Freethought Today*, September 2007.

33. Ibid.

34. See studies cited in Kimberly Blaker, "God's Warrior Twins," *Toward Freedom*, Fall 2003.

35. Scheeres, *Jesus Land*, p. 360.

36. Erica Etelson, *For Our Own Good: Real Family Values for an Ailing Society* (forthcoming), chap. 9. Dobson's book *Dare to Discipline* sold more than 3.5 million copies.

37. Philip Greven, *Spare the Child* (New York: Knopf, 1991), pp. 91–92, passim; Donald Capps, *The Child's Song: The Religious Abuse of Children* (Louisville, KY: Westminster John Knox Press, 1995).

38. Etelson, *For Our Own Good*, chap. 9.

39. Jeff Sharlet, "Inside America's Most Powerful Megachurch," *Harper's*, May 2005.

40. Blaker, "God's Warrior Twins"; Kimberly Blaker, ed., *The*

Fundamentals of Extremism: The Christian Right in America (Plymouth, MI: New Boston Books, 2003).

41. Bruce R. McConkie, *Mormon Doctrine* (Salt Lake City: Bookcraft Inc., 1966), p. 844.

42. Deborah Laake, *Secret Ceremonies* (New York: Dell, 1993), pp. 108, 118, 176, passim; Jessica Longaker, "The Role of Women in Mormonism," http://www.exmormon.org/mormwomn.htm.

CHAPTER 11: GOD, LEFT AND RIGHT

1. Heinrich Bornkamm, *Luther in Mid-Career, 1521–1530* (Minneapolis: Fortress Press, 1983), p. 375.

2. See Luther's "Against the Robbing and Murdering Hordes of Peasants," in *Luther's Works*, ed. Robert C. Schultz, vol. 46 (Minneapolis: Fortress Press, 1967), pp. 49–55.

3. Leo Gershoy, *The French Revolution and Napoleon* (New York: Appleton-Century-Crofts, 1933), pp. 30–33.

4. Reinhard Bendix, *Work and Authority in Industry* (New York: Harper & Row, 1963), p. 68; Sidney Fine, *Laissez-Faire and the General Welfare State* (Ann Arbor: University of Michigan Press, 1965), pp. 117–25; Liston Pope, *Millhands and Preachers* (New Haven, CT: Yale University Press, 1942).

5. Walter Rauschenbusch, *A Gospel for the Social Awakening* (Eugene: Wipf & Stock Publishers, 2008), compiled by Benjamin E. Mays.

6. *New York Times*, July 21, 2007. For one evangelical's critique, see Randall Balmer, *Thy Kingdom Come: How the Religious Right Distorts the Faith and Threatens America* (New York: Basic Books, 2007).

7. Anita Gates, "Evangelicals Discover Environmentalism," *New York Times*, October 11, 2006; Sally Bingham, "Should Religion Have a Voice?" *San Francisco Chronicle*, February 16, 2005.

8. Marilynne Robinson, "Hallowed Be Your Name," *Harper's*, July 2006.

9. Quoted in Neela Banerjee, "Liberal Denomination Fires Salvos at Right," *New York Times*, April 7, 2006. For liberal Catholic views, see such publications as *Pax Christi*, *National Catholic Reporter*, and *America*. For a radical pacifist viewpoint, see the *Catholic Worker*.

10. *Peoples Weekly World*, April 30, 2005, and *Louisville Courier-Journal*, April 25, 2005.

11. *New York Times*, December 27, 1984.

12. *Los Angeles Times*, September 4, 1984; *Washington Post*, September 4, 1984; *Guardian*, April 19, 1989; Jane Kramer, "Holy Orders," *New Yorker*, May 2, 2005; Gary MacEoin, *The People's Church* (New York: Crossroad Publishing, 1996).

13. Barry Healy, "Pope John Paul II, a Reactionary in Shepherd's Clothing," *Green Left Weekly*, April 6, 2005.

14. *New York Times*, July 27, 1988.

15. Penny Lernoux, "Opus Dei and the 'Perfect Society,'" *Nation*, April 10, 1989; Curtis Bill Pepper, "Opus Dei, Advocatus Papae," *Nation*, August 3–10, 1992.

16. Mark Engler, "John Paul II's Economic Ethics," *ZNet Commentary*, April 7, 2005.

17. Jason Berry and Gerald Renner, *Vows of Silence: The Abuse of Power in the Papacy of John Paul II* (New York: Free Press, 2004).

18. Special report, *Newsweek*, April 18, 2005.

19. Paul Wilkes, "The Reformer: A Priest's Battle for a More Open Church," *New Yorker*, September 2, 2002.

20. Larry Rohter, "As Pope Benedict Heads to Brazil, Rival Theology Retains Its Appeal," *New York Times*, May 7, 2007.

21. Joe Garofoli, *San Francisco Chronicle*, February 28, 2005.

22. "Left Behind: The Skewed Representation of Religion in Major News Media," report by Media Matters for America, May 2007.

23. John C. Green, Mark J. Rozell, and Clyde Wilcox, eds., *The Christian Right in American Politics* (Washington, DC: Georgetown University Press, 2003); Adam Piore, "A Higher Frequency," *Mother Jones*, December 2005; Michael Parenti, *Superpatriotism* (San Francisco: City Lights, 2004), chap. 6.

24. Warren St. John, "Sports and Salvation on Face Night at the Stadium," *New York Times*, June 2, 2006.

25. Adam Green, "Standup for the Lord," *New Yorker*, August 9 and 16, 2004.

26. Matthai Chakko Kuruvila, "Christian Teens Flock to BattleCry," *San Francisco Chronicle*, March 11, 2007.

27. *San Francisco Chronicle*, December 12, 2006.

28. Laurie Goodstein, "Pentecostal and Charismatic Groups

Growing," *New York Times*, October 6, 2006; see also Harvey G. Cox Jr., *Fire from Heaven: The Rise of Pentecostal Spirituality and the Reshaping of Religion in the Twenty-first Century* (Cambridge, MA: Da Capo, 2006).

29. Alex Hogan, "Grassroots Uprising? The Marriage of the Christian Right and the Republican Party," *Left Turn*, February/March 2005.

30. Pat Robertson, undated fund-raising letter, summer 1992.

31. Pat Robertson, *The New World Order* (Nashville: Thomas Nelson, 1992), p. 228.

32. Pat Robertson, *The 700 Club*, Christian Broadcasting Network, August 22, 2005.

33. *Z Magazine*, July/August 2007; *San Francisco Chronicle*, November 20, 2005, and May 18, 2007.

34. Charles Marsh, "Wayward Christian Soldiers," *New York Times*, January 20, 2006.

35. Stephanie Hendricks, *Divine Destruction* (Brooklyn, NY: Melville House, 2005).

36. All Haggard quotations in Jeff Sharlet, "Soldiers of Christ," *Harper's*, May 2005.

37. So concludes the documentary film *The Tailenders* (2006), produced and written by Adele Horne, American Documentary Inc. For an overview of reactionary fundamentalists, seeing Chris Hedges, *American Fascists: The Christian Right and the War on America* (New York: Free Press, 2007).

38. For an early critique of the privatized view of evil, see sociologist E. A. Ross, *Sin and Society: An Analysis of Latter-Day Iniquity* (Boston: Houghton Mifflin, 1907).

CHAPTER 12: PIOUS PREDATORS

1. Robert G. Anderson, "The Two Faces of George Roche III, Part II," December 1999, Religious Freedom Coalition, http://www.tylwythteg.com/enemies/roche2.html.

2. Robyn Meredith, "Scandal Rocks a Conservative Campus," *New York Times*, November 15, 1999.

3. John A. Baden, "When Leaders Lie," *Bozeman Daily Chronicle*, December 1, 1999; *Imprimes*, June 2006.

4. Mona Charen, "The Truth and Hillsdale," November 24, 1999, http://www.jewishworldreview.com.

5. *New York Times*, October 15, 18, and 19, 1991. The prostitute in question gave a complete exposé in *Penthouse*, July 1988.

6. *New York Times*, March 21 and April 27, 1987; Clint Willis and Nate Hardcastle, eds., *Jesus Is Not a Republican* (New York: Thunder's Mouth Press, 2005), p. 319.

7. Dory Turner, Associated Press, November 20, 2007.

8. *New York Times*, November 4, 2003.

9. Jeff Sharlet, "Soldiers of Christ," *Harper's*, May 2005; CNN.com, November 4, 2006; MSNBC, November 5, 2006; Mike Jones, *I Had to Say Something: The Art of Ted Haggard's Fall* (New York: Seven Stories Press, 2007).

10. *Denver Post*, February 6, 2007.

11. *Denver Post*, December 11, 2006.

12. *Oklahoman*, January 5, 2006.

13. "Vatican Official Insists He's Not Gay," Associated Press, October 14, 2007.

14. Sharon Smith, "The Hypocrites in the Catholic Church," *Socialist Worker*, March 5, 2004.

15. Karen Liebreich, *Fallen Order* (New York: Grove Press, 2004), pp. 258–62.

16. David France, *Our Fathers: The Secret Life of the Catholic Church in an Age of Scandal* (New York: Broadway, 2005).

17. *San Francisco Chronicle*, January 30, 2008.

18. *Pittsburgh Post-Gazette*, September 23, 2005. Several of these were reported in *Freethought Today*, various issues. For wrenching accounts of abuse and cover-up, see France, *Our Fathers*, passim.

19. JoAnn Wypijewski, "The Roman Inquisition," *Mother Jones*, December 2005.

20. Dahlia Lithwick, "But Why Isn't Bernard Law in Jail? (Part 2)," *Slate*, December 19, 2002.

21. Liebreich, *Fallen Order*, pp. 263, 266.

22. *Boston Globe* investigative staff, *Betrayal: The Crisis in the Catholic Church* (Boston: Little, Brown, 2002), p. 162.

23. Christopher Brauchli, "Rome on $12,000 a Month: The Return of Cardinal Bernard Law," *Counterpunch*, June 3, 2004.

24. *New York Times*, November 3, 2007; *Chicago Sun-Times*,

October 24, 2007; and Kay Jones, "Catholic Church Aware of Donald McGuire's Abuse of Young Boys," October 29, 2007, http://www.associatedcontent.com/article/430455/catholic_church_aware _of_donald_mcguires.html.

25. Associated Press, July 17, 2007; *Los Angeles Times*, July 15, 2007.

26. *Milwaukee Journal Sentinel*, November 4, 2005; Keloland TV, November 2 and 3, 2005.

27. Jason Berry in *San Francisco Chronicle*, April 10, 2005.

28. Jason Berry and Gerald Renner, *Vows of Silence: The Abuse of Power in the Papacy of John Paul II* (New York: Free Press, 2004).

29. Berry and Renner, *Vows of Silence*, and Berry's report, *San Francisco Chronicle*, April 10, 2005.

30. *San Francisco Chronicle*, May 21, 2003.

31. See Ron Russell's articles in *San Francisco Weekly*, July 13, 2005, and January 4, 2006.

32. Quoted in Robert Scheer's column, *San Francisco Chronicle*, May 25, 2005; also see anonymous, *Against Ratzinger* (New York: Seven Stories Press, 2007).

33. Thomas P. Doyle, A. W. Richard Sipe, and Patrick Wall, *Sex, Priests, and Secret Codes: The Catholic Church's 2,000-Year Paper Trail of Sexual Abuse* (Santa Monica, CA: Bonus Books, 2006), pp. 1, 60, passim.

34. Ibid.; Liebreich, *Fallen Order*.

35. Frank Bruni and Eleanor Burkett, *A Gospel of Shame: Children, Sexual Abuse, and the Catholic Church* (New York: Norton, 2002), esp. chaps. 7–10.

36. Liebreich, *Fallen Order*, p. 258.

37. Bruni and Burkett, *A Gospel of Shame*, p. 161.

38. *Deliver Us from Evil*, Disarming Films, 2006, produced by Amy Berg and Frank Donner.

39. Bruni and Burkett, *A Gospel of Shame*, passim; Doyle et al., *Sex, Priests, and Secret Codes*, pp. 242–49.

40. See Kevin G. Hall, McClatchy Newspapers, September 5, 2007, http://www.mcclatchydc.com/homepage/story/19483.html.

41. *USA Today*, October 10, 2007.

42. *Belfast Telegraph*, May 20, 2009; *Los Angeles Times*, May 21, 2009; and *New York Times*, May 21, 2009.

43. *Los Angeles Times*, April 16, 2008.

44. Rose French, Associated Press, February 22, 2007.

45. NBC News, January 20, 2006.

46. *Chicago Tribune*, July 2, 2005; *Palm Beach Post Staff*, October 11, 2006; *Advocate* (LA), October 19, 2006; *Dayton Daily News*, November 22, 2006; Associated Press, February 22, 2007.

47. *Sacramento Bee*, July 15, 2006.

48. *Independent* (UK), August 24, 2007.

49. *New York Times*, March 12, 2005; Bruce Falconer, "The Torture Colony," *American Scholar* 77 (Autumn 2008).

50. Associated Press, October 3, 2007; *Deseret News* (Salt Lake City), January 23, 2007; http://www.boyscoutabuse.com/abuse-case-successes/#MormonAbuseSuccesses.

51. *San Antonio Express-News*, November 13, 2005.

52. *New York Daily News*, September 9, 2006.

53. Russell Shorto, "Contra-Contraception," *New York Times Magazine*, May 7, 2006.

CHAPTER 13: POLITICOS AND OTHER PHARISEES

1. See Froma Harrop, "Naughty Conservatives: Stick to Your Own Foible; They Should Their Noses in Their Own Dirt," *News & Record*, December 1998; Jim Abrams, Associated Press, November 30, 2007.

2. CNN.com, December 19, 1998.

3. As reported by Rev. Jerry Falwell, Associated Press, March 10, 2007.

4. "Florida Randall Admits Fathering Child," *Roll Call*, October 26, 1998.

5. CNN, January 12, 1999, and *Newsweek*, February 27, 2004.

6. *Washington Post*, July 17, 2007; Associated Press, July 17, 2007; *New York Times*, September 12, 2007.

7. *Washington Post*, May 9, 2008.

8. *Washington Post*, June 9, 2002.

9. Associated Press, August 31, 2004.

10. *Orlando Sentinel*, July 22, 2007.

11. *Washington Post*, August 28 and 29, 2007.

12. Rachel La Corte, "GOP State Rep Resigns amid Sex Scandal," October 31, 2007, http://www.usatoday.com/news/nation/2007-10-31-3507873937_x.htm.

13. David Brock, *Blinded by the Right: The Conscience of an Ex-Conservative* (New York: Three Rivers Press, 2002).

14. See Anthony Summers, *Official and Confidential: The Secret Life of J. Edgar Hoover* (Kirkwood, NY: Putnam, 1993); John Cooney, *The American Pope: The Life and Times of Francis Cardinal Spellman* (New York: Times Books, 1984).

15. *Republican-American* (CT), October 21, 2004; CNN, March 29, 2003.

16. *Herald Journal* (Spartanburg, SC), July 28, 1995.

17. *Seattle Times*, October 10, 2005; Associated Press, August 16, 2006.

18. http://www.armchairsubversive.org.

19. *Boothbay Register*, April 15, 1999.

20. All the examples in that paragraph are cited in http://www.recoveringliberal.com/?page_id=765. See also Jane Ann Morrison, "Officials Report More Crimes in Candidate's Past," *Las Vegas Review-Journal*, October 30, 2002.

21. *Spokesman-Review*, May 5, 2005, and *New York Times*, December 8, 2005.

22. http://www.armchairsubversive.org.

23. http://www.democraticunderground.com/top10/05/217.html.

24. http://www.urbandictionary.com/define.php?term=Republican+pedophiles.

25. *Washington Post*, October 5–10, 2006; ABC News, October 5, 2006.

26. NBC News, October 13, 2006; *Washington Post*, October 18, 2006.

27. http://www.armchairsubversive.org/Patrick_Lee_McGuire.htm.

28. http://www.nytimes.com/2007/09/29/us/29florida.html; *New York Times*, October 6, 2007.

29. Win McCormack, *You Don't Know Me: A Citizen's Guide to Republican Family Values* (Portland, OR: Tin House Books, 2008).

30. Lou Dubose and Jan Reid, *The Hammer Comes Down: The Nasty, Brutish, and Shortened Political Life of Tom DeLay* (New York: Public Affairs, 2006).

31. *New York Times*, January 10, 2006.

32. *New York Times*, December 2, 2005, and March 8, 2006; Andrew Wheat, "Not Kosher: The Ralph Reed–Jack Abramoff Connection," *Multinational Monitor*, January/February 2006.

33. Michael Kinsley, "Bill Bennett's Bad Bet," May 4, 2003, http://www.slate.com/id/2082526.

34. Congresspedia, http://www.sourcewatch.org/index.php?title =Bill_Frist#Named_one_of_the_.22most_corrupt.22.

35. CNNMoney.com, June 13, 2002; Alan Saracevic, "Gimme That Old Time Religion—And Arrogance," *San Francisco Chronicle*, July 28, 2002.

36. CNNMoney.com, June 20, 2005.

37. *Austin American Statesman*, May 25, 2006.

38. CNNMoney.com, March 15, 2005; Saracevic, "Gimme That Old Time Religion."

CHAPTER 14: CHURCH *IN* STATE

1. *New York Times*, January 28, 1992; *Asheville Global Report*, April 14–20, 2005.

2. *Dallas Morning News*, June 4, 2006.

3. Robert Weitzel, "Religious Tests for Public Office," *Freethought Today*, October 2007.

4. Letter to William Bradford Jr., April 1, 1774, selection reprinted in Marvin Meyers, *The Mind of the Founder* (Indianapolis: Bobbs-Merrill, 1973), p. 6.

5. See Madison's note regarding a religious test, in Max Farrand, ed., *The Records of the Federal Convention of 1787* (New Haven, CT: Yale University Press, 1966), vol. 2, p. 468; Paul Boller Jr., *George Washington and Religion* (Dallas: Southern Methodist University Press, 1963), pp. 88–89.

6. In a letter to Jefferson, see Brooke Allen, *Moral Minority: Our Skeptical Founding Fathers* (Chicago: Ivan R. Dee, 2006).

7. Carl Van Doren, *Benjamin Franklin* (New York: Viking Press, 1938), p. 777.

8. Allen, *Moral Minority*, passim.

9. Farrand, ed., *The Records of the Federal Convention of 1787*, vol. 1, p. 452; see also Virginia delegate Edmund Randolph's comments, vol. 3, p. 310.

10. Alexis de Tocqueville, *Democracy in America* (Garden City, NY: Anchor Books, 1969), vol. 1, pp. 295–98.

11. *San Francisco Examiner*, August 29, 1992.

12. *New York Times*, August 30, 1992; see also Clint Willis and Nate Hardcastle, eds., *Jesus Is Not a Republican* (New York: Thunder's Mouth Press, 2005).

13. Martin E. Marty, "The Sin of Pride," *Newsweek*, March 10, 2003.

14. *San Francisco Chronicle*, October 7, 2005; see also "Bush's Messiah Complex," *Progressive*, February 2003.

15. Lewis Lapham, "Notebook," *Harper's*, April 2005.

16. Howard Fineman, "Bush and God," *Newsweek*, March 10, 2003; Elisabeth Bumiller, "Anti-war Clerics Find Access to Bush Barred," *International Herald Tribune*, March 11, 2003; Stephanie Salter, commentary in *Terre Haute Tribune*, July 10, 2007.

17. Robyn Blumner, *St. Petersburg Times*, July 1, 2007.

18. Anna Bates, "Church-*Dictated* Health Care Policy?" *Political Affairs*, May 2007.

19. Michelle Goldberg, *Kingdom Coming: The Rise of Christian Nationalism* (New York: Norton, 2007).

20. *New York Times*, May 13, 2007.

21. Diana B. Henriques, "Religion-Based Tax Breaks," *New York Times*, October 11, 2006.

22. Diana B. Henriques, "In the Congressional Hopper," *New York Times*, October 11, 2006.

23. Esther Kaplan, *With God on Their Side* (New York: New Press, 2005); *New York Times*, July 17, 2006; Chris Mooney, *The Republican War on Science* (New York: Basic Books, 2005).

24. Neil A. Lewis, "Justice Dept. Reshapes Its Civil Rights Mission," *New York Times*, June 14, 2007.

25. David Antoon, "The Cancer from Within," *Truthdig Report*, November 7, 2007, http://www.truthdig.com/report/item/2007.

26. *New York Times*, June 11 and October 25, 2005; Associated Press, May 4, 2005.

27. Antoon, "The Cancer from Within"; Kate Randall, "Whitewash of Christian Fundamentalist Bigotry at US Air Force Academy," June 27, 2005, http://www.wsws.org/articles/2005/jun2005/acad-j27.shtml.

28. Antoon, "The Cancer from Within"; Gustav Spohn, http://www.yale.edu/divinity/notes/050516/notes_050516_kl.shtml.

29. *New York Times*, July 12, 2005.

30. Michael L. Weinstein and Davin Seay, *With God on Our*

Side: One Man's War against an Evangelical Coup in America's Military (New York: Thomas Dunne, 2006), passim.

31. David Kelly, "Loosening Religious Grip at Air Force Academy," *Los Angeles Times*, April 24, 2005.

32. "Military Proselytizing Continues," *Freethought Today*, August 2008.

33. Antoon, "The Cancer from Within"; *Star-Bulletin*, May 22, 2008, http://starbulletin.com/2008/05/22/news/story10.html.

34. Jason Leopold, *Freethought Today*, December 2007.

35. Weinstein and Seay, *With God on Our Side*.

36. Joe Parko, "US Government Training Clergy to Quell Dissent in Martial Law," *Atlanta Progressive News*, September 3, 2007, http://www.atlantaprogressivenews.com/news/0220.html. First reported to the Web site prisonplanet.com in May 2006.

37. "I'm Free to Submit to Authority," timeofgrace.com; http://www.youtube.com/watch?V=3KGD14Dxa4; see also http://www.youtube.com/watch?v=e-BtWhs8qlg.

38. *New York Times*, December 10, 2006.

39. *Washington Post*, June 3, 2006.

40. *New York Times*, December 10, 2006.

41. *New York Times*, August 23, 2005.

42. Roy Schotland of Georgetown University, quoted in Margaret Ebrahim, "The Bible Bench," *Mother Jones*, May/June 2006; see also *Washington Post*, April 12, 2005; *San Francisco Chronicle*, August 11, 2007.

43. Stephanie Simon, *Los Angeles Times*, December 25, 2006.

44. Jacqueline Salmon, *Washington Post*, December 25, 2007.

CHAPTER 15: THE RETURN OF TOTALITARIAN THEOCRACY

1. Michael Parenti, *History as Mystery* (San Francisco: City Lights Books, 1999), pp. 44–45.

2. Ibid., pp. 97–103; Charles Freeman, *The Closing of the Western Mind* (New York: Vintage Books, 2005), pp. 120, 149, and passim.

3. Luciano Canfora, *The Vanished Library* (Berkeley: University of California Press, 1987), p. 192.

4. Parenti, *History as Mystery*, p. 97.

5. 1 Corinthians 6:9; Romans 1:26–32.

6. *New York Times*, April 3, 2006.

7. Chris Hedges, *American Fascists: The Christian Right and the War on America* (New York: Free Press, 2006).

8. Quoted in Kimberly Blaker, ed., *The Fundamentals of Extremism: The Christian Right in America* (Plymouth, MI: New Boston Books, 2003), p. 25.

9. John Sugg, "A Nation under God," *Mother Jones*, December 2005.

10. http://www.skepticfiles.org/fw/terry.htm; http://www.source watch.org/index.php?title=Randall_Terry.250.

11. http://en.wikipedia.org/wiki/Gary_North.

12. North and Kennedy's comments in Bob Moser, "The Crusaders," *Rolling Stone*, April 21, 2005.

13. Ellen Bulf, "Roots of the Religious Right," *Committees of Correspondence for Democracy and Socialism*, January/February 2008.

14. See Aayan Hirsi Ali, "Islam's Silent Moderates," *New York Times*, December 7, 2007; Khaled Abou El Fadl, *The Great Theft: Wrestling Islam from the Extremists* (New York: HarperOne, 2007).

15. Koran 2:98; 16:2.

16. Koran 3:125.

17. See Ibn Warraq, *Why I Am Not a Muslim* (Amherst, NY: Prometheus Books, 2003); Robert Spencer, *The Truth about Muhammad* (Washington, DC: Regnery, 2007).

18. Koran 9:30; 5:51; 5:12–18; 9:31–35.

19. Zachary Karabell, *Peace Be Upon You: Fourteen Centuries of Muslim, Christian, and Jewish Conflict and Cooperation* (New York: Vintage, 2008); Abdullah Yusuf Ali in *The Holy Qur'an* (Elmhurst, NY: Tahrike Tarsile Qur'an, Inc. 2001), p. 447, n. 1281.

20. Tim Wallace-Murphy, *What Islam Did for Us: Understanding Islam's Contribution to Western Civilization* (New York: Watkins Publishing, 2006).

21. Daniel Cooney, Associated Press, March 24, 2006.

22. Jason Straziuso and Amir Shah, Associated Press, January 24, 2008.

23. *New York Times*, May 7, 2007.

24. Melissa Buckheit, "Taliban Has Made Afghan Women Virtual Prisoners," *People's Weekly World*, January 23, 1999.

25. Reports by Jason Straziuso, Associated Press, December 10, 2006, and January 24, 2008.

26. Ali al-Fadhily, "Iraq: 'Bad' Women Raped and Killed," Inter Press Service, December 18, 2007; *Washington Post*, December 13, 2007.

27. Examples from Nigeria and Iran in *New York Times*, March 13, 2005. For similar instances in northern Iraq, see *Los Angeles Times*, May 22, 2007; *New York Times*, January 11, 2008.

28. *San Francisco Chronicle*, December 13, 2000.

29. Jehangir Pocha, "Pulling Back the Veil," *Utne*, March/April 2005.

30. Camelia E. Fard, "Unveiled Threats," *ZNet Commentary*, June 6, 2001.

31. "Justice, Saudi Style," *USA Today*, November 27, 2007.

32. Donna Abu-Nasr, Associated Press, June 3, 2005; *Washington Post*, December 25, 2006.

33. *New York Times*, May 24, 2006.

34. All these examples were reported in *New York Times*, March 13, 2005.

35. Ibid.

36. Nicholas Kristof, *New York Times*, March 28, 2006.

37. *New York Times*, December 7, 2006.

38. Robert F. Worth, *New York Times*, June 29, 2008.

39. "Pakistani Girls Shortchanged," *Freethought Today*, June/July 2007.

40. Lawrence Wright, "The Rebellion Within," *New Yorker*, June 2, 2008.

41. Mary Anne Weaver, "A Fugitive from Injustice," *New Yorker*, September 12, 1994; *Los Angeles Times*, August 10, 2007.

42. See, for instance, Irshad Manji, *The Trouble with Islam* (New York: St. Martin's Press, 2004); Asra Nomani, *Standing Alone* (New York: HarperOne, 2006); Ayaan Hirsi Ali, *Infidel* (New York: Free Press, 2008).

43. Among the most notable are Afschineh Latifi, Roya Hakakian, Nahid Rachlin, Azadeh Moaveni, Marina Nemat, Zarah Ghahramani, and Marjane Satrapi.

44. Lorraine Adams, "Beyond the Burka," and Sarah Wildman, "Caught in the Ayatolla's," both in *New York Times Book Review*, January 6, 2008. On Kazemi's death, see http://www.cbc.ca/news/background/kazemi.

45. *San Francisco Chronicle*, July 3, 2007.

46. Joel Brinkley, *San Francisco Chronicle*, December 9, 2007. See also *New York Times*, February 4 and 6, 2006.

47. Hanif Koya, letter to *San Francisco Chronicle*, February 4, 2006.

48. *Los Angeles Times*, June 3, 2008.

49. Photographs of London protesters sent to me by Barry Lituchy, February 2007.

50. Associated Press, July 12, 2005; Jane Kramer, "The Dutch Model," *New Yorker*, April 3, 2006.

51. *New York Times*, December 8, 2005.

52. *Wall Street Journal*, February 15, 2008.

53. Jane Kramer, "The Pope and Islam," *New Yorker*, April 2, 2007.

54. *Freethought Today*, March 2008.

55. James Brandon and Salam Hafez, *Crimes of the Community: Honor-Based Violence in the UK* (London: Center for Social Cohesion, 2008), http://www.socialcohesion.co.uk/pdf/CrimesOfThe Community.pdf.

56. PBS special, *Islam vs. Islamists*, KQED-TV, August 30, 2007.

57. See Jane Kramer, "Taking the Veil," *New Yorker*, November 22, 2004; Hassan Fattah, "Radicalism among Muslim Professionals Worries Many," *New York Times*, July 14, 2007; see also Robert Dreyfuss, *How the United States Helped Unleash Fundamentalist Islam* (New York: Metropolitan Books, 2005).

58. *New York Times*, October 15, 2007.

59. David S. Pena, "Judging the Importance of Religious Teachings," *Nature, Society, and Thought* 17, no. 3 (2004).

CHAPTER 16: FOR LORDS AND LAMAS

1. Mark Juergensmeyer, *Terror in the Mind of God* (Berkeley: University of California Press, 2000), pp. 6, 112–13, 157; see also Rungrawee Pinyorat, Associated Press, August 8, 2007.

2. Kyong-Hwa Seok, "Korean Monk Gangs Battle for Temple Turf," *San Francisco Examiner*, December 3, 1998.

3. Dalai Lama quoted in Donald Lopez Jr., *Prisoners of Shangri-la: Tibetan Buddhism and the West* (Chicago: University of Chicago Press, 1998), p. 205.

4. Erik D. Curren, *Buddha's Not Smiling: Uncovering Corruption at the Heart of Tibetan Buddhism Today* (Buena Vista, VA: Alaya Press 2005), p. 41.

5. Stuart Gelder and Roma Gelder, *The Timely Rain: Travels in New Tibet* (New York: Monthly Review Press, 1964), pp. 119, 123; Melvyn C. Goldstein, *The Snow Lion and the Dragon: China, Tibet, and the Dalai Lama* (Berkeley: University of California Press, 1995), pp. 6–16; Pankaj Mishra, "Holy Man," *New Yorker*, March 31, 2008.

6. Curren, *Buddha's Not Smiling*, p. 50.

7. Stephen Bachelor, "Letting Daylight into Magic: The Life and Times of Dorje Shugden," *Tricycle: The Buddhist Review* 7 (Spring 1998). Bachelor discusses the sectarian fanaticism and doctrinal clashes that plague certain sectors of Buddhism.

8. Pradyumna P. Karan, *The Changing Face of Tibet: The Impact of Chinese Communist Ideology on the Landscape* (Lexington: University Press of Kentucky, 1976), p. 64.

9. Gelder and Gelder, *The Timely Rain*, pp. 62, 174.

10. As skeptically noted by Lopez, *Prisoners of Shangri-la*, p. 9.

11. Melvyn Goldstein, William Siebenschuh, and Tashì-Tsering, *The Struggle for Modern Tibet: The Autobiography of Tashì-Tsering* (Armonk, NY: M. E. Sharpe, 1997).

12. Gelder and Gelder, *The Timely Rain*, p. 110.

13. Melvyn C. Goldstein, *A History of Modern Tibet, 1913–1951* (Berkeley: University of California Press, 1989), p. 5 and passim.

14. Anna Louise Strong, *Tibetan Interviews* (Beijing: New World Press, 1959), pp. 15, 19–21, 24.

15. Ibid., p. 25.

16. Ibid., p. 31.

17. Gelder and Gelder, *The Timely Rain*, pp. 175–76; Strong, *Tibetan Interviews*, pp. 25–26.

18. Gelder and Gelder, *The Timely Rain*, p. 113.

19. A. Tom Grunfeld, *The Making of Modern Tibet*, rev. ed. (Armonk, NY: East Gate Book, 1996), pp. 9, 7–33; Felix Greene, *A Curtain of Ignorance* (New York: Doubleday, 1961), pp. 241–49; Goldstein, *A History of Modern Tibet*, pp. 3–5; Lopez, *Prisoners of Shangri-la*, passim.

20. Strong, *Tibetan Interviews*, pp. 91–96.

21. Waddell and Chapman are quoted in Gelder and Gelder, *The Timely Rain*, pp. 123–25.

22. Heinrich Harrer, *Return to Tibet* (New York: Schocken, 1985), p. 29.

23. See Kenneth Conboy and James Morrison, *The CIA's Secret War in Tibet* (Lawrence: University of Kansas Press, 2002); William Leary, "Secret Mission to Tibet," *Air & Space*, December 1997/January 1998.

24. On the CIA's links to the Dalai Lama and his family and entourage, see Loren Coleman, *Tom Slick and the Search for the Yeti* (London: Faber and Faber, 1989).

25. Leary, "Secret Mission to Tibet."

26. Hugh Deane, "The Cold War in Tibet," *CovertAction Quarterly* (Winter 1987).

27. George Ginsburg and Michael Mathos, *Communist China and Tibet* (1964), quoted in Deane, "The Cold War in Tibet." Deane notes that author Bina Roy reached a similar conclusion.

28. Greene, *A Curtain of Ignorance*, p. 248 and passim; Grunfeld, *The Making of Modern Tibet*, passim.

29. Foster Stockwell, "Essays on Tibet: Myth and Reality," *Chinese American Forum*, April 2008.

30. Karan, *The Changing Face of Tibet*, pp. 36–38, 41, 57–58; *Times* (London), July 4, 1966.

31. Harrer, *Return to Tibet*, p. 54.

32. Gelder and Gelder, *The Timely Rain*, pp. 29, 47–48.

33. Tendzin Choegyal, "The Truth about Tibet," *Imprimis* (publication of Hillsdale College, Michigan), April 1999.

34. Karan, *The Changing Face of Tibet*, pp. 52–53.

35. Jean-Paul Desimpelaere, "La CIA sponsor du Dalaï Lama," http://www.michelcollon.info/articles.php?dateaccess=2007-12-18%2006:32:03&log=lautrehistoire.

36. Elaine Kurtenbach, Associate Press, February 12, 1998.

37. Goldstein, *The Snow Lion and the Dragon*, pp. 47–48.

38. *San Francisco Chronicle*, January 9, 2007.

39. Report by the International Committee of Lawyers for Tibet, *A Generation in Peril* (Berkeley, CA: 2001), passim.

40. Ibid., pp. 66–68, 98.

CHAPTER 17: GOOD-BYE, SHANGRI-LA

1. This comparison is drawn by Stuart Gelder and Roma Gelder, *The Timely Rain: Travels in New Tibet* (New York: Monthly Review Press, 1964), p. 64.

2. Michael Parenti, *The Culture Struggle* (New York: Seven Stories Press, 2006).

3. John Pomfret, "Tibet Caught in China's Web," *Washington Post*, July 23, 1999.

4. *Los Angeles Times*, September 15, 1998; *New York Times*, October, 1, 1998.

5. Heather Cottin, "George Soros, Imperial Wizard," *Covert-Action Quarterly* 74 (Fall 2002).

6. Melvyn C. Goldstein, *The Snow Lion and the Dragon: China, Tibet, and the Dalai Lama* (Berkeley: University of California Press, 1995), p. 51.

7. Tendzin Choegyal, "The Truth about Tibet," *Imprimis* (publication of Hillsdale College, Michigan), April 1999.

8. Christopher Hitchens, "The Divine One," *Nation*, July/August 1998.

9. The Dalai Lama in Marianne Dresser, ed., *Beyond Dogma: Dialogues and Discourses* (Berkeley, CA: North Atlantic Books, 1996).

10. These comments are from a book of the Dalai Lama's writings quoted in Nikolai Thyssen, "Oceaner af onkel Tom," *Dagbladet Information*, December 29, 2003 (translated for me by Julius Wilm). Thyssen's review (in Danish) can be found at http://www.information .dk/Indgang/VisArkiv.dna?pArtNo=20031229154141.txt.

11. "A Global Call for Human Rights in the Workplace," *New York Times*, December 6, 2005.

12. *San Francisco Chronicle*, January 14, 2007.

13. *San Francisco Chronicle*, November 5, 2005.

14. *Times of India*, October 13, 2000; Samantha Conti, Reuters, June 17, 1994; Amitabh Pal, "The Dalai Lama Interview," *Progressive*, January 2006.

15. Erik Curren, "Not So Easy to Say Who Is Karmapa," August 22, 2005, www.buddhistchannel.tv/index.php?id=22.1577,0,0,1,0.

16. Erik D. Curren, *Buddha's Not Smiling: Uncovering Corruption at the Heart of Tibetan Buddhism Today* (Buena Vista, VA: Alaya

Press 2005), passim. For books favorable toward the Dalai Lama's faction, see Lea Terhune, *Karmapa of Tibet* (Somerville, MA: Wisdom Publications, 2004); Gaby Naher, *Wrestling the Dragon* (New York: Rider, 2004).

17. "Dalai Lama and Dorje Shugden," www.dalai-liar.com/videos.htm.

18. Kim Lewis, personal correspondence, July 15, 2004.

19. Kim Lewis, correspondence, July 16, 2004.

20. Foster Stockwell, "Essays on Tibet: Myth and Reality," *Chinese American Forum*, April 2008.

CHAPTER 18: SECULAR TOLERANCE RISING?

1. Karl Marx, introduction to his *Contribution to the Critique of Hegel's Philosophy of Right.*

2. PBS special, *Islam vs. Islamists*, KQED-TV, August 30, 2007.

3. Burton L. Mack, *Who Wrote the New Testament?* (HarperSanFrancisco, 1995), p. 199.

4. Adrian Reddy, "A Plan? A Man? The Quran," October 26, 2007, http://www.butterfliesandwheels.com/articles.php.

5. See observations by Christopher Hitchens, "God Bless Me, It's a Best-Seller!" *Vanity Fair*, September 2007.

6. Laurie Goodstein, "More Atheists Are Shouting It from Rooftops," *New York Times*, April 27, 2009.

7. Hitchens, "God Bless Me, It's a Best-Seller!"

8. Pew Research Center's Forum on Religion and Public Life, June 2008, http://religions.pewforum.org/reports.

9. See correspondence by Lori Lipman Brown, *Nation*, December 17, 2007; Goodstein, "More Atheists Are Shouting It from Rooftops."

10. Jim Wallis quoted in *San Francisco Chronicle*, July 21, 2005.

11. *San Francisco Chronicle*, July 24, 2008.

12. Bill Berkowitz, "Is the Religious Right Wounded or in Transition?" *Z Magazine*, June 2008; see also E. J. Dionne, *Souled Out: Reclaiming Faith and Politics after the Religious Right* (Princeton, NJ: Princeton University Press, 2008); Christine Wicker, *The Fall of the Evangelical Nation* (New York: HarperOne, 2008).

13. The information and quotations in that paragraph are from

Lawrence Wright, "The Rebellion Within," *New Yorker*, June 2, 2008.

14. See Ingrid Rowland, *Giordano Bruno: Philosopher/Heretic* (New York: Farrar, Straus & Giroux, 2008).

15. James Carroll, *Constantine's Sword* (Boston: Houghton Mifflin, 2001), p. 374; *New York Times*, February 18, 2000.

16. Michel de Montaigne, "On Cato the Younger," in *The Complete Essays* (New York: Penguin, 2003), p. 257.

INDEX

belief in existence of, 19
Bible as the word of, 20–21
gender of, 13, 46
as the intelligent designer, 80–82.
	See also creationism
		imperfections in the design,
		83–85
	and Job, 29–31
	names of, 13, 15, 26, 49, 83
	omnipotence of, 22, 23, 66,
		69–70, 84, 217
	omniscience of, 22, 23, 217
	See also Bible; Jesus; Yahweh
Gogh, Theo van, 192
Gomorrah and Sodom, 23–24, 32–33,
	42
Gone with the Wind (movie), 53
GOP. *See* Republican Party
Gorman, Martin, 141
government
	faith-based initiatives, 171–72
	political agendas and religion, 14
		of John Paul II, 131–33
		of the religious Right, 137,
		155–64, 182–85
	providing tax exemptions to reli-
		gious groups, 172
	religious involvement in politics
		and government, 127–29,
		131–33, 134–35, 170–73,
		182–85
	See also church and state
Government Accountability Office, 171
Graham, Billy, 100
Grant, W. V., 103–104
Grassley, Charles, 36–37
Great Designer as a name of God, 83
Great Ineffable as a name of God, 15
greed. *See* monetary malfeasance

Greek Orthodox Church, 130
Grunfeld, Tom, 200
Guatemala, 136
Guyana, 116
Gyalo Thondup, 202

Hagee, John, 68
Haggai 2:8, 99
Haggard, Ted, 137, 142, 220
Harrer, Heinrich, 203
Harris, Sam, 84–85
Haught, James, 71
Hawking, Stephen, 12
Hay, Malcolm, 58–59
healing power of prayer, 68–70
Heavenly Father as a name of God, 49
Hegel, Georg Wilhelm Friedrich,
	12–13, 81
Heldreth, Howard Scott, 161
Hillsdale College, 140–41
Hinduism
	deaths on route to worship Shiva,
		66
	and sexual abuse, 152
	violent and repressive acts of, 72,
		73–74, 196
Hitler, Adolf, 60–61, 62
Hittites, 29
Holocaust, 60–62
Holy Bible. *See* Bible
Holy Roman Rota, 147
Home for the Dying (Calcutta, India),
	90–91
homophobia, 39, 116, 141–43, 159
	scandals involving those who de-
		nounce homosexuality, 141–43
		Catholic priests, 142–43
		megachurch leaders, 142
		Republicans, 158–60, 161

ABOUT THE AUTHOR

Michael Parenti is the author of hundreds of articles and twenty-one books, including *The Assassination of Julius Caesar* and *Contrary Notions: The Michael Parenti Reader.* He lectures frequently across North America and abroad. He lives in Berkeley, California. Visit him online at www.michaelparenti.org.